Sociability and
Its Enemies

Sociability and Its Enemies

German Political Theory After 1945

✦

Jakob Norberg

NORTHWESTERN UNIVERSITY PRESS
EVANSTON, ILLINOIS

Northwestern University Press
www.nupress.northwestern.edu

Printed in the United States of America

10 9 8 7 6 5 4 3 2 1

Library of Congress Cataloging-in-Publication Data

Norberg, Jakob, 1975– author.
Sociability and its enemies : German political theory after 1945 / Jakob Norberg.
pages cm.
Includes bibliographical references and index.
ISBN 978-0-8101-2936-8 (pbk. : alk. paper) — ISBN 978-0-8101-2970-2 (cloth : alk. paper)
1. Political science—Germany. 2. Political sociology. 3. Social sciences—Philosophy. 4. Germany—Intellectual life—20th century. 5. Schmitt, Carl, 1888–1985—Political and social views. 6. Arendt, Hannah, 1906–1975—Political and social views. 7. Koselleck, Reinhart—Political and social views. 8. Habermas, Jürgen—Political and social views. I. Title.
JA84.G3N67 2014
306.2094309045—dc23
2013031514

∞ The paper used in this publication meets the minimum requirements of the American National Standard for Information Sciences—Permanence of Paper for Printed Library Materials, ANSI Z39.48-1992.

Till mamma och pappa

CONTENTS

Introduction
Sociability and Its Enemies 3

Chapter One
Sociability as Reeducation: The Program of *Die Wandlung* 29

Chapter Two
Conversations and Interrogations: Carl Schmitt 57

Chapter Three
The Mob of Bourgeois Society: Hannah Arendt 81

Chapter Four
Sociability and Hypocrisy: Reinhart Koselleck 107

Chapter Five
Saving Bourgeois Sociability: Jürgen Habermas 127

Chapter Six
Among the Rotarians: Sociability in West Germany 157

Notes 181

Bibliography 219

Index 235

Sociability and Its Enemies

Introduction

Sociability and Its Enemies

In the fall of 1946, the young Swedish writer Stig Dagerman traveled through the British- and American-occupied zones of Germany and filed journalistic reports for the Stockholm-based tabloid *Expressen.* In his accounts, he kept his eyes on the immediately visible devastation. The series of articles, which came out in book form in 1947, portrays starving and freezing Germans inhabiting water-filled basements in destroyed and desolate cities. Dagerman describes Germany as one continuous "cold, rainy, and ruinous hell," its train stations chock-full of unceasing streams of refugees from the East.[1]

These vivid observations of the material conditions also inform Dagerman's evaluation of the Germans' postwar political beliefs. Unlike fellow journalists primarily concerned with whether Germans were still "infected by Nazism," Dagerman argues that it would be unrealistic to expect a population plagued by constant hunger to examine the causes of their plight and confront their own participation in "Hitler's politics."[2] Hunger is, he writes, a "very bad teacher."[3] This particular kind of realism earned him criticism from contemporary reviewers, many of whom felt that Dagerman's literary skill in evoking concrete details came at the cost of a responsible discussion of how to best reorient Germany and reeducate the Germans.

But despite Dagerman's sensitivity to the dreariness of day-to-day struggles, the people depicted in *German Autumn* do not disappear in a haze of equalizing suffering. Dagerman had ties to Syndicalist groups, had published in left-wing journals in Sweden, and, in his encounters with Germans, was particularly keen to point out the persistence of class differences. For all his attention to the effects of material destruction, he contests the idea that widespread shortage of food and shelter would have eroded distinctions among classes, a claim he attributes to "bourgeois ideologists."[4] It is wrong, he writes, to confuse poverty and classlessness, because there are still significant differences between the most and the least poor; the general economic collapse may even have "sharpened rather than blurred" the differences.[5] He makes this point most clearly in an article that describes a visit to a lawyer fortunate enough to live in a spared villa on the outskirts of Hamburg, a city that is otherwise nothing but an enormous wasteland.

Dagerman's account of his visit is something of a study in the careful maintenance of a class identity with a checkered past and an uncertain future. First he enters the hallway and the lounge and takes note of the typical, and intact, signs of wealth and cultivation, such as an umbrella stand, "metres of gold-edged morocco-bound volumes in the bookshelves," a dense carpet, and leather armchairs.[6] Sitting down for a conversation, his host offers him tea and cake, in keeping with social conventions in better-class households. And finally, he listens to the unnamed lawyer and his friend, apparently a writer of picaresque novels, voice worked-out opinions about the various aspects of Germany's current state. They speak about how disappointed they are in the English after an initial phase of enthusiastic welcome, or the obscure character of the emerging political parties, whose election meetings are virtually indistinguishable from one another. Dagerman's main host seeks to present himself as generous and concerned with the protocols of correct interaction, but also as a man of considered opinions, one who is able to offer comments on current political developments and life chances in Germany. Dagerman conveys how fine objects such as furniture and fragile porcelain cups, rituals of hospitality, and the articulation of viewpoints belie the notion that all the demarcations of class have been dissolved through war and defeat.

Dagerman also notices, however, that the Hamburg lawyer is under some strain to put on this display. The tea is served without sugar, and "beneath the layers of carefully counterfeited cream" the cake turns out to be "the usual bad German *ersatz* bread."[7] The cake, the visiting reporter concludes, is more a "symbolic cake" than a real one, a feat of presentation designed to indicate the distance between people with a solid background and good breeding and the poor, who would not consume their bread that way.[8]

In his portrayal of his Hamburg hosts, Dagerman shows how the lack of commodities—sugar, cream, bread—makes itself felt in the salon of the educated upper-middle class. This puts the lifestyle into crisis. If the members of this class cannot remain relatively well maintained and relatively well dressed, it will perhaps cease to exist altogether. At the same time, Dagerman indicates how this lifestyle can be upheld, at least for the time being, with the help of symbols and practices. Even when the tea is bad and there is no sugar, a visitor is invited to tea. The general state of deprivation may have penetrated the once-affluent residential areas, but its inhabitants can at least try to foreground their knowledge about how to welcome guests, their sense of what entertaining people would typically entail, and their skills of conversation. The state of reduced resources does not compel them to relinquish their sense of what circles they belong to; rather, it intensifies their efforts to maintain appearances. Under dire economic circumstances, the burden of performing an already established class identity, of persuading others of one's continued membership in the German *Bürgertum* as a stratum of continued relevance, shifts away from actual wealth toward proper social and discursive conduct, from goods toward learned behaviors. Socializing, knowing how to engage in the style of behavior that the Germans call *Geselligkeit*, is an immaterial resource that can be deployed in a time of material desolation.

In her book on the networks of mining and manufacturing executives, bankers, and daring entrepreneurs in the era of the German economic miracle, Nina Grunenberg presents a couple of *Urszenen*, or "originary scenes," of the postwar market economy.[9] Days after the currency reform in June 1948, for instance, a fish trader from Braunschweig traveled to the restored Volkswagen plant in Wolfsburg with a carton of fresh bills collected from his customers in order to buy one of the new cars, most of which until then had been made and delivered to the administration of the British-controlled zone. Moments such as these, Grunenberg states, epitomize the reemergence of a strong domestic economy based on the revival of industrial production and a mass of consumers eager to purchase durable goods such as cars, refrigerators, stoves, and radios.

In a similar way, one can perhaps speak of Dagerman's encounter with relatively well-to-do, well-informed, and slightly pretentious members of upper-middle-class circles as an *Urszene* of postwar sociability. After the war was over and the Nazi regime removed, new or old acquaintances greeted each other, invited others into their drawing room for a light lunch or tea and cake, and began to articulate their very own personal opinions on the state of the world while being (somewhat) mindful of what could blatantly offend their interlocutors. Or, to phrase it a little more abstractly, people began again to engage in polite face-to-face interactions in spaces beyond those reserved exclusively for intimate, familial life on the one hand, and goal-oriented professional or political interactions on the other, often in a conscious effort to return to or symbolically enact the resumption of a genuinely civil life.

What we are seeing in Dagerman's article, through the eyes of the skeptical observer with left-wing commitments, is the somewhat nervous demonstration of an intact upper-middle-class identity through the medium of *Geselligkeit*, or sociability. The trivial nature of the encounters around the coffee tables may seem to prohibit further explorations of their meaning, but, as we shall see, quite a few writers, intellectuals, and theorists in the postwar period would invoke the spaces and behaviors that constitute sociability in their attempts to envision a possible future for Germany. Not infrequently, they would speak of the special significance of small networks of friends or regularly convening discussion groups, and above all, they would look back at an idealized history of nonprofessional academies and sophisticated salons for people who wanted to gather and enjoy each other's company while relieving themselves of the burdens of clearly purposive (administrative, economic, or political) activities in structured and stratified organizations, enterprises, bureaucracies, and parties.

But what could be the appeal of scenes of sociability or performances of politeness to those engaged in the earnest business of reforming the political culture of Germany? Only a much-abbreviated answer can be offered here, an answer to be explored and expanded upon throughout the entire book. Implicitly disputing the idea that sociable interaction is merely a means to bourgeois self-presentation and impression management, intellectuals and engaged theorists looked to how sociability draws together and coordinates individuals in shared activities that could be presented as civil rather than martial, voluntary rather than coercive, sustained by self-monitoring individuals rather than imposed by an external agency, tied to quiet and peaceful circumstances rather than emergency and war, and based on reciprocity rather than narrow self-interested pursuits.

Sociability with roots in a bourgeois context of life, then, represented a nonmilitaristic and nonhierarchical sphere of action, for it depends on each participant's supple and circumspect attunement to others in a placid setting. As such, it could be reintroduced and welcomed after 1945 as a much-needed contrast to Nazi rule and world war, and even as a key strategy in the simultaneous recuperation and reformation of German (upper-middle-class) culture at a time when an identity defined by material possessions was under threat. The immediate postwar period was, among many other things, an era of revivified sociability.

Sociability and Postwar Political Thought

By focusing on different, and indeed conflicting, conceptions and interpretations of bourgeois forms of sociability in postwar Germany, this book offers readings of works by thinkers such as Hannah Arendt, Jürgen Habermas, and Carl Schmitt in order to present a new interpretation of

German intellectual history after 1945. Arendt, Habermas, and Schmitt are all known as contributors to modern political theory. Their names are frequently invoked in discussions about the nature and value of political action, the character of democracy and deliberation, and the political pathologies and possibilities of modern societies. The situation in Germany after 1945 has attracted considerable scholarly attention, too, but mostly in slightly different contexts and disciplines. Historians, sociologists, and psychologists have explored how (West) Germany sought to come to terms with, or repress, the immediate past, or how the people of a collapsed and defeated totalitarian state made the transition to Western democratic and liberal politics.

This book seeks to make a contribution both to contemporary studies of political theory and the discourse on postwar Germany, and does so by reconstructing the arguments of Arendt and others concerning the role and value of sociability or *Geselligkeit* as a form of interaction and interconnection particular to modern bourgeois society or the *bürgerliche Gesellschaft*. The works of Arendt, Habermas, Schmitt, and the historian Reinhart Koselleck can partly be viewed, I argue, as divergent responses to a hitherto neglected question or point of contention, namely whether or not bourgeois sociability should serve as a therapeutic practice and politically relevant ideal for postwar Germany. Reconstructing the context of this argument will shed light on previously neglected historical and conceptual connections among political theorists and enrich the established narratives of postwar intellectual history.

The focal issue in this project, then, is the ongoing critical engagement with particular historical types of sociability. Essays and reflections by Arendt and Schmitt from the late 1940s contain recurrent observations and comments on the forms of interaction and coordination peculiar to bourgeois society. In the late 1950s and early 1960s, the influential historian Reinhart Koselleck and the young Habermas would publish academic studies devoted to the emergence and character of bourgeois society, with particular attention to bourgeois modes of interaction. And both Koselleck and Habermas would refer to the works of Arendt and Schmitt at crucial junctures. When read carefully, this constellation of texts yields a series of arguments concerning the complex relationship of bourgeois sociability to the (variously defined) conduct of politics.

Without necessarily entering into a direct debate with one another, these prominent theorists sought to respond to the same set of questions. Does bourgeois sociability serve as the matrix of a new kind of deliberative political conversation in which people participate by offering their calm and well-informed judgments? Or does it rather erode the understanding of how collective decisions are reached through vigorous and sometimes anarchic contestation and conflict? Does bourgeois sociability that takes place in extrafamilial and extraprofessional venues provide a much-needed egalitarian, nonauthoritarian, and inclusive form of social integration? Or does it establish a specious kind of harmony that prevails by raising barriers to the outside and neutralizing oppositional voices within? Is there a path from convivial exchange, so popular among certain intellectuals in the immediate postwar period, to vigorous debate? As the questions imply, this group of theorists consisted of both advocates and critics of the idea of sociability.

But why—the question must be posed again—would a concern with something so trivial and apparently marginal as the bundle of practices and values associated with sociability occupy an important place in postwar intellectual and political life? Bracketing the various individual experiences and preferences of the thinkers involved, there are a handful of general reasons for the turn to bourgeois sociability, some of which have already been indicated. After 1945, German academics and publicists entrusted with reeducational tasks faced the problem of having to formulate the principles of a future collective that had been stripped, or finally relieved, of the myths of a transcendent state or a racially homogeneous people. How, they were compelled to ask, do we conceive of a political formation without falling back on notions of race or popular unity under a leader and, at least temporarily, without the ordering and stabilizing presence of the state and its institutions?[10] What practices of social integration are still available and acceptable? How can we speak of some unity and cohesion among ourselves when a host of traditional concepts used to signify and exhort the collective, such as *Volk, Nation,* or *Gemeinschaft,* have been irrevocably tainted under National Socialism?[11]

In response to this situation, figures such as the philosopher Karl Jaspers and the journalist and political scientist Dolf Sternberger searched for terms and symbols of noncoercive and nonauthoritarian forms of cohesion, which would still be recognizable to Germans and thus potentially hold some appeal for their audience. With the literary and political Heidelberg journal *Die Wandlung* as his platform between 1945 and 1949, Sternberger in particular invoked *Geselligkeit* as a viable model, or at least a suitable strategic self-description, for a future Germany. In a series of articles, some programmatic and some anecdotal, Sternberger described postwar associational life in idealized terms and spoke of the virtues of politeness, affability, and civility, all with the aim of reintroducing a nearly ruined tradition of bourgeois conduct and self-reflection.

The historical bourgeoisie, Sternberger proposed, had developed stable patterns of interaction enlivened by desires for companionship and diversion, shaped by protocols of circumspection and politeness, and informed by values of mutual respect and moderation.[12] Members of the bourgeoisie had, if not in Germany then in other nations, convened voluntarily for the sake of pleasurable conversation, acquired virtues of tact and toleration toward others, and come to accept and promote a fair distribution of opportunities to speak. This model showed that societies of interdependent individuals are able to sustain themselves through ongoing acts of non-economic cooperation such as free conversation. They do not, Sternberger suggested, require the constant intervention and management of an external supervising authority such as the state.

Not knowing the political future of a German state and facing volatile and uncertain circumstances, Sternberger highlighted practices of contact and communication that could not be confounded with the subjection of the many to a state with coercive resources.[13] Moreover, he couched his vision in the language of *bürgerliche* virtues and habits, perhaps in the hope that it would appeal to a war-weary readership eager to find comfort in a reconstituted form of everyday life. Yet he also argued that the type of interaction he depicted could help foster a commitment to egalitarian and participatory discussions, which in turn would provide a foundation for active citizenship.

In other words, Sternberger introduced bourgeois sociability as a form of reeducation in a moment of perceived institutional and conceptual vacuum. Instead of a radical, even revolutionary transformation of Germany, he hoped for quiet adoption of democratic and liberal forms of life through the gradual rebuilding and further cultivation of particular modes of bourgeois sociability.[14] If people could come together in small circles of discussion and begin to interact with each other tactfully and respectfully in relaxed social settings, they would also slowly gain exposure to the demands of reasoned deliberation about political matters. In a period in which "German public identity" was "up for grabs," Sternberger promoted sociability as a recognizably bourgeois form of interaction that would help Germans turn into citizens.[15]

In 1962, a little more than a decade after Dolf Sternberger's journal *Die Wandlung* ceased publication, Jürgen Habermas published *The Structural Transformation of the Public Sphere,* his influential book on the historical emergence and sociological composition of the bourgeois public sphere. It is in this work that Habermas outlines how a model of conversation and rationally oriented debate developed among members of the bourgeoisie who gathered in clubs, salons, and coffeehouses and consumed reading materials such as journals and pamphlets. Distinct from the procedures of market exchange that knit the bourgeoisie together in economic networks, and located above the more secluded sites of familial reproduction and intimate life, these institutionalized forms of assembly and interaction eventually yielded an addressee and vocal interlocutor for the modern, territorially delimited state. In this examination of the emerging public sphere as a "category of bourgeois society," as the subtitle reads, Habermas offered a historical reconstruction of how the habits of discussion particular to the bourgeois social venues could assume political significance and even present a paradigm of argumentation unencumbered by inequalities in wealth, power, and prestige. Bourgeois sociability in drawing rooms used as salons, or coffeehouses and semiprivate clubs, could forge a modern political subject.[16]

Viewed against the backdrop of Sternberger's postwar project, Habermas's 1962 book looks somewhat like an elaborate and more academic version of an already established idea of bourgeois sociability as a possible transitional and educational practice for Germans on the path toward a more deliberative polity. With this juxtaposition of Sternberger and Habermas, bourgeois sociability emerges as a positive ideal of the postwar period with more than one supporter. At the very least, both writers accorded value to the notion of a bourgeois society (*Gesellschaft*) and thus avoided standard German invocations of the infrangible bonds of an organic community supported by structures of kinship and custom (*Gemeinschaft*),[17] or the special mission of the German state in ordering and ethically guiding the otherwise dispersed and merely self-interested subjects.[18]

Yet Habermas was not building directly on the work of the journal *Die Wandlung*, although he was socialized as a researcher and intellectual in the immediate postwar period, spent some time at the University of Heidelberg, and would later invoke Sternberger's concept of "constitutional patriotism."[19] There is no clear line from Sternberger's efforts to conjure up some credible vision of a future community in the precarious years 1945–49 and Habermas's 1962 attempt to provide an image of a politically efficacious rational discourse anchored in historically specific, bourgeois sites of sociable intercourse. However, both endeavors can be seen as belonging to the same domain of postwar reflection, along with interventions and works by Schmitt, Koselleck, and Arendt. As we shall see, multiple ties link Habermas and Sternberger together via sociability's skeptics and critics. The present book seeks to delineate and describe this domain or nexus of intellectual connections and pay particular attention to the critical assessments of sociability or *Geselligkeit* as a set of integrative, discursive practices understood to be peculiar to bourgeois society as separate from the state.

The notion of a bourgeois brand of sociability as a seemingly tenuous but direly needed form of nonauthoritarian coordination of diverse individuals is understandable against the backdrop of the postwar circumstances and the fear of fragmentation. Yet it immediately attracted a host of critics. In articles, essays, and scholarly publications, Arendt, Schmitt, and Koselleck devised a series of counterarguments to this model or, rather, presented starkly contrasting accounts of some fundamental structural characteristics of bourgeois society. Interestingly, they all entertained at least an indirect relation to *Die Wandlung*. Arendt herself published multiple essays in Sternberger and Jaspers's journal, which became her most important German outlet in the immediate postwar period. She used the publication opportunities, however, to articulate a relentless condemnation of bourgeois society and its dissolution of all genuinely political forms of collectivity. Schmitt experienced the postwar years in imposed silence after collaboration with National Socialism but commented privately on the intellectual climate of 1945 to 1950, for which he saw Karl Jaspers and his fellows as typical representatives. Finally, Koselleck studied in postwar Heidelberg, where *Die Wandlung* was published; openly declared his debt to Carl Schmitt's thought and personal guidance; and studied Arendt's early work on bourgeois society and its historical relationship to totalitarianism with great interest.

What are, in brief, the arguments *against* sociability? While Schmitt, Arendt, and Koselleck presented a multiplicity of critical viewpoints, they all denied that an orientation toward values other than profit or class domination even existed in bourgeois society, or they pointed to bourgeois sociability's concealed political costs.[20] There are, they asserted in different idioms and with radically different purposes, elusive but pervasive forces of influence and correction or organizational imperatives in bourgeois society that inhibit the articulation of dissent and therefore prevent the complex of habits, attitudes, and ideas that constitute sociability from ever performing a constructive political role. The reliance on particular kinds of discursive transactions among bourgeois society's members to sustain a cohesive and tranquil community was branded as unrealistic, manipulative, self-delusional, or inimical to the unpredictable diversity distinctive of genuinely political communities. For Schmitt, Arendt, and Koselleck there was simply no path from interaction in the sphere of bourgeois sociability to genuine political life.

The critical arguments can be presented in abbreviated form to indicate the diversity of the skeptical positions. First, the vision of self-managing circles of discourse with low levels of contention seemed symptomatic of a society that avoided or neglected the inescapable realities of conflicts of interests and whose apparently self-moderating members were actually unable to muster the energy to display an upright and virile resolve and instead indulged in dreams of more peaceable solutions. To some extent, this is actually the position sketched out by Sternberger himself in his articles on bourgeois sociability, as he set up a foil for his own proposition to strengthen the bourgeois tradition of sociable interaction, of *Geselligkeit,* in Germany. As we shall see, one of Sternberger's aims was to break the idolatry of the stern, manly character in German emotional life.

In his guarded and often esoteric postwar writings, Schmitt developed a different approach. The trust in forms of integration not dependent on structures of command and personally held power could, Schmitt implied, be seen as a form of disavowed authority. Contrary to the image of harmonious interaction among sociable individuals who all subscribe to an ethos of conversational tolerance, partisan groups continued to direct larger communities of people, but by the covert and even conspiratorial means of hegemony, through which a small group manages to make its agenda the agenda of all.

In a related but still distinct critique primarily formulated by Koselleck, bourgeois hegemony depends not so much on deception as on self-deception. The historical bourgeoisie, Koselleck claimed, was initially shielded within the absolutist state and grew accustomed to interactions in the relatively conflict-free fields of economy, scientific inquiry, and pleasant sociability. As a result of this experience, its members became prone to misapply the principles of civil interaction to the realm of politics defined by lines of conflict between factions contending for power.

Finally, Arendt argued that processes of efficient and production-oriented collaboration within bourgeois society continually demand the adjustment of each individual to everyone else. She conceded that the historical bourgeoisie might possess an idea of how individual subjects compose larger collectivities without the ordering effort of a coercive authority, but that it remains oblivious to the significance of political interaction that exceeds the demands of material production, with fatal results for the public spirit. Schmitt, Arendt, and Koselleck thus criticized the notion of bourgeois sociability as a foundation for politics from multiple angles, by claiming that it was an ideological illusion, a hypocritical move in a concealed struggle for power, or simply a groundless claim.[21]

These critical arguments formulated by Schmitt, Arendt, and Koselleck form an important intellectual backdrop to Habermas's work on the social and historical conditions of free and rational discourse in bourgeois society. Read in this context, his highly influential account of the crystallization of a bourgeois public sphere emerges as a reevaluation of an already established area of critical thought, which in turn is bound to particular responses to the relative conceptual and institutional vacuum of the postwar situation. Habermas's book represents an attempt to save bourgeois sociability from its detractors by integrating it in an overarching narrative of the public sphere, in which it plays a significant historical role by paving the way for discursive situations not structured by hierarchies of rank. Habermas not only disputes the claims of Koselleck, a scholar of the same generation whose work he reviewed in 1960, but also explicitly and quite systematically seeks to overturn the positions of Schmitt and Arendt. For him, the idea that bourgeois forms of social conviviality can function as a platform for a politics by argumentation rather than by coercion is not a spurious attempt to mask actual power grabs behind a vocabulary of cooperation, to deny the spread of conformity, or to elide the underlying economic organization of bourgeois society. It is instead an inspiring political vision buried in history that his German contemporaries should be made to recall.

To summarize, an important but previously neglected postwar debate took place among the proponents and skeptics of bourgeois sociability. After 1945, Sternberger and other intellectuals introduced bourgeois sociability as a practice of beneficial therapeutic and political value to a disoriented Germany. But the concept also came under attack by an array of thinkers including Schmitt, Arendt, and Koselleck, only to finally receive a vindication in the early work of Habermas, an intellectual with deep knowledge of the critical arguments.

Images of the Postwar Period and the Role of Sociability

Let us review yet another sample of postwar sociability, but now look at a proposal for cultural reform rather than a single, concrete scene, such as the one found in Dagerman's dispatch from Hamburg. In 1946, the historian Friedrich Meinecke suggested, in a book entitled *The German Catastrophe,* that Germans must turn away from world-political ambition and instead quietly devote themselves to their cultural heritage. Meinecke even recommended founding "Goethe congregations [*Goethegemeinde*]" in every German city and town, small communities of the culturally interested who would meet to listen to Bach, Beethoven, Mozart, and Schubert and read poetry by Hölderlin, Mörike, and Rilke.[22]

The suggestion that the "road to German salvation would be the establishment of 'Goethe communities'" has often been singled out for criticism and even ridicule.[23] In his *Society and Democracy in Germany* from 1965, for instance, the liberal sociologist Ralf Dahrendorf dismissed Meinecke's work as a series of vague musings on hypostasized world forces such as technology, power, and modern humankind. Without any analysis of the particular social structure and political constitution of Germany, Dahrendorf argued, Meinecke did not have the means to formulate an empirically grounded and plausible account of how National Socialism was possible in Germany and cast recent history as an outburst of people's demonic impulses. Meinecke subsequently came to the most hackneyed and unhelpful of conclusions. Rather than identifying specific failures in the political system and ways to begin the work of reform, he proposed that Germans should retreat from politics altogether and care for the sacred heritage of Goethe's time.[24] The idea of founding "Goethe congregations" encapsulated the postwar obliviousness and evasiveness of traditionalist German thinkers and academics writing on the recent past, their combination of "disbelief and denial."[25]

Without wanting to redeem Meinecke's faith in the healing powers of Goethe, one can still pay a little more attention to the way in which he thinks the return to the cultural heritage should be organized and mediated. And here we can discern the neglected significance of ideas of sociability in postwar visions of Germany. Meinecke first disputes that individuals in isolation from one another can initiate the cultural renewal, although it may seem that profound reflection and art appreciation requires a sphere of solitude. In fact, the reconnection with sacred heritage of Goethe's time must include a sense of how its great representatives explored and realized the idea of spiritual education together. They came together freely in friendships that constituted "small circles," and when they devoted themselves to musical performances, for instance, they did so in free, unceremonious, and spontaneous ways.[26] Such a mode of voluntary and relaxed association in intimate circles, Meinecke continued, can hardly be reproduced in an organizational age with a bureaucratic system of schooling and examination or state-funded symphony orchestras offering regular concerts. Yet some compromise between the unforced association of individuals and stable organizational structure must be found, he maintained, because the institutions of cultural life have been disrupted or closed due to the war and less regulated gatherings must now take the place of ruined institutions. Meinecke's solution was weekly meetings of local "Goethe congregations" all over Germany, apparently without designated leaders, at which people would listen to poetry and music, perhaps inspired by one of the suggested programs in a yet-to-be-written handbook.

As the overview makes clear, Meinecke's call for a return to Goethe possesses a distinctly social dimension. His proposal looks back to a golden age of small circles of friendship and reflects concerns about the postwar lack of books and venues. He wants the Goethe congregations to imitate or at least commemorate the social interactions of Goethe's age, find the right level of organization to ensure stability and regularity without stifling spontaneity, and compensate for the paucity of cultural offerings in the aftermath of war. The resulting body would come quite close to but not pass into the form of the *Verein,* defined as a legally recognized voluntary association or club whose members are devoted to the pursuit of some common activity or goal, be it charity, the preservation of local traditions, or art appreciation. Not coincidentally, Meinecke admitted that his Goethe communities might seem to compete with the already established *Goethegesellschaft,* a Weimar-based association founded to promote Goethe's legacy, but argued that no one group could monopolize Goethe. He wanted the Goethe communities to recapitulate not only the friendship networks of the luminaries of the Goethe age, but the bourgeois forms of clubs and organizations in what the historian Thomas Nipperdey has called the "age of associations," the late eighteenth and early nineteenth centuries, during which, as enterprising economic agents with no designated position in old feudal or religious orders, individuals began to satisfy their need for fellowship by voluntarily forming or joining *Vereine.*[27]

In sum, Meinecke did not simply suggest a return to Goethe the author of works of unparalleled greatness. Rather, he found in the age of Goethe, or in the age of the association, a form of casual but regularized interaction, a social life of "small circles" tied together by multiple friendships, some modified version of which would be necessary in the present moment. He was first and foremost a traditional custodian of the German high cultural canon and especially of the heritage of the *Weimarer Klassik,* but it is not unimportant that the encounter with that culture was to take place in the domain of free association, in *Gemeinden* or *Gesellschaften,* which are voluntary, noncoercive, and depend on the self-organized coordination of interested individuals. In the absence of a settled cultural life with stages and orchestras and political groups such as parties, and most significantly, in the absence of independent German statehood, Meinecke was exploring available models of what he called the generation of community. What provides unity, he asked, when the German state had been "shattered [*zerschlagen*]"? And his answer was voluntary associations beyond the family but without explicit economic or professional goals. Some form of sociability would help reconstitute Germany.[28]

Contrary to standard judgments, then, Meinecke was not just a custodian of culture, hopelessly out of touch with the demands of the postwar situation, but did envision, in a vocabulary that may seem antiquated, a specific form of social life that could operate despite the lack of an intact German state. Like Sternberger and other contemporary intellectuals, Meinecke saw in sociability a possible response to the problems of the postwar period. And it is by focusing on the previously overlooked importance of further scenes and visions of bourgeois sociability that the present book seeks to make a number of interrelated points. It connects the work of political theorists such as Arendt, Schmitt, and Habermas in a new way by introducing them as advocates or critics of bourgeois sociability as a protopolitical form of association. It recasts Habermas's seminal study *The Structural Transformation of the Public Sphere* as the end point of a discussion on the form and role of sociability in the history of bourgeois society rather than as the foundational text for a succeeding debate on the public sphere. Finally, it uncovers a postwar intellectual conflict beyond the left/right division by looking at the multifaceted non-Marxist or non-socialist accounts of bourgeois sociability.

The cumulative result of this enterprise is a narrative that differs from the prevailing accounts of German intellectual life after 1945. The constellation of thinkers who offer probing examinations of the character and value of practices of sociability cannot, for instance, be easily divided along traditional political or ideological lines. Familiar dichotomies such as the open or the closed society, restoration or renewal, conservative nationalist Germans, or progressive non-nationalist Germans do not necessarily capture the questions that animate the projects under consideration and therefore may not do full justice to the thinkers' multiple affinities and alignments. We can come to a more differentiated understanding of the central intellectual concerns and disputes of postwar Germany once we recognize the collection of thinkers as exponents of, or opponents to, key aspects of sociable interconnection in bourgeois society.

To understand how this project deviates from established narratives and customary polarities, it is necessary to look at the literature on the period. Much of the research on postwar German history is structured by a widespread interest in two confluent concerns, namely the imperative to confront, directly and without reserve, the National Socialist past and the will to found a truly participatory, tolerant, and rationally oriented liberal-democratic culture in Germany. The intellectual historian Anson Rabinbach speaks of two central tasks after 1945, namely "the confrontation with the Nazi past and the renewal of democratic culture."[29] Interestingly, Rabinbach also considers the journal *Die Wandlung* as a prime example or exponent of these two tendencies: "*Die Wandlung* was the most democratically oriented [journal], and the most emphatic in its insistence on a moral and spiritual reckoning with the Nazi past."[30] To speak in the established shorthand, Germans had to come to terms with the past, a process often referred to as *Vergangenheitsbewältigung*, and emerge as an involved and responsible citizenry in a vivacious public sphere or *Öffentlichkeit*.[31] The first of these moves entailed breaking the silence about the atrocities committed by Germans and talking about past ideological commitments, and the second entailed speaking up as an egalitarian collective to scrutinize political decisions according to a standard of rationality.[32] Without these processes, Germans would be trapped in a state of emotional inertia, unreformed callousness, and political apathy.[33]

These two motifs also belong together in that they both issue in demands for openness and discussion. Germans must disclose rather than deny or repress the crimes they had committed, and the political developments to which they were subject must be transparent and amenable to their influence. In line with this, a leading contemporary scholar of postwar intellectual life calls the development of common values in the Federal Republic an "open process" founded in "open discussions in which rival claims about the meaning of the past were made, modified, and rejected."[34] These demands for openness, with connotations of moral sincerity, political pluralism, and accountability are, moreover, associated with the specific contributions of intellectuals in the 1960s, fifteen or more years after the end of the Second World War. As mentioned above, Habermas published his *The Structural Transformation of the Public Sphere* in 1962, and his Heidelberg friends Alexander and Margarete Mitscherlich came out with *The Inability to Mourn* five years later.[35] If Habermas called for a more deliberative politics in Germany to vitalize the otherwise fragile democracy, Mitscherlich observed how an emotionally stunted German population unable and unwilling to work through the past remained silent when confronted with the fact of German crimes.[36] The political-historical analysis and the psychoanalytic approach to the German postwar silence yielded overlapping ideas about reform: authoritarian habits and sentiments could only be dissolved by means of sustained discussions. It was important to move uncomfortable and demanding topics out of the realm of "undiscussables" and break the "social construction of silence," to quote a recent study of the sociology of pervasive denial and stubborn reticence in troubled societies such as postwar Germany.[37]

This established view of postwar Germany suggests, finally, a clear narrative of at least potential progress along an outlined route. As observers we can plot the collective's successful, or not so successful, trajectory toward a kind of greater loquaciousness in the form of admissions of guilt as well as political transparency and democratization. While commentators have differed in their optimism about the robustness of West Germany's achievement, their estimate of the likelihood of fascist recidivism, or their judgment of the authenticity of direct acknowledgments of past crimes, they have tended to agree on the underlying aim, namely that the nation should transform itself into a more open society able to sustain and productively manage conflicts. Here Ralf Dahrendorf can yet again serve as an example. In his study from 1965, he spelled out the tenets of an open and liberal society and expressed his skepticism of West Germany's ability to satisfy the criteria. His liberal political position can be summarized in the following way: since no one person or group can claim full knowledge or certainty about the world and the best policies for the future, people must allow for and even cultivate a socially rooted political pluralism of political ideas, let multiple factions or parties compete for influence, and ensure that minority positions come to enjoy institutionalized protection.[38] However, in Germany, Dahrendorf continued, the dogmatic enshrinement of one limited and necessarily flawed ideology in the name of harmony and unity had regrettably taken precedence over the responsible articulation of disagreements among groups with different views and interests.

By means of a reconsideration of Sternberger, Schmitt, Arendt, Koselleck, and Habermas, this book suggests a slightly different way of organizing and presenting the intellectual life of the immediate postwar period.[39] Rather than assuming the utility and centrality of the value dichotomy of "open" and "closed," with its connotations of dynamic and static, democratic and undemocratic, rational and irrational, this work brings to the fore a series of more historically textured questions. Do the practices that constitute bourgeois sociability offer a viable template or useful point of departure for a discredited nation on its way to reform itself as a political collective? More specifically, does the kind of discursive interaction that accompanies bourgeois sociability serve as a preparatory stage toward potentially contentious political deliberations, or does it preclude such deliberations? Is there, again, a path from a reintroduced bourgeois sociability, as envisaged by Sternberger, Meinecke, and others, to the desired democratic and liberal polity? Once retrieved as an issue that animates and connects seemingly disparate intellectual projects, the focus on sociability can help us recover a richer sense of the intellectual tendencies and needs of the postwar period, scramble customary divisions of figures into opposing groups, and reconsider established narratives of improvement (or the absence thereof).

To begin with, the focus on sociability as a mode of integration with a discursive dimension will enable us to gain a finer sense of the historical conditions and generic diversity of "talk." Standard invocations of beneficial discussions will then yield to a more detailed look at the character and constraints of conversations, debates, interrogations, and other forms of discursive interactions.[40] How, for instance, does sociable talk in a relaxed atmosphere differ from disciplined deliberations on political issues (an issue addressed in chapter 6)? Or how do interrogations both simulate and subvert genuinely egalitarian conversations (a question dealt with in chapter 2)? Any survey of the postwar discourse in Germany should, this book suggests, include a close look at how diverse conceptions and genres of talk were brought into play, identified as located in and inflected by historical conditions, and assessed for their political content. The intellectuals of the period were themselves engaged in an ongoing scrutiny of the multiple meanings and directions of conversations.

Once sociability emerges as an ambivalent practice, analyzed, coded, and evaluated in different ways, the opposition between the champions of an open versus a closed order, or between silence and speech, becomes somewhat less useful. And when these polarities are complicated and the question of bourgeois sociability comes to guide the study of political thought in the postwar period, the narrative outlined above also undergoes change. A society that returns to the discourse genres particular to bourgeois sociability is not necessarily the most open society, and the most loquacious society not necessarily the most improved. The focus on sociability as a particular mode of integration thus does not generate a story about a collective German journey to greater openness, transparency, and volubility. Instead, it directs us to an analysis of different kinds of discursive mediation and interpersonal talk with different purposes and effects. Can the type of milieu-specific talk that accompanies sociable interaction serve to educate its participants for explicitly political and hence potentially conflict-ridden discussions and engagements? How porous are the boundaries between different types of discourse, such as polite and friendly conversations, on the one hand, or argumentative or polemical debates, on the other? What is the relationship between sociable talk and political argumentation?

As proponents and critics of bourgeois sociability as a foundation for political interaction, the diverse figures dealt with in the chapters—Sternberger, Schmitt, Arendt, Koselleck, and Habermas—complicate a clear-cut division of left-wing and right-wing political thought. Such divisions are entirely legitimate when applied to other intellectual cohorts, and historians of postwar intellectual life have often pitted left against right, or, to offer specific examples, Western Marxists against liberals or neoliberals.

The Frankfurt School intellectuals with Horkheimer and Adorno, for instance, have been credited with the intellectual founding of the Federal Republic. With their moral authority as returning émigrés, their institutional structure within the growing field of social sciences, and their continuous mass media presence, they were able to offer a postwar student generation an encompassing and communal ethos structured around the resistance to modern commodity culture and the moral duty of coming to terms with the past.[41] The critical rationalism of Karl Popper and the market-oriented liberalism of Friedrich Hayek have been suggested as a counterpoint with a significant presence in Germany. While enjoying less immediate resonance than the Frankfurt School, the postwar period saw the mobilization and rejuvenation of various strands of liberal thought that invoked the paradigms of the scientific community of permanent criticism or unregulated market exchanges as foundations of good societies.[42] Popper proposed a society engaged in an open-ended process of trial and error, conjecture and refutation, where policy makers were ready to admit errors and adjust beliefs or actions in response to results. Hayek advocated the dismantling of centralized state planning in favor of a legally protected market as a guarantee against totalitarian developments.

In contrast to these left/right divisions, the collection of thinkers studied in this book are not quite as easily divided into recognizable ideological groups. The works of Schmitt, Koselleck, and Arendt under consideration below are driven by a critical engagement with aspects of bourgeois society, but they do not rely on left-wing or Marxist arguments. They are neither proponents of a liberal order of competing opinions in a marketplace of ideas, nor advocates of a free market of competing economic agents, nor do they employ the vocabulary of class struggle. Even those who value bourgeois sociability, such as Sternberger and Habermas, do not only identify society with strictly economic types of coordination. Bourgeois society, they argue, possesses arenas for both economic and social types of relations, both commerce and conversation, and the latter should receive more attention for its political value than the former. It follows that this study does not primarily treat Habermas as the most important heir of Frankfurt School critical theory, although he of course occupies that role.[43] Rather, Habermas's work on the public sphere is introduced as an informed and ingenious response to preceding analyses of the history and forms of bourgeois sociability.

It has often been claimed that the German economic miracle provided the Federal Republic with a source of pride and identity,[44] that the astonishing prosperity of the postwar period was conducive to political stability and even furnished the German state with legitimacy,[45] and that societal conflicts frequently crystallized around the distribution of wealth. While this book does not dispute the centrality of the economy in the West German imagination, it reconstructs a context of reflection on a parallel mode of integration deemed typical of bourgeois society, namely (noneconomic) sociability. Again, the thinkers treated below look closely at both commerce and conversation and primarily promote, or critique, social rather than economic activity.

The historian Dirk Moses has introduced yet another way of characterizing postwar intellectual groups, one based on a "dualism of subjectivities" generated by divergent responses to a stigmatized German nation.[46] While some intellectuals such as Habermas were horrified by German crimes and called for a profound and lasting transformation of the collectivity in order to make it worthy of any continued solidarity, others sought to make the "national past bearable," for instance by denationalizing the origins of the Nazi disaster and claiming that it represented a pathological modernity rather than a particularly German development.[47] This very illuminating categorization of German intellectuals is, however, a less useful tool by which to understand the range of specific positions covered below. The authors discussed below do frequently speak of Germany as a belated or an exemplary modern nation. The Nazi catastrophe is ascribed to either backwardness or excessive modernization, to either Germany's fateful failure to catch up with Western nations or its corruption by modern pathologies. Yet the diverging assessments of Germany's advancement along a path toward modernity often reflect on prior judgments on the resources of typical bourgeois societies. The passionate advocates of bourgeois sociability as a good school of political conduct, Sternberger and Habermas, are likely to argue that important potentials of bourgeois sociability have remained tragically unrealized in a backward Germany. The equally passionate opponents of bourgeois society, such as Arendt, tend to claim that Germany is in fact a perfectly modern society and that this modernity is the nation's root problem.

To be sure, the thinkers brought together here also differ greatly in the intensity of their affective attachment to Germany. One needs only to think of Schmitt's tortuous apologetics for himself and Germany next to Arendt's sobering postwar observations. Yet the arguments for and against bourgeois sociability do not always correspond to an underlying structure of political emotions aroused by Germany, and the dividing line in the debate over sociability does not quite run between nationalist and non-nationalist Germans. For this reason, the positions will be analyzed as complex arguments rather than manifestations of problematic emotional attachments.[48] A particular affective relationship to the past and the future of the German nation as the source of identity does not necessarily predetermine the approach to the issue of bourgeois sociability and its political potentials.

This leads us to a final comment about the approach of this study. *Sociability and Its Enemies* rereads thinkers concerned with the formation and maintenance of particular kinds of social cohesion, who all in some way posed the question of how the authority or stability immanent in the habits of interaction or forms of interconnection in bourgeois society can allow for or minimize contestation, or how it encourages or eliminates disagreement. This means that Arendt, Koselleck, and Habermas, for instance, do not principally address diversity in terms of a multiplicity of ethnic, cultural, or sexual identities. Their common emphasis on opposing interests or argumentative disputes no doubt reflects the social conditions in Germany before significant developments, such as the influx of immigrant labor or the rise of the feminist movement.[49] Yet Schmitt and Arendt in particular also analyze how dissident positions are sometimes attributed to specific and in some cases pathologized identities, a technique that leads one to neglect the autonomous dynamic of conflictual engagements.

Overview of the Book

The chapters follow a chronological order but employ slightly different interpretive approaches. While the two first chapters, on Sternberger and Schmitt, look more closely at the historical situation in which the authors wrote, and seek to embed their writings in a broader analysis of the conditions of public speech immediately after 1945, the third and fourth chapters analyze the complex structure of historical and theoretical arguments in texts by Arendt and Koselleck. The fifth chapter is similar to the two immediately preceding sections and presents a rereading of Habermas's work on the public sphere in the bourgeois era. The final chapter returns to the historical situation in postwar Germany to review the decline of conviviality in the Federal Republic.

A more detailed description of the chapters will let the overarching trajectory of the book emerge in sharper relief. The first chapter, "Sociability as Reeducation," reconstructs how Karl Jaspers and Sternberger, editors of and prominent voices in the postwar journal *Die Wandlung* in Heidelberg, set out to formulate the principles of a future German community. Using Sternberger in particular, the chapter also explains why the postwar situation led to a turn to bourgeois sociability, or the endeavor to revive *Geselligkeit.*

Equipped with the license to publish an intellectual journal in the American zone in 1945, Jaspers and Sternberger confronted the task of stating the principles of a nonauthoritarian Germany. Given the lack of institutional structures and the uncertainty of the future, this was not an easy task. In their publication, they wanted to distance themselves from National Socialist concepts of a homogeneous race or cohesive German *Volk* and promote an egalitarian and tolerant participatory democracy, but because they collaborated with and were supervised by the American authorities, they also had to temper their claims about the future political shape of Germany. From the outset, they were entrusted with a purely reeducational task and could not appear as lawgivers. Navigating this precarious situation, Sternberger in particular chose to introduce the idea of bourgeois sociability or *Geselligkeit* as a viable transitional ideal for Germans. Conversational practices that embodied ideals of politeness, civility, and friendliness, *Höflichkeit* and *Umgänglichkeit,* would tie people together and thus ensure the continued coherence of Germany in the absence of other institutional supports, but without in itself being openly political. Sociability would even teach Germans to relate to each other smoothly and respectfully and pave the way for some more robustly institutionalized polity still invigorated by nonanonymous deliberations. However, the reeducational program of bourgeois sociability seemed less and less feasible as increasingly vicious disagreements surfaced in and around the pages of the journal. *Die Wandlung* folded in 1949.

Chapter 2, "Conversations and Interrogations," offers a clear contrast to the project of *Die Wandlung.* After 1945, the political theorist and jurist Carl Schmitt, who had joined the Nazi Party and emerged as its most prominent legal scholar before being attacked by flanks within the movement, was interned and interrogated by the American military administration. When released and allowed to publish again in 1949–50, he presented a bitterly critical account of the political and intellectual climate of the immediate postwar period. In his reluctant and strangely self-undermining autobiographical essays, the severely compromised Schmitt critiqued the developing culture of loquacious sociability for its inability to acknowledge its boundaries and its means of managing and neutralizing disagreement. He deemed the seeming absence of visible coercive authorities as either regrettable or illusory and implied that those who did not adhere to the canon and the terminology of the reigning conversational culture were scrutinized and branded as deviant. In short, he viewed the spirit of tolerance promoted by figures such as Jaspers (whom he mentions in his diary) as a screen for hegemony. The Allied forces determined who was allowed to speak and who was not, and thus the invitation to an open discussion about Germany's future was delimited by licenses and other constraints.

More importantly, Schmitt contrasted the call for a civil conversation—a *Gespräch*—with the practice of interrogations that he himself had experienced. The conversation is an egalitarian form of communication in which the interlocutors calmly consider each other's arguments in a polite, respectful, nonconfrontational manner. The interrogation, in contrast, sets up an asymmetrical situation in which all aspects of the questioned person's behavior is inspected for what it reveals about his criminal past, general attitude, and concealed motivations. Schmitt argued that the true form of communication of the postwar period was not the cautious dialogue but the psychologically informed examination. The reeducational imperative undermined the spirit of sociability, a point that Schmitt connected to his earlier, prewar critique of liberal societies.

The third chapter, "The Mob of Bourgeois Society," analyzes how Hannah Arendt presented a dramatic narrative of the disarticulation of traditional communities and their reaggregation as functionally organized composites of estranged atoms in the era of the bourgeoisie. After the war, Arendt resumed contact with her former teacher Karl Jaspers and published an entire series of articles (with titles such as "Organized Guilt") in Sternberger's journal *Die Wandlung*. In fact, her presence in the journal's pages confirmed its openness. Arendt was a Jewish woman writing in America and thus exemplified the editors' efforts to create a more inclusive intellectual community. Yet Arendt's articles did nothing to nurture bourgeois sociability. On the contrary, her dense essays on the historical background of totalitarianism and her polemical interventions in the debate on collective guilt assigned a startling amount of blame to the European bourgeoisie. In her view, the historical bourgeoisie had seen individuals as essentially abandoned and isolated creatures and therefore viewed any collective as a merely temporary and convenient aggregation of discrete units for the purpose of greater productivity or accumulated power. In one of her articles, she even claims that bourgeois society replicates the basic structure of a mob—an organization formed by social outcasts to increase their ability to inflict violence. For Arendt, bourgeois society did not supply a vision of friendly reciprocity that could serve as a transitional ideal on the road toward liberality and democracy in Germany. The most authentic symbol of bourgeois society was, for Arendt, not the salon but the pack of outsiders.

Chapter 4, "Sociability and Hypocrisy," focuses on Reinhart Koselleck, the young historian who studied in Heidelberg, the seat of *Die Wandlung*, and found inspiration in Arendt's early theses on bourgeois society but also entertained intellectual contact with Schmitt. His dissertation, "Critique and Crisis," finished in 1954, reflected the interventions of the preceding years in the coded form of a skeptical history of the rise and outlook of bourgeois society. Indeed, Koselleck's arguments reveal his multiple connections to thinkers such as Schmitt and Arendt. In his work, he reconstructed how the emerging bourgeoisie began to claim that it represented a society freed from arbitrarily imposed dictates. Conditioned by their own experiences in new settings of peaceful sociability, members of the bourgeoisie envisioned how associations could form spontaneously and harmoniously without the coercive rule of a sovereign. Yet Koselleck also claimed that this view involved the misapprehension and disavowal of stark political conflicts. Bourgeois sociability, he argued, does not mend but rather tends to deny fractures between opposing factions, which deepen when they are misunderstood and ignored. Like Schmitt, Koselleck sought to unmask the vision of sociable harmony typical of the bourgeoisie, but without inviting the paranoid suspicions of concealed agendas present in the work of his mentor. Partly following the route of Arendt, Koselleck instead looked at how bourgeois forms of association in the realm of commerce and conversation could not form the basis of a political collective aware of irreconcilable conflicts over principles and values. The ease of sociability could not, he maintained, be extended to cover all modes of activity without a descent into self-deception or hypocrisy.

The fifth chapter reads Jürgen Habermas's early work *The Structural Transformation of the Public Sphere*, published in 1962, as a masterly encapsulation and reassessment of the preceding arguments over sociability. While Habermas's study more or less founded a discourse on the "public sphere," now a standard concept in political theory, history, and media studies, its subtitle—*An Inquiry into a Category of Bourgeois Society*—indicates Habermas's relationship to a preceding discussion. His study is indeed deeply rooted in the intellectual debates covered in the preceding chapters. The germ of Habermas's book was a severely critical review of Koselleck's study, in which he tied Koselleck to Schmitt's polemical approach to politics. Moreover, in the introduction to *The Structural Transformation of the Public Sphere*, Habermas explicitly delineates his concept of the bourgeois public sphere in contrast to

Arendt's and Schmitt's idealizations of the Greek polis and the (medieval) Roman Church, respectively. On the whole, Habermas's book can be read as an attempt to validate the idea that forms of bourgeois sociability—conversations about art and proper conduct in the salons, clubs, and coffeehouses of the early bourgeoisie—did pave the way for an egalitarian and democratic politics, in which governmental decisions were subjected to rational discussions among citizens. There is, Habermas proposed, a continuum between the sites and conventions of bourgeois conviviality and rational, egalitarian politics.

The formidable success of Habermas's book testifies to his skill at saving sociability, thus delivering a late confirmation of attempts by intellectuals such as Sternberger to introduce bourgeois sociability as a preparatory stage of democratic politics. Thanks to the structural clarity of his argument as well as his suggestive historical explorations, Habermas managed to lay the foundations for a debate that would to some extent eclipse the concern with what he himself referred to as "bourgeois forms of sociability."[50] Yet his phenomenal framing did come at some cost. In many ways, Habermas fails to address some of the arguments against bourgeois sociability developed by Schmitt, Arendt, and Koselleck.

As a whole, *Sociability and Its Enemies* recovers and analyzes a vital discussion among major figures of recent political theory, alters established accounts of the central questions and directions in postwar intellectual life, and finally embeds one of the most influential and popular pieces of modern historical sociology in this reconstructed context. Habermas's study of the rise and regrettable decomposition of the bourgeois public sphere reveals itself as an extension of a previously neglected prior discussion of bourgeois sociability and its political meanings and uses.

The sixth and final chapter draws on the research on the cultural and social life in early West Germany to determine whether it was an era of revived bourgeois sociability. The material is ambiguous. Intellectuals might have called for and sought publicly to demonstrate civility and propriety in the immediate postwar period, but the work of cultural historians on West German life points to important counterdevelopments. The early years of the Federal Republic was a time of retreat into the domestic sphere and unprecedented levels of private consumption. Germany after World War II was not a nation of the lively salon or the coffeehouse, despite the initial appeal of such a vision for intellectuals. The chapter ends with a final assessment of the political value of sociability and with a close look at a short story by Alexander Kluge from 1962 that can be seen as a report on bourgeois social life in the 1950s and early 1960s. The story, which describes a typical Rotary meeting, suggests a rather ambivalent picture of postwar German sociability. Kluge's laconic text asks whether the gathering Rotarians are open to multiple arguments or instead convene for the sake of enjoying the comfort of shared prejudices. Thus Kluge's story from 1962 can profitably be read as a coda to the preceding debate on sociability as a basis for political life in Germany.

Chapter One

✦

Sociability as Reeducation: The Program of *Die Wandlung*

"We have lost almost everything: state, economy, the secure conditions of our physical existence, and much worse than that: we have lost the valid norms that bind us together, the moral dignity, the unifying consciousness of a people."[1] Published in November 1945, Karl Jaspers's introductory statement to the first issue of the journal *Die Wandlung* begins with an inventory of losses.[2] In a sense, Jaspers first posits a remaining collective that he then, in the course of the sentence, deprives of content. He invokes a unified "we," but the list of vanished institutional supports that follows is so long that one must wonder what, if anything, holds this collective together.

The collective is no longer guaranteed by a state that embodies its agency, and it does not have the shape of a national household consisting of interdependent parts; it lacks the norms that would connect its members and the consciousness that would meld them together. The "we" that Jaspers invokes is not sustained by some shared possession or spirit, and it may not even enjoy the sense of a shared past, a bundle of recollections to which its former members could look even at the brink of their dispersion.[3] What, in this situation, saves the invoked German collective from irredeemable dissolution? What attenuated bonds still enable and permit the address with which the statement opens?

Jaspers's opening remarks to the journal *Die Wandlung* poses the question of the possible and proper sources of cohesion in a moment of near-total desolation. His own response to this question lies in the rhetorical operation with which he starts off his text. There is still an integrated collective that can be and is addressed, even though it seems defined in the most fragile fashion, by its having lost everything that would ensure its continued existence. If it does linger on, however, it assumes the tenuous and temporary form of a discursive construct. This is in fact Jaspers's project; his statement suggests the persistence of a collective in and through enunciations such as his own, one that has no other substance than the conversation in which its members are still able to engage. The response to the urgent problem of societal cohesion is contained in the words with which Jaspers announces the publication of a journal: "We are allowed to speak to each other publicly. Let us see what we have to say to one another!"[4]

The collective will endure in the exchange of words that Jaspers himself has just commenced. Of course, Jaspers may seem to overemphasize the difficulties and losses that threaten to fragment it in order to downplay a continuity of language and identity that he nonetheless relies on. Yet his voice is neither assured, as if a common future could be taken for granted despite the talk of disintegration, nor anxious, fearful of dissolution. He simply enumerates the foundations that have now been swept away: citizenship, economic ties, established or preconceived notions of moral worth. And then he tries to derive a possible sense of togetherness out of the resulting sparseness. Describing the conditions of institutional vacuum, he even draws an ethos of egalitarian conversation out of the attending disorientation. In circumstances of radical uncertainty, he writes, no single person can assert an authority grounded in superior knowledge, therefore no one can claim the position of a leader. He observes that "no one is a prophet, who can say definitively, what is happening and what must be done."[5] The break with dictatorial party rule and charismatic or prophetic leadership follows from the unpredictability of the situation, which does not allow for anything but a hesitant and nonhierarchical community of speech.

Jaspers grasped the fragility of the postwar moment as an opportunity to form a collective not dominated by an overbearing ruler.[6] This appeal stood in a complex relationship to the contemporary political landscape and the forces that effectively dominated it; it was at one and the same time the expression of a positive vision of renewed intellectual exchange and a response to exigencies.

The journal *Die Wandlung* was published in Heidelberg, the university town located in the American zone. The publication was a so-called license journal. Its editor Dolf Sternberger, a journalist with an academic background and a liberal outlook who had been all but silenced during the years of National Socialism, had contacts with the American administration and managed to secure the right to publish a cultural magazine.[7] The resulting publication was a fairly typical example of the reeducation period. It rested on cooperative efforts between previously censured and marginalized members of a local academic and intellectual elite in search of opportunities to reemerge in the public arena after National Socialism, and a foreign military administration that regulated access to key offices and media but was interested in forming working alliances with native non-Nazi groups in order to gather information and build legitimacy in Germany.[8] *Die Wandlung* was, in other words, a mutually beneficial arrangement, a channel for Germans to speak to Germans, under the supervision of Americans. And due to the general lack of reading material in the immediate postwar months and years, the publication initially enjoyed a readership of tens of thousands of people, rather impressive numbers for a journal that featured scholarly articles by sociologists and philologists, translations of modernist poetry, and some frank discussions of German guilt.

The enthusiasm of the editorial board, its sense of bearing an unparalleled responsibility for the future of the German polity, is evident in the title of the publication, which resonates with an expressionist pathos.[9] The aim of *Die Wandlung* was, according to its editor, nothing less than a transformation of the German spirit.[10] This sense of an ambitious and even exhilarating departure is understandable. In the open and seemingly malleable institutional landscape of 1945–49, groups of intellectuals and writers could understand themselves as the only available and perhaps the only legitimate centers of social and political renewal. For at least a moment, traditionally marginal coteries of scholars and publicists operated in surroundings no longer and not yet completely dominated by established parties and interest groups, and as a consequence, these loose formations of interlocutors joined by personal ties could present themselves as important sites of social organization.

As we shall see, the immediate postwar period seemed to be a time of what we can call miniature institutions, of small cells such as salons, clubs, and voluntary associations, all engaged in conversation. However, the dedication with which the board of *Die Wandlung* approached its perceived task, and the unusually large readership for a journal of its kind, did not necessarily persuade the foreign military administration of its importance. The American officials who oversaw the broader reeducation programs discerned the rather minor place of a "magazine for the intelligentsia" alongside the major sources of news and pedagogic material for the bulk of the German population and accorded it more of an ornamental function. In the words of Robert Wolfe, the American censor stationed in Heidelberg, *Die Wandlung* was a short-lived journal for the intelligentsia "adorned" with contributions by figures such as Jaspers.[11]

The ongoing transactions between German intellectuals and American officials typical of the era of reeducation form the backdrop to the announcements and articles of *Die Wandlung*. Indeed, they remain readable in the texts themselves. Jaspers's opening words, for instance, did more than propose a model of interpersonal communication that had become possible in a space beyond the destroyed or dismantled structures of statehood, commerce, and a taken-for-granted moral culture. He also noted the presence of a foreign administration in Germany and hinted at its role for the prevailing conditions of articulation. He spoke of "the dependence of everything we do on the will of the occupying forces" and admitted how this dependence delimited the journal's project.[12] "Our initiative," he wrote, "is limited to the space [*Spielraum*] that the occupying forces grant us."[13] The fact that *Die Wandlung* received its publication license and, like all similar publications, was continually monitored by American representatives thus entered the announcement of the journal as its basic premise. In wanting to fully exhaust the opportunity for free speech, Jaspers did not forget that it was provided by a foreign government able to guarantee a measure of peace and tranquility after "the end of independent German statehood."[14]

This meant that those who were finally allowed to speak publicly were in a sense *only* allowed to speak. In Jaspers's own words, the "opportunity [*Chance*]" to address each other relied on and was determined by a fixed "permission [*Erlaubnis*]."[15] Jaspers advanced the ideal of a collective that had no foundation external to discourse, but he also revealed how this was a vision structured by the situation. After all, only public discussion was allowed; actual decisions about the future of Germany were not. The definition of the collective as a purely discursive one was a liberating vision but also a consequence of clear constraints. The conversation envisaged by Jaspers would instantiate a spirit of tolerance and negotiation, yet it owed as much to the particular political conditions established during the era of supervised reeducation as it did to the stated goals of this educational process. Liberalization, one could say, was a feature of the transitional process itself.

Dolf Sternberger and the Idea of Postwar Sociability

The fact that Germany was put on hold until its learning period was over gave form to the future collective imagined at the time. Liberality was not just an import from other, more democratic and liberal countries, but to some extent was also an effect of the constraints imposed by those nations during the phase of managed importation. This becomes clear in the articles of Dolf Sternberger, the editor of *Die Wandlung* and its most prolific exponent of the need for fundamental reorientation in Germany. Much like Jaspers, he devoted himself to defining the principles of a viable nonauthoritarian German collectivity, and in the process he had to respond to the same complex of requirements. Sternberger set out to delineate and support an ethos of conversation that could hold Germans together while also preparing them for responsible citizenship and democratic self-governance, but one that would still stop short of any explicit pretension to immediately reconstituted nationhood. The solutions he found to this problem—his vision of a postwar collective—owed their shape to the prevailing demands.

Without the academic background and status of Jaspers, but equally dedicated to a reform of Germany that would meet the peculiar demands of the period, the journalist and publicist Sternberger sought to invoke a resilient impulse of human solidarity. He did this by recalling an idiom of sociability and making frequent use of concepts such as *Umgänglichkeit* (affability), *Höflichkeit* (politeness), and *Geselligkeit* (sociability). He, too, wished to promote discursive exchange, but he embedded his call for interpersonal talk in depictions of civil and refined behavior in specific, recognizably *bürgerliche* settings. Inclined to find an evocative source of inspiration for a desolate present, he chose to promote sociability as a habit of enjoyable and circumspect social interaction, which he took to have a specifically bourgeois provenance.[16]

Sternberger's program, which we will explore in more detail below, is summed up in a 1949 essay on aspects of the *bürgerliche* character: "The more we become 'Bürger,' who determine our own fate and form our own state in society and through sociability . . . the more civil things will become [Je mehr wir Bürger werden, die in Gesellschaft und Geselligkeit ihr Geschick selber machen und ihren Staat selber bilden . . . desto ziviler kann es zugehen]."[17] Sternberger envisioned Germans gradually becoming citizens, but imagined how they would initially be drawn and held together through conviviality or mutual friendliness. Voluntary interaction informed by an ideal of civility would help independent individuals to congregate without reliance on some preconstituted, external source of authority. There could be, Sternberger suggested, a path from sociability to collective self-determination.

Looking back on his efforts in another 1949 intervention, in full knowledge that the journal was about to fold owing to financial difficulties, Sternberger even pointed to the publication itself, *Die Wandlung*, as an exemplary locus of polite and sociable interaction. The relationship between the journal's contributors and its readership was, he claimed, characterized by a sense of friendliness, a "Moment der Geselligkeit."[18]

Indeed, when calling the editorial board a "free group"[19] and describing the connections between German-speaking writers inside and outside Germany in terms of a "tender net of beneficial friendship,"[20] he quite consciously recalled the notion of people convening for the enjoyment of company and discussion in places separate from those reserved for the pursuit of material interests. *Die Wandlung* had been produced within an intimate but not exclusive "circle," a "net" in which every member was concerned above all with the cultivation of friendly reciprocity.[21]

This self-description, formulated at the end of *Die Wandlung*'s existence, may seem hopelessly vague, but as indicated, it had been preceded by a series of diagnostic and anecdotal texts in which Sternberger tried to connect the adumbrated ideal of interpersonal talk to a more concrete and recognizable historical context. In articles with titles such as "Aspects of the Bourgeois [*bürgerlichen*] Character," he claimed that the ideal of civilized conduct and conversational reciprocity, the comportment specific to *Geselligkeit,* had its proper home in the era of the *bürgerliche Gesellschaft*. Even though the conventions of politeness (*Höflichkeit*) may have originated around courts (*Höfe*), it was still a mode of behavior sustained and refined within a class committed to genuine conversation and tactful interaction among equals rather than to the ostentatious display of rank.[22] Pressed, like Jaspers, to conjure up a mode of integration in a time of institutional uncertainty, Sternberger tried to evoke a social world of circles and networks where membership would be freely chosen and where all interactions would be tolerant and civil, but tied it more closely to a particular sociohistorical epoch. Sociability was, or at least ought to be, an essential feature of postfeudal or nonaristocratic society.

Sternberger's interest in the *Geselligkeit* particular to *bürgerliche Gesellschaft* may seem to involve little of substance, and mostly results in somewhat bland celebrations of the journal's amiable character: "Every one of the journal's editors and contributors stepped forward as an individual, a person. And yet they formed with one another, and with the readers whose participation was always to be felt, a society [*Gesellschaft*]."[23] Yet a dismissal of Sternberger's project would be unfair, for it does not capture the full reeducational significance of sociability. With his insistence on *Geselligkeit,* Sternberger in fact wanted to address specifically German pathologies that, to his mind, had contributed to the National Socialist seizure of power. His wish to reinvigorate social discourse was not simply a way to acquaint the readership with a historically grounded ideal of conversation, but also included a program of psychosocial treatment that would undo the historical deformation of the German *Bürger.*

How, according to Sternberger, was sociability supposed to work as a therapy for the figure of the German *Bürger*? In agreement with many later diagnosticians of the German problem, Sternberger subscribed to the idea that Germany had taken a "separate path" and been delayed in its movement toward modernity and that the major deficiency of his nation consisted in the weak political assertiveness of the native bourgeoisie.[24] This rudimentary analysis of the peculiar social relations in Germany was unremarkable in itself. Many analysts have claimed that territorial fragmentation or a state bureaucracy in the hands of a traditional aristocracy had prevented the emergence of political liberalism in the German lands, which in turn entailed a lag in the relationship between economic and political development. Ralf Dahrendorf, for instance, writes about the German bourgeoisie's willing submission to older and more established authorities, its failure to commit to a coherent set of liberal values throughout its unfulfilled historical existence, and even calls it the "bourgeoisie that wasn't one [*jene Bourgeoisie, die keine war*]."[25] However, Sternberger's solution to this pernicious belatedness, or his outline of a reeducational therapy, centrally involves the promotion of sociability. It is in this context that his notion of sociability receives clearer contours and emerges as a consistent program.

In his journal articles on the features of Prussian pedagogy or aspects of the bourgeois character, Sternberger claimed that the prototypical German *Bürger* had stiffened in his commitment to affect-control, self-discipline, and incorruptibility and that these values had ultimately made him vulnerable to the lure of dictatorial rule. Only dictatorship, the German *Bürger* had falsely thought, would embody the values of discipline and strong rule. When tracing the genesis and evolution of this character ideal, Sternberger first claimed that the German bourgeoisie's search for a cultural identity set apart from the aristocracy had compelled it to embrace sobriety and sexual purity as markers of good, ethical conduct. The bourgeois attempt to claim a specifically moral legitimacy entailed something like the formation of a distinct corporeal disposition. Sternberger again and again refers to the "fortified fear of touch [*gepanzerte Berührungsfurcht*]"[26] particular to the *Bürger* armored with moral character, or this figure's fearful resistance to "foreign influences."[27] These ideals were, he claimed, clearly on display in early bourgeois tragedies, dramas that typically revolved around the fantasy of princes and aristocrats seeking to seduce the virgin daughters of bourgeois families.

The corporeally coded means of self-definition in an ongoing conflict with an aristocratic class may seem irrelevant to the twentieth century, which also saw other conflicts, for instance between the bourgeoisie and the working class. Yet Sternberger argued that the early phase of bourgeois society had far-reaching political consequences, well into the modern period. Sternberger observed, one could say, a feudal overhang in German history. As the traditional, aristocratic groups continued to monopolize the affairs of government in Germany into the nineteenth century—all according to the thesis of a separate path—the bourgeoisie defensively associated them with intrigue and deception and sought comfort in their own purely moral superiority, most forcefully demonstrated on the level of sexual control.[28] Politics in the sense of an ongoing search for influence over legislation through persuasion and alliance building, arguing and bargaining, came to be seen as a perennial threat to a commendably upright and austere character. In other words, once the libertine conduct of the aristocracy had become entwined with the practice of political governance, the typical *Bürger* could tell himself that he opted out of politics in order not to have his character spoiled.

The resulting bourgeois admiration for icons of integrity such as Bismarck was, Sternberger concluded, politically disastrous, insofar as it made the class receptive to the early propaganda of the National Socialist movement, with its promises of steely resolve beyond the bickering of Weimar party politics. The German bourgeoisie's acceptance of an extremist movement intent on abolishing citizen participation was nearly automatic because of its historical roots in an embodied set of values. The German *Bürger*'s insistence on frugality, rectitude, and continence—at bottom a historically conditioned "secret position of class warfare" against an overbearing and excessive aristocracy[29]—proved all too easy to manipulate by a party leadership that claimed to want to eliminate all political tactics.

In light of Sternberger's analysis of the bourgeois fear of physical contact and its long-term political effects, it becomes clear that the idea of revivified sociability in the postwar period has a therapeutic and even bodily dimension. To remove the inculcated impediment to active participation in common affairs, Sternberger did not set out to divorce politics from any unfortunate sexual connotations and instead present it as a worthwhile, ascetic pursuit. Rather, he exploited the established association and proposed means by which the German bourgeoisie, or what was left of it, could come to accept the previously refused sensuality within the frame of its own (unfulfilled) tradition and, by this route, come to engage more in politics. Sternberger in fact sought to insert the pleasant and variegated conversation implied by sociability as a means to a postwar defrosting of the *bürgerliche* character, to making it more open to light sensuality.

The primary historical site of *Geselligkeit* was for him the salon, which he conceived of as a mixed-sex setting located in a middle ground between familial and public zones. As a venue that draws together people from different walks of life and provides them with the opportunity to engage in conversation with one another, salon sociability allows for a kind of tangential contact between various fields of experience, something Sternberger captures in the phrase "touching spheres [*Berührung der Sphären*]."[30] Yet the metaphor also alludes to the promise of lightly tactile encounters in a space that is not strictly gendered. Genuine sociability, Sternberger implied but did not quite spell out, requires the presence of women. This separates his program from the tradition of exclusively male sociability, represented by, for instance, the Masonic lodges. As the historian Stefan Ludwig Hoffmann has noted, the German Freemasons constructed, through the use of special venues and intricate rituals, intimate and exclusive social spaces for both leisurely relaxation and sincere edification, *Vergnügen* and *Bildung*. But these allowed for the bonds of fraternity or sociability only among men.[31]

Sternberger's covert therapeutic move thus involved breaking the spell of the bourgeois character and dissolving the constitution of the German body, with its "armor,"[32] by exposing it to the mildly sensual practice of *Geselligkeit* as a scenario with a (frustrated) bourgeois history.[33] If only the German bourgeoisie, or those who considered themselves the legatees of this class, could interact a little more fluidly and perhaps even flirtatiously, Sternberger maintained, the rigid ethos of character that ultimately prepared the ground for dictatorship could be remedied for the future. In his concluding article in the final issue of *Die Wandlung,* Sternberger underscores that the editorial board wanted to eschew poses of (manly) struggle and cultivate instead the free and "floating" connections among friends as well as disparate themes of discussion.[34] This, then, was Sternberger's paradoxical postwar narrative of German culture: in the case of the Germans, a greater acceptance of some degree of promiscuity within the unthreatening frame of light sociability could promote a greater willingness to take political responsibility. There was, in other words, a path from bourgeois sociability to political action.

Writing just after the Second World War and the fall of Nazism, Sternberger wanted to stress the importance of free and egalitarian discussion, much like his fellow editor Karl Jaspers, but with the difference that he tied this ideal to a conception of *Geselligkeit*. This makes his reeducational program rather complex. In his writings for the journal, sociability appears as a form of discursive exchange with a concealed sensual dimension designed to dissolve the inflexible character ideal of the German bourgeoisie. *Geselligkeit* would entail discursive exchange and public or semipublic discussion, which both Jaspers and Sternberger deemed crucial after 1945, but it was also attached to a therapy targeted at the fortified body of the anxious German *Bürger.*

Postwar Sociability and the Redefinition of the *Bürger*

In his writings in *Die Wandlung,* Sternberger hoped that the *Bürger* of some future and independent Germany would first be able to come together in sociability, "in Gesellschaft und Geselligkeit," but he simultaneously ascribed to this sociable activity a crucial pedagogic value. In effect, he invoked sociability as a possible relaxation therapy for anxious and rigidified members of the German bourgeoisie, who throughout the nineteenth and twentieth centuries had fatally written off politics as a source of corrupting influence.

Yet Sternberger's focus on sociability harbored further culturally strategic advantages. What could have been the attraction of sociability for Sternberger right after 1945, beyond the hoped-for therapeutic effect? The answer to this question possesses several dimensions, which can be uncovered with the help of recent historical research on the pressures of the immediate postwar period. A *bürgerliche* form of conviviality could first of all serve as a soothing practice after years of war, and a civil antidote to a quasi-military hierarchy, but also as an immaterial practice that could be maintained in spite of economic precariousness. In addition, voluntary interactions among cultured individuals could provide a desirable ideal for an intellectual who set out to generate a sense of collectivity despite the dissolution of clearly defined and independent German statehood. In other words, *Geselligkeit* could help redefine the identity of apprehensive members of the German bourgeoisie, while at the same time providing a much-needed mode of social cohesion not reliant on the integrity of an intact German state. In sum, sociability represented a sort of comprehensive package of cultural reforms, a bundle of values and outlined behaviors that fit the economically and politically turbulent times.

Sternberger's move was to speak of the resurrection, or belated emergence, of the German *Bürger,* but in his articles he tied this figure to a life of *Gesellschaft und Geselligkeit* (association and sociability). The program may have resonated with the readership precisely because of the turn away from a hortatory rhetoric of endless struggle and heroic sacrifice. "The fighter," Sternberger wrote, "may find a following [*Gefolgschaft*], but no companionship [*Gesellschaft*]."[35] After years of National Socialist rule predicated on the subservience of all areas of life to a totalitarian project and incessant mobilization, the notion of a *bürgerliche Gesellschaft* conjured up associations of a calmer order with walls separating personal and professional spheres, as well as a life of moderation and modest pleasures, such as conversations among good friends and acquaintances.[36]

But while an idiom of militancy and urgency may have been ill suited to the war-weary public of the postwar period, a return to some of the comforts of an earlier incarnation of the German *Bürgertum* also risked sounding like an empty promise. After 1945, there were many nervous *Bürger*, self-identified members of a destabilized economic and academic elite, who wondered if they still belonged to a coherent social formation.[37] A future Germany may continue to need the services of executives, bankers, judges, governmental officials, professors, physicians, and ministers, but many nonetheless asked whether the people in these professions and positions would still inhabit a contoured social world permeated by traditions. Would they be united by a sense of a common value-based identity and specific set of societal duties? Would they enjoy wide recognition as a coherent formation with a special and indeed enviable status, distinct from other groups in German society? And most crucially, would they be able to count on the security and independence afforded only by protected private property? After all, the first half of the twentieth century had done much to erode the very idea of economic security.

The historian Klaus Tenfelde, among others, has recounted the multiple twentieth-century crises and indicated how each one seemed to hollow out the substance of the *Bürgertum*. The inflation of the interwar period eliminated the savings of countless upper-middle-class families and ruptured lines of inheritance; a further world economic crisis strained incomes; war bombings destroyed homes and estates; mass deportations involved, among other things, expropriation; and the many businessmen and academics who had supported the NSDAP had to face denazification procedures that, at least temporarily, barred them from work.[38] In the immediate postwar period, then, the traditional *Bürgertum,* defined by its intellectual and economic capital, its *Bildung und Besitz*, seemed a severely damaged and decimated class.

A rather nervous article published in the *Frankfurter Allgemeine Zeitung* in 1950 captured the prevailing postwar mood by asking whether the German bourgeoisie was finished ("Hat der deutsche Bürger ausgespielt?")[39] Moreover, the article explicitly referred to the problem of economic autonomy. Even though the immediate threat of poverty had begun to lift around 1950, the prospect of working in a large-scale corporation or an anonymous bureaucracy still seemed to prevent the reemergence of the *Bürgertum* in the classical sense. "We do not possess anything any longer," the newspaper's editor wrote, "and we have ended up in the insecure material existence of dependent wage earners."[40]

This lament presupposes that genuine individual agency must be grounded in command over private property. Personal self-determination can only become efficacious, and also manifest to and acknowledged by others, when an individual enjoys full freedom to enjoy private possessions rather than be subject to the will and generosity of others.[41] Moral and political autonomy must be grounded in indisputably exclusive ownership. It follows, then, that half a century of economic upheavals would have injured the self-image of the *Bürgertum*'s members. If only a handful of people in German society could enjoy the stability of private property, a larger social class traditionally defined by its exclusive control over a clearly demarcated material domain would surely meet its demise.

In part, the widespread concern with the material basis of a *bürgerliche Gesellschaft* explains Sternberger's focus on civil discussion as a practice that should be claimed and fully explored by the German *Bürgertum*. To be sure, he is not insensitive to the importance of possessions for self-identified *Bürger.* In a brief 1948 article entitled "Bürgerlichkeit," he observed how "erratic and careless" his generation has become in its handling of "possessions of all kinds," a symptom of its having lost faith in the durability and significance of property.[42] Yet Sternberger's emphasis on sociability was a consciously crafted response to the greater vulnerability of *Besitz* as a pillar of the German *Bürgertum.* Focusing more on the demands and benefits of social conduct than on issues of material independence, Sternberger tried to circumvent the issue of economic autarchy and security and its possible foundational importance for the realization of and commitment to individual freedom. He even declared the survival of *Bürgerlichkeit* after the probable disintegration of a *Bürgertum* defined exclusively in terms of economic autonomy (*wirtschaftliche Selbstständigkeit*).[43] A *bürgerliche* society, he insisted, should be most prominently characterized by voluntary, noncoercive sociability, or qualities such as "companionableness [*Umgänglichkeit*]." In an uncertain economic situation, conversation and politeness could and should take precedence over commerce and property as essential facets of bourgeois society.

Sternberger's attempt to detach the *Bürger* from the ties to property and promote sociability thus represents an effort to calm an embattled constituency by reorienting its identity around a different set of values. When the confidence in material assets has been eroded, his statements imply, there are immaterial ones of conduct and performance encoded in the concepts of politeness, companionableness, and sociability. But Sternberger's shift in emphasis from property to protocols of behavior was simultaneously meant to broaden the appeal of this program, to make it less class-based and more malleable and inclusive. In a sense, the conduct of sociable interaction can be more widely distributed and shared than private property, and thus Sternberger's emphasis on sociability over ownership, or on *Bürgerlichkeit* over *Bürgertum,* was also designed to enhance the integrative potential of his proposed ideal. Indeed, Sternberger actively worked to lessen the polemical force lodged in the very notion of the *Bürger.* He wanted, he quite explicitly indicated in his central article on the history of the antipolitical character, to abandon the idea that the *Bürger* was the label for a class identity in the socialist sense and make it more encompassing.

This move, too, can be better understood against the historical changes of the time. As the journalist Stig Dagerman reported in his portrait of the Hamburg lawyer (discussed in the introduction), the general situation of scarcity and need in Germany had, at least according to some "bourgeois ideologists," served to flatten class hierarchies and make the German people more homogeneous. While this economic situation clearly put the identity of self-identified individual *Bürger* under pressure, it also arguably helped to diminish the salience of class antagonism in postwar society, a development with a paradoxical consequence: the borders of the *Bürgertum* seemed to become more open to what the historian Manfred Hettling has termed a kind of social "osmosis."[44] As discrepancies faded, Hettling asserts, a more softly defined *Bürgertum* could become a more widely affirmed identity.

In a similar vein, the historian Hans Ulrich Wehler has argued that the notion of a *Bürgertum* ceased to function as the name for a particular cohort sharply distinguished from the nobility and the proletariat after 1945, mostly because these two latter classes seemed to fade away somewhat in postwar Germany. When two traditional "enemy camps," the aristocracy and the working class, increasingly lost definition, the notion of the *Bürgertum* or a *bürgerliche Gesellschaft* did not so much lose relevance or disappear as become more integrative.[45] In the early postwar period, these two concepts seemed vague enough to function as points of identification of broad segments of the population, but were still exclusive enough to retain some power of definition. The notion of a *bürgerliche Gesellschaft* could, for example, continue to serve as a welcome contrast to the socialist ideal of a society of laborers.

Sternberger's use of sociability in redefining the German *Bürger* represents a combination of reassurance and expansion. By highlighting the virtues of conviviality, he sought to preserve a distinct *bürgerliche* form of life while at the same time making it less obviously exclusive. The apprehensive members of an old *Bürgertum* were told that their identity still mattered, yet that identity was also gradually opened up to others.

Finally and importantly, Sternberger's investment in the idea of sociability was also a response to the contemporary institutional vacuum. Like Jaspers, Sternberger was searching for a model of collective life that seemed separate from more robust political structures, such as a clear center of power equipped with the monopoly of violence over a specified territory. By invoking the idea of *Geselligkeit* as a mode of interaction within an idealized *bürgerliche Gesellschaft,* Sternberger found a way of speaking about those "dimensions of social life which cannot be confounded with, or swallowed up in the state."[46] Knowing very well that he was active in an uncertain period of interregnum, he turned to a notion of collective self-organization that did not necessarily require a centralized source of agency.

With his insistence on *Gesellschaft und Geselligkeit,* association and sociability, Sternberger could even lean on the history of political thought. The notion of civil or bourgeois society appeared and gained currency at a specific historical moment, as a mode of integration dependent neither on the state and its means to ensure cohesion, nor on purely economic or contractual relations.[47] Indeed, the notion in many ways constituted a response to a crisis in the political imagination.[48] In the seventeenth and eighteenth centuries, an epoch of collapsing monarchical governments, political philosophy could no longer plausibly invoke sources of transcendent order such as a divine will or a dynastic regent to make claims about the organization of increasingly autonomous individuals. Instead it tried to counteract centrifugal forces by locating mechanisms of coherence in the workings of the social community itself. Political thinkers began to picture society as a self-sustaining entity, held together by myriad interpersonal loyalties as well as people's natural inclination toward gregariousness and a fundamental need for relationships of mutual regard. Authority was transferred from traditional institutional bodies and attributed to autonomous processes of interaction among people. In the resulting vision of a self-adjusting social whole, the foundation of a unified world of human affairs resided not in an entity external to that world, but in the spontaneous mutual attraction and coordination of its members—an answer to the problem of reimagining communal stability in the modern world.

In need of concepts of cohesion, Sternberger could turn to sociability as a viable model of integration. Society or the *Gesellschaft*, he claimed, could survive and acquire a modicum of stability in the rarefied medium of respectful conversations between people bonded by mutual sympathy. Behind his invocations of politeness and companionableness, one discovers a model of society able to sustain its own existence without the aid of an outside political agency.[49] Or, to put it differently, in a time when Germany was being divided up, war had laid the country to waste, the organization and distribution of political or state authority seemed unclear and unstable, and recent concepts of strong national unity such as the National Socialist *Volksgemeinschaft* had become politically impossible, *Geselligkeit* could provide at least a flickering sense of meaningful cohesion. Neither economic insecurity nor political uncertainty would completely cancel out conviviality.

In his extended discussion of the *bürgerliche* character, Sternberger imagined that the *Bürger* who would come to accept sociability as a practice with a sensual dimension could also be persuaded to participate more in political deliberations, something that this rigid figure had previously deemed corrupting. In the proposed narrative of (belated) development, postwar *Geselligkeit* would finally lure the stiffened German *Bürgertum* out of its shell of purity and soften its rigid stance against erotically coded contaminations. Yet looking at the challenges of the postwar period more broadly, Sternberger's promotion of sociability emerges as a multilayered strategy of cultural reform. The program allowed Sternberger to address the need for intact realms of bourgeois identity in a situation of economic hardship, to make this identity more mobile and less exclusive, but also to indicate sources of societal cohesion in the absence of independent German statehood. Germans would be able to come together in *Geselligkeit,* a sphere of companionship and interaction of which they could not be deprived, despite foreign occupation and a frayed sense of secure ownership. The notion of the *bürgerliche Gesellschaft* characterized by sociability suggested the possibility of an ostensibly weak and noninstitutional but nonetheless resilient self-organizing capacity of societal interaction, one that would also contrast with endless military struggle and even serve to prepare Germans for a common future of political responsibility.

As we shall see, however, there were also a number of problems with this program, for the integrative function of *Geselligkeit* would prove to be at odds with the task of training Germans politically, if this training would in any way include the management and resolution of conflicts rather than their supple evasion. The short history of the journal *Die Wandlung* itself would reveal that the capacity of sociable discourse to integrate diverse individuals ultimately depended on the possibility of containing, or denying, the existence of schisms.

Sociability After 1945

After this review of Sternberger's vision of how Germans would first forge bonds through the conduct of *Geselligkeit* to gradually emerge as responsible *Bürger* willing to participate in political affairs and determine their collective fate, one might impatiently ask whether his proposals corresponded to any actual development in postwar Germany. Did Germans in fact begin to long for sociable interaction, form circles of friendly discussion, or join clubs for light companionship? And did such trends in any way constitute a kind of internal reeducation process, through which people became accustomed to vigorous debates over shared problems? Sternberger's ideas for a broadened notion of *Bürgerlichkeit* defined by sociability may have been tailor-made for the time but still not resonated with their intended audience.

To begin with, Sternberger was certainly not alone in his enthusiasm for the small circle of amiable but earnest discussion. The years of the immediate postwar period were an age of proliferating communities of discourse. The historian Dirk van Laak depicts how German intellectuals and academics eager to reconstruct some form of intellectual infrastructure and orient themselves in an uncertain political situation frequently gathered in associations to conduct conversations, often in a ruminating, existentialist tone. The postwar period was, he writes, the great era of more or less stable circles of conversation.[50] This trend was noticeable across the political spectrum, and often enough, the point of the circles was precisely to bring together representatives of different persuasion in an atmosphere of mutual goodwill and ecumenical exchange beyond petty squabbles.

In his survey of the intellectual climate of the immediate postwar period, van Laak even claims that intellectual collectives tended to recapitulate the development of bourgeois society from the early Enlightenment formation of local clubs, lodges, and salons to the eventual crystallization of a coherent bourgeois public sphere as the medium for the articulation of public opinion. (From the perspective of this study, van Laak applies a Habermasian concept to a historical situation that may actually have influenced, in a highly mediated way, the very formation of Habermas's theory itself.) Van Laak's examples of such miniature institutions and circles include the Gesellschaft Imshausen, initiated by left-wing Catholic journalist Walter Dirks and Eugen Kogon, the author of *Der SS-Staat,* and devoted to themes such as the future possibility of a Christian socialism. He also mentions the Heidelberger Aktionsgruppe zur Demokratie und zum freien Sozialismus, which included members such as Alexander

Mitscherlich and Max Weber's brother, the sociologist Alfred Weber, who also served on the editorial board of *Die Wandlung*. After 1947, this Heidelberg group started organizing conferences with over a hundred participants.

The most famous of these postwar circles of discussion, however, is no doubt Gruppe 47, which would later emerge as the dominant literary grouping of the 1950s and 1960s, its name serving as a constant reminder of its roots in the early postwar period. The group is best known for organizing yearly gatherings with some of the most prominent authors of the Federal Republic, such as Heinrich Böll, Hans Magnus Enzensberger, Günter Grass, and Martin Walser, and acting as a sort of "literary stock exchange" that determined the success of young authors invited to give readings and respond to criticism from the colleagues and professional literary critics that made up the audience. But this ambulating literary capital of West Germany began as a small group of friends welded together by their shared experiences as soldiers and prisoners of war in American camps.[51] In other words, Gruppe 47 represented yet another coterie devoted to conversations on culture and literature with a disposition of brooding sincerity, and as such it was affiliated with Sternberger's vision of how "tender net[s]" of friendship would be crucial to the return to civil life and the reconstitution of a demilitarized German collective. For the members of Gruppe 47 as for Sternberger, the organizational template was not the political party, the cohort of fighting ideological comrades, the productive profit-driven enterprise, or the family, but the egalitarian cluster of friends dedicated to conversations.

To inscribe Gruppe 47 in a history of postwar *Geselligkeit* in this way may of course seem to ignore the literary group's austere focus on the craft of writing as well as the left-wing commitments of many of its members. (Günter Grass and Hans Magnus Enzensberger would hardly have regarded themselves as legatees of the sociable *Bürgertum*.) Yet the present book is not the first to remark on the dimension of sociability in the group's constitution. Looking back at his own participation in the Gruppe 47 meetings, the author and filmmaker Alexander Kluge, to whom we will return in the sixth and final chapter, has suggested that its central figure, the writer Hans Werner Richter, solved the "question of organization" by keeping the numbers of attendees manageable, skillfully blocking any debates that would fracture the group, and always playing the jovial host.[52] According to Kluge, Richter assumed the role of someone who was inviting friends and acquaintances to meetings and remained responsible for the event yet was never inclined to exercise authority in a hierarchical fashion. However committed individual authors may have been to radical political agendas, the meetings were couched in the "habits" and "rituals" of sociable interaction.[53]

Circles of discussion and literary clubs with regular meetings represented a preferred mode of association among authors and intellectuals in the postwar period. The year 1947 was, one could say, the year of the group. While this may seem to be a phenomenon in a relatively exclusive segment of society, historians have also noted that larger groups of Germans came together in similar ways to pursue mundane leisure activities that can nonetheless be understood as examples of *Geselligkeit*.

In a recent book, Klaus Nathaus argues that the immediate postwar period witnessed a reemergence of "organized sociability," a label referring to permanent associations devoted to some shared nonpolitical and noneconomic activity that allow individuals to enter into contact and form bonds with others outside their immediate families.[54] As soon as they received permission from the administrations of the occupying forces, Nathaus shows, people in small towns and even larger cities began to refound and revive the associational life that had come to a halt after 1933. "The local association," he writes, "experienced a renaissance."[55] Choirs, gymnastic clubs, rifle clubs, and volunteer fire brigades sprang up again and could rely on enthusiastic interest. In 1950, the umbrella organization of gardening associations counted about a million members, and around the same time, about 750,000 people had joined the coordinating association of local choirs, the Deutsche Sängerbund. Generally, these voluntary associations rooted in particular localities had been subject to increased state control under the National Socialist regime and also suffered disruptions during the war. After 1945, then, founding or refounding a local club symbolized a return to normality, a life of local traditions and enjoyable social intercourse with people with similar hobbies and interests. In this light, Sternberger's insistence on the need for Germans to affirm an existence in *Gesellschaft und Geselligkeit* may no longer stand out as an anomaly; it was a feature of "post-totalitarian" social life.

According to the sociologist Lewis Coser, clubs and associations such as the ones documented by Nathaus are not examples of a "greedy institution," a type of organization that makes total claims on its members and attempts to encompass within its circle the whole personality or seeks the "exclusive and undivided loyalty" of its supporters.[56] A totalitarian regime is precisely such an omnivorous institution in that the party state organizes almost all aspects of life, wants to harness all the energy of its population, and consequently leaves little room for weekly meetings with the church choir. The association or *Verein,* in contrast, is located at a remove from politics and can perhaps only flourish when it remains focused on shared, nonideological interests. As we shall explore below, this constitutive feature of organized sociability may make it less useful as a training ground for political deliberation, a problem with which Sternberger himself had to contend.

The postwar era was thus an age of voluntary associations, collectivities that operated neither in the market nor in the political sphere, but provided venues for individuals to gather freely to discuss some particular topic or pursue some particular activity in a spirit of companionship. In an unstable and changing institutional landscape, in which the future of German statehood was yet to be determined, a plethora of circles of discussion and clubs emerged as a socially integrative phenomenon. While small-town rifle clubs may seem to have very little to do with the cooperation of earnest young writers, they nonetheless conform to an underlying pattern of association: the postwar period belonged to the extrafamilial and extraprofessional group, or to forms of "organized sociability." And, to add a final note, there were also organizations that came to occupy the middle ground between hobbies and highbrow literature by letting members of the upper middle class meet to discuss a range of loftier questions. A good example of such an association was the international Rotary Club, to which we will return in the final chapter. Having been dissolved in 1937 because of National Socialist misgivings about its commitment to internationalism, epitomized by its headquarters in Chicago, the former members of Rotary Germany, typically prominent professionals and businessmen, sought to resurrect their association in the Western parts of the country after 1945 under the name Club der Freunde von 1927.[57] Only with the founding of the Federal Republic in 1949, however, did Rotary International actually recognize the reconstructed circles as local embodiments of Rotary.

The Limits of Sociability and the End of *Die Wandlung*

Sternberger's peculiar vision of Germans coming together in *Gesellschaft und Geselligkeit* may not have been such an isolated phenomenon; it may have typified a general trend in the intellectual and social life of the immediate postwar period. After the war and the fall of the Nazi regime, people in different areas of society formed or recovered associations that allowed for friendly and regularized nonpolitical and nonprofessional interaction. Sociability proved to be an attractive form of collectivity symbolizing a return to calm conditions or a bourgeois form of life that did not rely on independent German statehood.

The question remains, however, whether this revival of organized sociability could ease the transition to a democratic and liberal Germany—or, to return to the question formulated in the introduction, whether sociable exchanges and polite conversation could progress to political deliberations on controversial issues. What is the relationship between sociability and politics?

In Sternberger's program, the appeal to sociability was supposed to draw people together and keep them in conversation with one another. And in general, the notion of *Geselligkeit* proposes a scheme according to which the responsibility for the unity of the social whole has devolved to its individual particles.[58] Yet this scheme of cohesion is based on the premise that everyone must refrain from noxious self-assertion. To support everyone's exercise of restraint in civil discourse, sociability unifies people by relieving them of any specific tasks, besides the one of maintaining an inviting and amiable atmosphere. Those who enjoy sociability therefore enter a state of purified gregariousness, in which little else matters than the shared desire to take pleasure in the leisurely company of others; they engage in the activity of convening for the sake of convocation.[59] The resulting unity among individuals rests on a common willingness to suspend interests and purposes that might otherwise divide the temporary group: everyone must agree to focus only on what is inoffensive to all.

Sociability is therefore a type of interaction contingent on the absence, or at least on the readiness to ignore, predictably polarizing issues. In the realm of the salon, no one is allowed to ask people to take sides or to confront them with a stark either/or decision.[60] Indeed, the friendliness that Sternberger invoked can be plausibly demanded in a space already securely drained of any material that could trigger conflicts, and the self-regulation required of the participants in sociable discourse consists of everyone's tactful avoidance of any explosive theme and the consequent reliance on safely commonplace notions.[61]

Against this backdrop, the bland nature of Sternberger's many assurances of friendliness can be viewed as strategic inoffensiveness. Perhaps we can even say that the precarious unity of the individuals around *Die Wandlung* rested on the ability of its members to speak about nothing in particular. This vision might be deemed a form of systematic evasiveness, yet Sternberger did conceive of a very different communal unity than the fictitious grounding of a people in a common racial origin. When he outlined the notion of sociability and friendliness, he implicitly departed from any idea of the primordial togetherness of the members of a race and retired the strict policies of inclusion and exclusion that follow from that notion. It is better to be integrated by conversational commonplaces than by the mysterious qualities of blood; the former collectivity has always been achieved through ongoing discourse among its potential members, whereas the latter is simply presupposed as a kind of presocial entity.[62]

However, Sternberger also knew that the practices of sociability are not in themselves directly political and that sociable intercourse is not necessarily the best organ for contests over collectively binding decisions.[63] Indeed, the playfulness that, according to Sternberger, qualified sociability for reeducational tasks also separated it from the collective decision-making process that he imagined to be the ultimate goal. In the end, the character of sociability seemed to make it unsuited as an education in the tasks of politics, at least if politics involved making decisions.

Writing after 1945, Jaspers and Sternberger both searched for viable concepts of nonauthoritarian cohesion, and both had to perform the trick of producing a corporate identity out of the very absence of institutional supports. In responding to this problem, they showed some facility in turning a necessity into a virtue: the nonavailability of stable institutions could be converted into an opportunity to form symmetrical and egalitarian communities of discourse. Their visions of togetherness after the deluge would soon be tested, however, in and around the pages of the journal itself. Jaspers proposed an egalitarian mode of conversation and was, in a series of vitriolic statements delivered by prominent scholars, assaulted for his irreverence toward tradition; Sternberger delineated a practice of sociable interaction, but in the course of the journal's existence he would witness the disintegration of his editorial board. The problems or attacks both men confronted were tied to the question of accessibility. Sternberger was accused of initiating a form of sociable conversation that was not as inclusive as it pretended to be, and Jaspers was accused of relinquishing proven standards of excellence and profundity, standards that inevitably produce rankings and judgments of distinctions and differences.

To be sure, both Jaspers and Sternberger had envisaged difficulties, the images of which corresponded to the particular direction of their projects. Jaspers could oppose obstinate insistence on a particular belief by describing a discourse where all participants must view their statements as preliminary and relative in an ongoing cooperative inquiry without a prophet, and Sternberger implicitly relied on the guidelines of sociable and hence noncombative conversation, a form of collaboration resting on every interlocutor's measured self-effacement and fluid avoidance of unnecessary confrontations. These two contributors to *Die Wandlung* thus imagined different kinds of obstacles: the presumptuousness inherent in dogmatic approaches in the case of Jaspers, and the inflexible assertion of the self and its parochial interests in the case of Sternberger. Yet whether the projected conversations were guided by the search for truth or the maintenance of tactful distance—or whether the implicit model was the seminar or the salon—both Jaspers and Sternberger could in reasonably good faith imagine discursive situations free from irresolvable tensions. They felt that they possessed means to forestall disruptive conflicts or, at the very least, that there were conciliatory mechanisms inherent to the outlined discourse models, which would serve to manage a degree of turbulence.

Developments would bring home how helpless the journal was to settle these conflicts, despite its mollifying tone. To begin with, Sternberger himself seemed to violate the protocols of sociability by overloading the journal issues with discussions of potentially polarizing issues. He invoked the ideal of sociability necessarily predicated on each participant's readiness to bracket their particular positions and interests, but did not remain sufficiently sensitive to how far he could possibly stretch the invocation of goodwill.

For instance, the American authorities from which Sternberger had received a publication license had insisted that the editorial board be made up of representatives from a range of political camps so as to constitute a broad coalition of anti-Fascist groups. Partly to fulfill this purpose, the Romance language expert Werner Krauss, a Marxist who would gain a position at the University of Leipzig, was invited and agreed to contribute to the journal. But over the first couple of years, Krauss progressively distanced himself from *Die Wandlung*. As each of the German regions became increasingly homogenized ideologically, leading among other things to the prevention of Krauss's publications in the American-occupied areas, the cooperative project across the zones seemed more and more tenuous.

This was not simply an unfortunate development outside the journal. Sternberger and Krauss also had differing standpoints on a number of political issues, which threatened to disturb the coalition. In a discussion over future electoral reform, for example, Sternberger wanted to stress the role of individual politicians in the political process, at the expense of parties organized around ideological programs, an idea in line with his hope of somehow preserving the intimate, face-to-face scale of *Geselligkeit*. Krauss, on the other hand, disputed that relationships of political representation could be meaningfully converted into ties between individual persons; he felt that such an emphasis on individual politicians would simply repeat the cultish admiration for exceptional personalities.[64] As this and other potentially divisive issues were introduced into the pages of the journal, the call for continuing friendliness only seemed to exploit the cohesion achieved through the practice of polite self-restraint. In his letters to Sternberger, Krauss noted a widening gap between Sternberger's continued appeals for solidarity, on the one hand, and a diminishing space for diverging opinions in the journal, on the other—a discrepancy that made the emphasis on sociability look like a screen for an agenda without complete support by all participants. "It is doubtful," Krauss wrote, "to what extent your desire to come forward in solidarity as a group actually is supported by a real convergence of views."[65]

Sternberger was conscious of the failure to hold the editorial group together, and he remarked on the silence of previous member of the community in the final issue of the journal: "Against our hope . . . the communication with Profesor Krauss has come to an end. . . . In this way, we experienced in a most intimate domain the powerful tendencies that work against our spirit of sociability."[66] The sociable spirit, Sternberger admitted, had been defeated within the publication itself. Pleas for sociability could not hold the initial anti-Fascist alliance together across ideological divides.

Sternberger proposed sociability as a mode of interaction that relied on each participant's circumspect exercise of self-restraint in the choice of themes, yet the journal sought to house debates on divisive issues, to the point where the tempering effect of sociable discourse revealed itself as illusory. In a similar fashion, Jaspers's ideal of public discussion met with resistance from scholars initially associated with the periodical. At the end of *Die Wandlung*'s short life, a handful of the periodical's major figures even became involved in a cultural debate so bitter as to seem almost designed to repudiate its appeal to civility. The conflict was triggered by a lecture by Jaspers, in which he did little more than draw out the concrete implications of his inaugurating statement for *Die Wandlung*.

In 1947, Jaspers received the Goethe-prize of the city of Frankfurt and gave a speech that was soon published in the journal. His lecture—titled "Our Future and Goethe"—sought to ascertain the extent to which the work and person of Goethe could still serve as an ideal for the present, a topic that followed from his 1945 claim that the Germans could no longer fall back on a secure legacy as a source of orientation. As the sequence of the title suggests, "our future" possessed a certain priority over the figure of Goethe. It indicated that the great author's work must be measured against the needs and possibilities of the present time rather than the other way around. Jaspers also came to the conclusion that Goethe, however formidable a poet and personality, could no longer serve as an "*ideal to be emulated.*"[67] While presented as a specific detachment from the German classical period, the farewell to Goethe was entirely consistent with Jaspers's earlier notion of an irredeemable break with the past. To echo his statement in the first issue of *Die Wandlung*, Germans had lost "almost everything," including the right and the ability to view Goethe as a guiding ideal.

The contentious quality of this more specified rejection of the German past comes into view when one considers how large circles were invested in Goethe as an untarnished icon of culture whose major drama, *Faust*, represented a portrait of the possibilities and dangers of the German national character, understood as the most tragic representative of the fate of mankind in general.[68] However vaguely Jaspers articulated the existential challenges of the contemporary world in his call for a new seriousness, his lapidary judgments of Goethe's diminished relevance—"Goethe's world is a thing of the past"[69]—effectively deprived countless German literati of the central source of their cultural identity. Jaspers's critique disqualified their means of personal association with an unquestioned and comprehensive model. In short, the Goethe speech, in which Jaspers sought to weed out unhelpful appeals to authority, amounted to something like a ban cast on a community maintaining itself by means of a shared code. In the postwar period, no person, Jaspers claimed, could seek validation in Goethe's corpus: "There may be no justification by appeal to Goethe."[70] No one could legitimately tell anyone else what to think or how to act with reference to a towering figure of German cultural history.

Jaspers's speech was a more concrete intervention in the contemporary discourse than his opening words for *Die Wandlung*, and it therefore clarified his overarching project of turning the postwar destruction into a kind of capital for the future German collective.[71] The central idea of the earlier statement was again that the de facto dismantling of all supporting institutional structures, including the sure grasp of a specific cultural heritage that circumscribes a specific national identity, would necessarily preclude claims to authority. No speaker, however erudite and well versed in the founding texts, may look at cultural or historical sources as repositories of validity. This absence of reliable sources of certification must, almost by default, lead to a flattening of the discourse situation. There can be no experts when there is nothing useful or important about which one could claim expertise. Jaspers in effect asked the members of his audience to shed their professional, historical, and cultural identities and reckon with the consequence of such an admission of poverty. This did not necessarily involve an assertion of some rival source of authority; Jaspers did not aspire to inform his fellows about something of which he possessed superior knowledge, only to clear future conversations of certain kinds of justification.

Even so, Jaspers's call to disregard the most cherished of cultural contexts and loosen the commitment to custodianship amounted to blasphemy. To Ernst Robert Curtius, the leading Romance language philologist in postwar Germany and an early contributor to *Die Wandlung,* Jaspers's attempt to disallow references to Goethe as a new rule for discourse seemed like an almost unintelligible impertinence. In a sense, Curtius perceived Jaspers's injunction correctly, as the closing of an established speech community, and responded with a similar type of declaration—that is, with a refusal to discuss. In Curtius's 1949 article "Goethe or Jaspers?" he stated his lack of interest in any further dialogue.[72]

In his short reply, Curtius mobilized and combined two schematic oppositions against Jaspers, that between the poet and the tyrant-philosopher,[73] and that between the supremely forceful personality and the moralizing philistine,[74] the latter being the standard mock image of the parochial bourgeois individual since Goethe's *The Sorrows of Young Werther.*[75] The resulting composite image of Jaspers was one of a dictatorial and petty moralist who delivered a futile but nonetheless infuriating "reprimand" directed at Goethe.[76] When attacking Jaspers's statements on Goethe, then, Curtius could set up a number of associations designed to discredit Jaspers's postwar project as a whole, associations based precisely on the kinds of justifications that Jaspers had wanted to prevent—references to Goethe's world.

When Jaspers extended his program of radical cultural reform to the conventional celebration of Goethe, it opened itself to critique and even ridicule. No one should ever aspire to cut the ties to Goethe. Curtius could use the name of Goethe as leverage to denigrate Jaspers's entire reeducational vision, namely the formation of a speech community of individuals without access to generally accepted sources of authority, and hence without a certain settled (hierarchical) distribution of learning and expertise.[77] The debate, or rather the mutual refusal to engage in discussion on the terms determined by the other, indicated the fading support for Jaspers's postwar attempt to initiate and guide an integrative discourse. Curtius was no doubt aware of the fact that his polemics ruptured this model. In his reactions and replies to Jaspers, he repeatedly announced his turn away from conversation—"you cannot discuss with him [Jaspers]"[78]—and moreover pointed to Jaspers's envisioned speech situation: "You cannot discuss with Jaspers—he usually speaks of 'communication'—because he does not know Goethe, regardless of how much he has read by him."[79] The prerequisite for any debate among Germans,

Curtius claimed, is knowledge of Goethe—precisely the criterion Jaspers sought to displace.[80] Jaspers never did deliver a response directly to Curtius, but published an explanation as to why he deemed such a response impossible: "You kindly give me room for further reflection. But you will understand when I find it inappropriate to reply to a pamphlet, the author of which also says that one cannot 'discuss with Jaspers.'"[81] In this way, the Curtius/Jaspers controversy, not so much a debate as declarations of withdrawal from further debate, marks the further disintegration of *Die Wandlung*'s "circle" of contributors and their vision of a collective held together by nothing else than their conversation.

If Jaspers was the first to speak in the journal, and the person who outlined the premises and goals of its precarious existence, Sternberger provided it with a conclusion in 1949, the final year of its publication.[82] His text, titled "Attempt at a Summary" ("Versuch zu einem Fazit"), is in many ways an effort to review the conversation envisioned by Jaspers four years earlier and to evaluate its accomplishments and failures. In fact, the journal's achievements, which Sternberger records at the brink of the establishment of two German states, even seem conditioned by the constraints imposed on the publication by the period from 1945 to 1949. Sternberger's article is written in a moment in which the constitutive limits of the hoped-for conversation of *Die Wandlung* emerge clearly, limits that were already visible in Jaspers's opening text.

In the first paragraph of his "Versuch zu einem Fazit," Sternberger immediately recalled the formulations of Jaspers's introductory statement, noting that *Die Wandlung*'s time of publication had coincided with the years of German statelessness, from the fall of the National Socialist regime in 1945 to the establishment of two separate German states: "It is curious that the decision of this journal to discontinue its publication coincides in time with the establishment of a German state—just as the journal's beginning four years ago was marked by the 'end of German statehood.'"[83] Following Jaspers further, who in his 1945 announcement at least indicated that the establishment of a new Germany was the task of the journal's discourse, Sternberger even half seriously claimed that the journal itself had generated not just a set of discourse formations but the nation-state itself: "The transformation [*Wandlung*] that we called for in the title of our publication is, one could say, now complete."[84]

But how, according to Sternberger, had the journal, with its proposed ideals of egalitarian and sociable conversation, contributed to the reestablishment of a German state? On closer inspection, the establishment of independent statehood looks rather more like the imposed termination of his project of *Geselligkeit* than its desired fulfillment. Sternberger cannot claim that *Die Wandlung* successfully prepared the formation of states that in fact tore the "circle" apart. After all, writers originally tied to the journal, such as Werner Krauss, now lived in an inaccessible zone at the other side of a geopolitical dividing line. Indeed, the constitution of two German states, which made Germany a split province of "competing, even antagonistic systems,"[85] represented just the kind of opposition between organized blocks that *Die Wandlung* had hoped to prevent by means of a sociability capable of neutralizing or softening conflicting agendas.

Yet the establishment of two states did not simply defeat the initial hopes of the journal. By putting a bracket around the brief period, it also exposed the journal's models of conversation as interim programs, solutions to a peculiar threshold situation.[86] Sociability filled a transient space just after 1945 by promising to bring people together in a situation in which they could do little else than converse with one another.

Not much more than a decade after the journal's last year, however, Sternberger's early postwar vision of sociability as a practice that could contribute to the political education of the bourgeoisie received a kind of vindication. In 1962, Jürgen Habermas published *The Structural Transformation of the Public Sphere,* in which he integrated a depiction of the conversations in coffeehouses, salons, and clubs into his narrative of the emergence of a politically active bourgeoisie. With Habermas, a systematic thinker emerged ready to ascribe a politically relevant and beneficial egalitarianism to the conduct of sociability. Habermas, too, pointed to a passage between bourgeois conviviality and an ideal of genuinely political deliberation.

Habermas did not refer to Sternberger, however, and may have been completely unaware of his work, although he would later appropriate and develop Sternberger's notion of constitutional patriotism. Yet, as we shall see, Habermas was intimately familiar with the work of the critics and skeptics of bourgeois sociability in the postwar period. It is to these contributions we must now turn—to the statements and interventions of Carl Schmitt (chapter 2), Hannah Arendt (chapter 3), and Reinhart Koselleck (chapter 4).

Chapter Two

✦

Conversations and Interrogations

Carl Schmitt

Let us begin with yet another scene of postwar sociability. In the fall of 1949, Martin Heidegger visited Bremen to hold a series of lectures entitled "Das Ding," "Das Gestell," "Die Gefahr," and "Die Kehre."[1] Those familiar with Heidegger will recognize in these titles major themes of his late philosophy. But he did not give these lectures for an audience of philosophers and students. Bremen, a Hanseatic city known as a hub of commerce, was not a university town, and Heidegger was no longer a professor with the right to teach at a university. In 1946, the French military administration, basing their judgment on a report by Karl Jaspers, removed Heidegger from his position at Freiburg University and stripped him of his right to conduct seminars, while allowing him a reduced pension.

In Bremen, Heidegger did not speak as a professor at a university. Instead he held lectures in the town hall for the members of the Club zu Bremen, an association of independent businessmen and civil servants in high positions that regularly organized lectures and events. The association or *Gesellschaftsclub* had been founded in 1783, an association of the Enlightenment period, and was reconstituted in 1947.[2] With no access to the university, Heidegger had accepted the invitation to speak before a group of wholesalers, shipping agents, captains, and dockyard directors, the people who constituted the "good society [*gute Gesellschaft*]" in a town known for trade.[3] And according to the businessman F. W. Oelze, a good friend of the poet Gottfried Benn, the response was enthusiastic; the famous thinker was viewed as a demigod. Prevented from reentering the realm of higher learning as a teacher and mentor, Heidegger appeared in a less regulated but not necessarily less exclusive venue, namely that of bourgeois "organized sociability."[4]

Writing in *Die Wandlung*, the editor Dolf Sternberger envisioned a future Germany both held together and reformed by revived sociability.

By appealing to people's inclination toward gregariousness and half-buried virtues of politeness and civility, Sternberger set out to redefine traditional German bourgeois identity by emphasizing performances of good and indeed elegant conduct instead of increasingly fragile concepts of private property and to reinvigorate a sense of German collectivity by highlighting self-organized associational life over notions of the *Volk*, or even the German state. Indeed, he even imagined how light conversational interaction would work as a therapy for the German *Bürger.* The mild and modest pleasures of sociability, he suggested, would help to dissolve the armored character of a class that, for complex historical reasons, had previously retreated into the sanctuary of family life and shunned political negotiations and deliberations as undignified bickering and bargaining. An increased appreciation for supple tactfulness in the extrafamilial but nonpolitical sphere of sociability would gradually serve to erase the stigma attached to tactics in the sphere of politics. Hence sociability would ideally fulfill the function of a preparatory stage toward liberal-democratic governance.

In his enthusiasm for the multiple benefits and advantages of the sphere of free sociability beyond the (then uncertain) terrain of the market and the state, however, Sternberger may not have discerned the tendency evident in the Bremen scene: unregulated and semiprivate sites of sociability could also constitute a refuge for vilified figures barred from their previous positions in institutions such as universities. After 1946, Heidegger was no longer allowed to lecture to students in Freiburg, but he was free to appear in the meeting place of a tradition-rich *Verein* in Bremen, an association of wealthy and locally influential members of good society. Trying to identify a loose organizational form that could fit the constraints and demands of the postwar period, Sternberger had embraced the small, nonanonymous circle of friends and the salon. But obviously, disgraced intellectuals and professionals could surround themselves with friends and acquaintances too, build small groups of companionship, and in this way find a sympathetic audience. For those who were compromised by their involvement with National Socialism, the spaces of sociability proved more receptive than institutions under the control of foreign administrations or untarnished elites.

This is true also for the jurist and political theorist Carl Schmitt, who in the immediate postwar period was first detained and questioned by the American military for his involvement with the National Socialist regime and, on his release, was removed from his academic position and temporarily banned from publishing.[5] Marginalized in official settings in much the same way as Heidegger, Schmitt could count on continued support from spontaneously forming networks of individuals meeting for discussion and reflection. As Dirk van Laak has reconstructed, friends and former students and assistants of Carl Schmitt started gathering regularly around 1948 with the idea of trying to preserve and promote his legacy, and in 1949 they formed a small unofficial "academy" that met over coffee for intimate discussions but also organized lectures in Cologne and Düsseldorf.[6]

As we shall see, however, Schmitt himself did not simply affirm this emerging culture of small discussion circles, although it provided him with some comfort and support. Intensely preoccupied with the diverging trajectories of academics and intellectuals after 1945, he repeatedly returned to what he deemed the inherently contradictory character of the postwar conversational culture. His posthumously published private notes from 1947 to 1951 are in fact filled with bilious attacks against the rhetoric of conversation in the immediate postwar period.[7]

Significantly, Schmitt pointed to the duplicity of a social and intellectual life that presented itself as open and spontaneous but relied on the presence of an authority with control over the means of coercion. Clearly aware of publications such as *Die Wandlung,* a journal entrusted with the task of introducing and exemplifying a practice of intellectual exchange, Schmitt spoke of the system of licenses put in place by the Allies to control access to the tools of dissemination. Time and again, he claimed that the "licensed public sphere"[8] was not as widely accessible as it pretended to be and that the outlines determined by numerous policies and restrictions were passed over by those invited to speak, noting that the person who "makes appearances in Berlin today can only do so with multiple approvals, licenses, passports, approbations and certifications. He will be cautious to speak critically about this situation."[9] The allegedly free and nonhierarchical conversation of the postwar period, Schmitt implied, was neither widely accessible nor genuinely prepared to make a place for critique. In a particularly poisonous statement, Schmitt refers to "the license holders of 1945 as the heroes of the free word!"[10] (Of course, *Die Wandlung* was a journal that had been given a license to publish.) At points, his contemptuous comments on the discussions that took place in such sponsored journals assumed the form of vituperations directed specifically at Karl Jaspers as one of the prominent "pinups of liberated Germany."[11]

But Schmitt's comments did more than berate the fact that Germans with a democratic and liberal outlook were finally allowed to speak in Germany, while those in some way associated with the National Socialist regime were questioned, censored, and sometimes incarcerated.

Proceeding from the alleged hypocrisy involved in the postwar suppression of illiberal voices and compromised persons, Schmitt also pointed to the denied oppositional value of the supposedly accessible discourse. The public discussions of the immediate postwar period, which often played out in journals put together by small circles of intellectuals, had an integrative intent.[12] As we have seen in the case of *Die Wandlung*, participants tended to emphasize a shared commitment to inclusive and open-ended dialogue and a welcoming sociability.[13] If anything, those publishers and essayists trusted to participate in reeducation were abstaining from agitation. Leading figures such as Jaspers were committed to deescalating and deintensifying any latent conflicts and promoting mutual tolerance and sympathy. This was partly a sign of caution and partly a remarkable shift in criteria for membership. Sternberger, for instance, wished to allow for a conversation across ideological divides and used a somewhat bland rhetoric of conciliation and friendliness, but in these publicist efforts, he also effectively retired any idea that common origin or racial homogeneity could or should be the basis for community. A group of people who come together in sociability differs from some imagined primordial community of blood.

In his postwar notes, Schmitt interpreted the often cautious and tentative tone of the mostly journal-based public conversations of the era as a strategic silence, a silence about excluded positions and a silencing of those who represented them. Highlighting the vocabulary of Enlightenment debates in which new generations of intellectuals challenged the pomp associated with the baroque court, Schmitt framed placidity as a cunning move in an ongoing battle between political factions: "noble simplicity and calm [*stille*] grandeur; yes, calm [*Stille*]! . . . I ask myself: Calm against whom? Calm becomes a polemical concept set against baroque noisiness."[14] In this and other statements, Schmitt was polemical and also insisted that every position should be viewed as a polemical one. The contemporary calm is deceptive, he claimed, and not simply because the people who would disturb it had been barred from speaking. Placidity itself was a political strategy and had to be branded as such. Schmitt sneered at those who were allowed to and did in fact publish immediately after the war, but also more specifically at those who denied that there were parties involved in a struggle over dominance. This struggle, he claimed, was conducted all the more effectively and insidiously the more completely it was denied.

Behind the broad postwar endeavor to contain and soften conflicts, Schmitt implied, one can detect a particular political-theoretical vision. More than maintaining the calm, the proponents of a sociable atmosphere sought to redefine the (German) polity in terms of a system of interacting forces rather than a binding of all to an awe-inspiring superintending authority. The emphasis on sedate conversations among mutually sympathetic interlocutors as well as a revitalized German economy revealed the desire to locate mechanisms of coherence in the workings of society itself rather than depending on the presence of a coercive state agency. As insufficiently trained in the virtues of kindliness and politeness, Germans should finally come to rely more on ostensibly weak but actually resilient self-organizing capacities of societal interaction.[15] The interest in sociability typified by Sternberger, including the skill of fluidly avoiding contentious topics, thus reflected the endeavor to derive societal cohesiveness from ongoing processes of commerce and conversation.[16]

The typical postwar liberal humanist, as Schmitt described him in a brief series of rhetorical questions, erroneously and naively assumed that peace is the natural state of affairs: "Enmity should be excluded from the essence of man? Man: this should mean peace, harmony, and unity?"[17] Following the cultural debate of the postwar period, Schmitt scornfully noted the belief in spontaneously emerging forms of harmonious interaction among human beings and likened the envisioned society to a buzzing beehive.[18] The stubborn fact that some people exercise power over others was, according to Schmitt, naively or deceptively elided.

For readers of Schmitt, this critique is familiar territory; he had already delivered analyses of the concealed political force of ostensibly apolitical discourses during the Weimar era.[19] In *The Concept of the Political,* for instance, he had claimed that liberalism sought to dissolve political struggles into economic competition and sociable or spiritual discussion. Carl Schmitt, one could say, had no new ideas after 1945.[20] For the older and embittered theorist, there was rarely anything new under the sun. But for Schmitt himself, the stasis was not necessarily evidence of a failing mind. In the postwar period, he often asserted that very few new developments surprised him and that he had already captured the problems of the contemporary moment.[21] To a large extent, his continued work in the postwar period was delivered as commentary and variations on earlier interventions, and he was inclined to present his prewar writings as far-sighted diagnoses ironically attracting condemnation.[22]

In the postwar period, moreover, his mode of analysis often included or took the shape of sustained reflections on the particular discursive forms in which he operated. If Schmitt's corpus of ideas was no longer augmented or changed in any substantial way and if his work exhibited no clear progression of thought in the postwar period, the formats in which his ideas are communicated nonetheless became subject to extended scrutiny. Facing a changed cultural climate partly shaped by a new set of authorities with particular agendas, Schmitt was concerned with what one can say, how one can say it, and in what forum.

Although it is obvious that Schmitt had to recontextualize and suppress part of his work to monitor impressions and cut connections to National Socialism, this pressing problem of presentation exceeded the need to make rhetorical adjustments in relation to a new or changed audience. To Schmitt, groups of texts with shared properties are molded by, and subsequently also project, particular structures of authority. The specific principles of textual organization that define different clusters of affiliated text are not, according to Schmitt, so many ways of conveniently and neutrally mirroring a given reality. Rather, they map the world in certain selective ways, or allow and facilitate certain approaches to it in accordance with particular ideological premises;[23] moreover, they prescribe relationships between the producer and the recipients of the text.[24] Genres are therefore never neutral media or convenient vehicles for messages; they provide sets of conventions that facilitate and constrain the production and interpretation of statements in ideologically relevant ways. This means that writing within a genre is itself a politically inflected practice.

From Schmitt's perspective, then, the postwar ideological culture did not ensnare him merely by conferring or withholding publishing rights while leaving everything else untouched; rather, it extended far into the domain of his writing, insofar as a host of explicit and implicit restrictions delineated a set of available genres that in turn embodied and conveyed certain commitments. The culture of the free word, meditative stillness, and inclusive conversation established and consolidated itself by introducing a repertoire of discursive rituals and types of texts, and Schmitt's engagement with the conditions of the period necessarily took the form of close attention to these procedures and their presuppositions.

When he engaged with the conditions of the postwar period, Schmitt not only rejected intellectuals such as Jaspers, nor was his critique exhausted in attacks on the preferred vocabulary and tonality of publications such as *Die Wandlung*. His attempted interventions took place at the level of a discussion, and a precarious enactment, of certain genre choices. But what kinds of texts did Schmitt confront and quarrel with when he challenged the prevailing postwar culture of kind sociability? The list would have to include the confession, the interrogation, the dialogue, and also the diary. In the first years after 1945, Schmitt was asked to complete questionnaires about his influence and activities in the Third Reich by university representatives, and he was also interrogated at various points during his detainment by the American authorities.[25] As he was allowed to publish his own texts again in the early 1950s, supposedly unconstrained by obligatory formats, he still returned to these first postwar experiences and often built on notes he took during the period of his incarceration. At various points, he opposed the way these formats framed him as a problematic and opaque subject that had to become known and reveal itself to an observer with the right to decide on punishment and therapy.

As a result, Schmitt's own writings often grappled with the problem of articulating an unwillingness to speak within the modes of a discourse that had achieved dominance or been imposed on him. He did not so much choose to use the genres of the diary or the questionnaire as he tried to write himself out of them, attempting to expose their enforced character, or the way they constrain and structure the reception of his speech. Yet Schmitt's point of departure in these textual forms also betrays a curious proximity to his object of scorn. He never sought to launch a critique from a point outside what he perceived as the contemporary horizon. Despite his attacks on the spirit of the age, he had, at least on the level of genre, already accepted it.[26]

Deliberation and Diagnosis: Schmitt on Postwar Discourse

At the turn of the decade, the publication ban was lifted and Schmitt could put his texts into circulation. Seizing the opportunity, Schmitt did publish a number of essays and tracts, many of which contained a coded critique of what he understood to be the reigning ideology of the time. Even when he could intervene in the public realm again around 1950, the form in which he did so was intimately linked to what he conceived of as the repertoire of sanctioned types of discourse. Indeed, Schmitt's most openly apologetic statements continued to circle around key categories of the postwar era, such as the notion of an egalitarian and inclusive conversation, a *Gespräch*. On the most basic level, he confronted the culture of conversation with his own experience of interrogations in order to show that the egalitarian discourse was not as open as it claimed to be.

Underlying this contrast between purportedly free conversations and strictly regulated and asymmetric forms of examination, however, lies a broader understanding of the elusive character of authority, which no longer declares itself through the imposition and enforcement of decisions channeled from above but rather resides in a regime of constant observation and therapeutic correction.[27] In Schmitt's analysis, people are indeed allowed and even invited to speak in modern society, but only because every conversation is already part of an ongoing examination, through which the speakers reveal and contribute knowledge about themselves to observers and institutions and in this process become available for psycho-pathological categorization and reform.

Much like Sternberger, but for radically different reasons, Schmitt thus viewed postwar sociability—the call for Germans to come together in a gentle conversation—as a form of reeducation. Schmitt wanted to reemerge through public statements and interventions, yet he was haunted by the thought that his self-directed public campaign of rehabilitation would turn into an extension of, rather than an effective counterstrategy to, the interrogations he had been subjected to during the time of censorship. The apparent absence of relationships of direct coercion hardly calmed him; instead they made him focus more intensively on the premises and the uses of the discourse he produced.

Schmitt's most unabashedly apologetic endeavor was the slim volume titled *Ex Captivitate Salus,* a collection that comprises a series of shorter, often elliptical reflections on his experiences and readings after the war. A date or a period is attached to each text, and taken together they establish a span from the summer of 1945 to April 1947, which was also the time during which he could not publish or move freely. The chronological structure indicates Schmitt's effort to recuperate the years of silence and to establish, retrospectively, a continuous presence of analysis and commentary. The first text also signals his engagement with the discourse of the postwar era, as it was developed in *Die Wandlung* and other publications devoted to an ameliorative and protopolitical practice of sociable discourse. Schmitt's account, consisting mostly of a glance back to 1945, bears the title "Gespräch mit Eduard Spranger," and it focuses on the concept of conversation.

Conversation was often a rejected or even ridiculed practice or notion in Schmitt's prewar corpus. Speaking of the romantic idea of the "infinite conversation [*unendliches Gespräch*]," Schmitt noted that conversations have a tendency to extend themselves indefinitely, since no force or mechanism internal to the conversation could allow it to issue in one outcome over another.[28] To engage in conversation is really to avoid taking sides, or even to dissolve any stark conflict into endless negotiations, if only by establishing the very possibility of a realm of potential exchange and conciliation. The meaning of the continual back-and-forth between contrary positions in a conversation is primarily that these positions can be related and brought into play with one another. The underlying premise of the conversation thus lies in the process of mediation as such, not in putting a definite end to the process of interpersonal talk. This turns each contribution to an ongoing discussion into a filibuster, and even if a final decision may correspond to an argument produced within the context of discourse, it does not emerge from it. There are never any decisive arguments, only interventions from outside the realm of argumentation, since the relative standing of arguing parties can always shift if the time frame is extended. In short, those who control *when* a decision is made effectively control *what* decision is made.[29]

Schmitt did not rehearse this critique of the infinite conversation in *Ex Captivitate Salus;* instead he sought to draw attention to the discrepancy between rhetoric and actual policy in postwar Germany. The opportunity to engage in genuinely open public communication was, he noted, hardly extended to all. He places the term "conversation" or *Gespräch* in the title of a prose piece dating back to summer 1945 and quickly makes clear that he was never invited to participate in conversation.[30] The essay describes how the conservative pedagogue Spranger, then the interim rector of the Friedrich-Wilhelms University in Berlin, presented Schmitt with a questionnaire designed to determine the extent of his involvement with National Socialism, his first encounter with attempts at denazification and reeducation.[31] Even though he might have approached Schmitt with the promise of an unrestricted dialogue, Spranger, portrayed with disingenuous respect as a "famous philosopher and pedagogue," does not expect dialogue but the "completion of a questionnaire [*Beantwortung eines Fragebogens*]."[32] When Schmitt does answer Spranger, as if the encounter stands at the beginning of a conversation, the dialogue ends, or it has already ended. Schmitt claims to have replied to Spranger "like a philosopher and not like a questionnaire . . . but no further conversation emerged out of this answer."[33] In this brief report, then, Schmitt insinuates that the postwar culture of conversation did not live up to its stated ideal, all the while conveniently eliding any mention of his own activities during the Third Reich.

Yet by focusing on the conversation that never occurs, Schmitt not only tried to point to an inconsistency between the postwar orientation toward inclusive dialogue and the interest in identifying, prosecuting, and removing the supporters of the National Socialist regime. He also inquired into the "thought premises [*gedankliche Voraussetzungen*]" of the form in which this identification and prosecution was carried out.[34] As he reflected on the questions delivered to him by Spranger, Schmitt asserted that the interrogation really aimed at profiling his person rather than ascertaining the details of his thought or reconstructing the chronological sequence of his actions.

In the realm of reeducation, Schmitt believes, what is at issue is never the clarity or logical form of an argument, or the structure and significance of a set of beliefs, but rather the transparency of a self. Spranger was someone who participated in the procedures of screening others, someone concerned with the "nontransparency [*Undurchsichtigkeit*]" of Schmitt's personality, and the purpose of the conversation that immediately shifted into an interrogation was to render him "completely transparent."[35] The interrogated person should above all be induced to verbalize the truth about his character traits and innermost motivations.[36] Schmitt claims that he was not invited to defend a particular position or to articulate an argumentative defense of his beliefs in an ongoing dispute but, rather, trapped in a situation designed to expose his personality as completely as possible so that it could be assessed or categorized as the bearer of a certain essence that must finally be made manifest.[37] Schmitt was asked to speak, and gently pushed to participate in an apparently noncoercive discourse between equals, for the purpose of a close observation that was actually designed to sidestep or hollow out the conversational relationship. In order for questioners to procure the necessary material for analysis, one could say, interrogations must be presented and conducted as a regular conversation.[38] The resulting conversation-interrogation constitutes a hybrid discursive form—the questioner must simulate the nonhostile and egalitarian communicative situation of the conversation in order to extract the truth about the subject, or must mask an asymmetry that nonetheless remains inherent in the purpose of the interrogation.

In Schmitt's account, his interrogator's interest in the lack of clarity of his essence demonstrated that the encounter took place beyond the space of any argumentative controversy. For Spranger, who approached a man associated with the National Socialist government, the time for a battle of ideas was over. This becomes visible in Schmitt's account as he speaks bitterly of Spranger's self-assurance: "He [Spranger] was completely possessed by the interest of having been and being in the right."[39] In this manner, Schmitt registers that he had, in the eyes of his interrogator, long removed himself from the realm of positions seen as worthy of any actual debate and deliberation and instead qualified only as an object of diagnosis. The objective of the conversation was not to debate beliefs but to understand a personality.[40]

More generally, the circle of topics and positions that can be discussed or argued for at any given moment is not endlessly expansive, and those who move beyond this circle are not required to supply a defense for whatever it is that they might believe but are asked to participate in a discursive format—the interrogation or the "screening," perhaps—that has already framed them as targets of psychological discernment and possibly also future reform. At a certain point an opponent ceases to hold a dissenting view, which must be confronted and addressed in a dispute and is instead treated as a pathological element.

Schmitt's tendentious record of his encounter with Spranger, as well as the further texts of *Ex Captivitate Salus,* represent an attempt to counter what he perceived as a narrowing down of the space of contestation for hegemonic purposes. Schmitt ultimately sought to convert the ongoing assessment of his person in talks and questionnaires, all of which rested on the assumption that he was not simply the perpetrator of a crime but a permanently suspect individual,[41] into a situation determined by antagonism. This is, for Schmitt, a problem of writing. He hesitates about how to articulate his protest, or how to try to make room for protestation, within the frame of the administrative screening that he knows he was subject to. It proves difficult to sustain a project of spitefulness strong enough to instigate antagonism against an apparatus with great interest in his person, capable of filing all his statements as material for an ongoing investigation, the legitimacy of which he wants to repudiate.

To transform the interrogation into contestation is a grotesque enterprise after Schmitt's support for National Socialism. His quarrels with the process of moral and legal screening ultimately serve a hideous purpose. But Schmitt's observations remain of interest in the context of this book because he examined how the culture of nonauthoritarian discussion, the culture of revivified sociability, was also a culture of diagnosis. Schmitt felt that whatever he said would be examined within the frame of an assessment of his person and rendered ineffectual as a declaration of opposition. As soon as he spoke or wrote, he satisfied a regime of observation that depended on his readiness to engage in "self-examination and self-recording [*Selbsterforschung und Selbstverdatung*],"[42] and he thereby helped sustain the diagnostic procedure that he at bottom wanted to reject, since it negated the dimension of conflict between political equals. Schmitt wanted to defend himself, yet he knew that his defense could also be read as so many replies to the question "Who are you?"—the question posed to him by his "interrogator."[43]

The discursive culture that Schmitt portrays, a culture that allowed for and even promoted civil exchange within the medium of a *Gespräch,* had its boundaries. It obviously did not endorse Schmitt's insistence on enmity as a fundamental political condition, but maintained the possibility of mediation. Faced with someone who crossed over the boundaries that delineate the area of accepted positions, however, it subjected the transgressing individual to intensified study as a deviant element, assuming a vantage point beyond the positions of the participants in a controversy or argument.

The shift from debate to psychological analysis was, however, not a fate that Schmitt alone confronted. He confronted it only because it had in some sense already enveloped everyone. As indicated above, Schmitt also focused on the reeducational function of discursive sociability, much like the major figures of the journal *Die Wandlung*. For Sternberger, the turn to sociable conversation in some imaginary salon space was partly an attempt to establish a notion of politics by discourse and partly an attempt to defrost a pathologically rigid German character ideal. But if *Die Wandlung* and specifically Sternberger enlisted conversational practices in an ambitious therapeutic project circumscribed by the conditions of the interregnum and put faith in the capacity of *Geselligkeit* to soften and mediate between oppositions as well as to dissolve the embodied ethos of the supposedly incorruptible German character, Schmitt argued that the reeducational project carried out by Americans and trusted Germans sought to stimulate individuals to talk about themselves, to reveal themselves, for the purposes of identifying nonliberal and nondemocratic elements. The postwar practice of sociability, then, was haunted by the need for screening, deliberation shadowed by diagnosis.

According to Schmitt, the postwar culture that he resisted could be economically described in terms of a relationship between conversations and interrogations. On the initial and polemical level of his texts, he implied that the liberal commitment to conversation was undermined and contradicted by the (mass) performance of interrogations. His scrutiny of the conduct of inquiries, however, also suggests the idea that every interrogation has to be presented as a conversation in order to be successfully carried out: the interrogation only works to the extent that the parties form a "human connection."[44] In this way, the practice of interrogation reaches into the realm of the civil dialogue or mimics it. Yet in the final analysis, conversations and interrogations begin to blur somewhat, both emerging as aspects of a type of governance in which the direct and undeniable imposition of authority through prohibition and coercion is replaced, or at least accompanied, by operations of assessment, labeling, and correction. Behaviors and beliefs are traced back to inner, hidden truths about subjects. The civility of the conversation-interrogation is the civility shown to a deviant element within a system that knows how to delineate and identify deviancy; there are no sharp edges because the challenge that Schmitt might have posed has already been safely voided and contained.

Ex Captitivate Salus was not Schmitt's direct defense of any past action or statement, but a consideration, often horribly self-pitying and resentful, of the peculiar or even impossible conditions of articulation for such a defense. Schmitt reflected on the fact that whatever he did say would be welcomed by a curiously distant interlocutor concerned with his person rather than his arguments, an interlocutor removed from the space of any argumentative or political struggle by virtue of already having claimed all righteousness and ruled out counterpositions, directing only a diagnostic gaze on the questioned person.

Interestingly, Schmitt was rather cautious in stating fierce opposition or proclaiming enmity where none was allowed or thought to exist. If he voiced dissatisfaction, it was more in the mode of sneers at the presumptuousness of those who required greater transparency from him. In a later text of *Ex Captivitate Salus,* Schmitt referred to the church's monopoly in all matters regarding the individual's confessions of sin—"If you want to confess, go and show yourself to the priest [Wer beichten will, gehe hin und zeige sich dem Priester]."[45] However, he himself documented how secular agencies had come to demand elaborate exercises in self-revelation and penitence, joining the methods of pastoral care with the determination of legal culpability. The "authorities and offices" that devised questionnaires wanted to probe the depths of the individual soul and enroll the subject in the production of knowledge through the means of self-examination, but they were also in the business of trying to discern points of reference for legal indictments.

Having delineated the presuppositions of any written statement he might make, Schmitt finally tried out an array of poses. In the pages of *Ex Captivitate Salus,* for instance, he claimed to be a man of inner emigration, disinterested scholarship and prognosis, and patient resignation in the face of the defeat of old Europe. His last line of defense, however, assumed the form of a discussion of the generic frame of his reflections. He may not have been able to completely remodel the discursive situation, and knew that he would be read and dealt with as a case with no means to neutralize the perceived need for a legal process, but he did try to repel the impression that he would deliver a confession. In the title essay of *Ex Captivitate Salus,* Schmitt summed up his attempt to negate the generic frames that his volume could not help but invoke:

> Here I have spoken about myself, for the first time in my life. A scientifically thinking human being rather speaks about objective issues and problems. . . . A jurist, who has brought himself as well as others to approximate an ideal of objectivity, tends to

> avoid narcissistic introspection. Any interest in literary confessions and avowals has been spoiled for me by the ugly examples of Jean Jacques Rousseau and poor August Strindberg. . . . I am speaking here without publicist or apologetic intent. It does not belong to the street or the stage, to the forum or the lectern.[46]

This passage is the clearest manifestation of how Schmitt struggled to remain in charge of the attribution of genre, or at least tried to evade modes of speech that would concede the legitimacy of the scrutiny to which he was subjected. As he piles up purely negative definitions of his publication—it is neither a rallying cry nor a performance, neither a political defense nor a lecture—it becomes clear that he could not so easily generate an appropriate category for his own discourse. Stretches of *Ex Captivitate Salus* come across less as a confession than an attempt to stage the refusal to make a confession. Schmitt did not completely deny that he was engaged in some process of self-investigation ("Here I have spoken about myself") but rejected the labels he knew he would inevitably conjure up, since his willing production of such statements would ultimately constitute responses to a question he claimed to want to escape: "Who are you?"

After 1945, Schmitt did not speak on his own terms and was forced to recognize this predicament again and again. Cultural and political premises that he opposed extended far into his writings. He attacked the reigning ideology of the age, yet he was conscious of how, on a textual level, he remained within its bounds. When he started writing after a few years of imposed silence, he knew he had to expose himself to diagnostic procedures and interpretations, cloaked as they were in the medium of conversation.

Interrogation and Self-Interrogation: Schmitt and the Genre of the Diary

In their work on the Frankfurt School, Andrew J. Perrin and Jeffrey K. Olick claim that postwar Germans had by 1949 become one of the "most surveyed populations in history."[47] It is easy to understand why. Determined to gauge the extent of any lingering commitment to National Socialism among Germans and the likelihood of recidivism, the Psychological Warfare Division of the U.S. Army, for instance, conducted numerous series of public opinion surveys, the results of which did suggest a "quick cultural turnaround" in Germany.[48] After 1945, it seemed, few Germans were explicitly declaring allegiance to the utterly defeated regime, perhaps partly because they had swiftly learned how to parrot the new official discourse.[49]

Viewing the results of this standard public opinion research in postwar Germany with some skepticism, members of the relocated Frankfurt School, among them Theodor W. Adorno, set out to conduct social science studies in West Germany to identify what they saw as the authoritarian and possibly protofascist but latent "*nonpublic opinion*" in an ostensibly denazified Germany, a durable and stable bundle of ideas and prejudices that could not be captured by means of the standard questionnaires.[50] The study was published in 1955 under the heading "Group Experiment," a title that referred to the assembly of 136 focus groups consisting of both men and women, often from different occupational groups, who were brought together to discuss a fictional letter by an American soldier designed to elicit attitudes to German guilt.

The Frankfurt School sociologists consciously set out to generate a friendly atmosphere in which the participating Germans would be more willing to express their opinions. For the social scientists, the ideal frame for the carefully arranged group discussions was that of a compartment of a long-distance train, in which travelers who happened to ride together would chat as the hours passed by and would eventually begin to let their guard down.[51] In the words of Perrin and Olick, the Frankfurt researchers aimed to create a sphere of "temporary sociality" as the space in which latent opinions would become manifest.[52] Analyzing the gathered data, the coauthors could then establish that the participants' voiced opinions first and foremost seemed formed by "the person's attachment to a social situation."[53]

Schmitt's sense of how the dialogues in which he was invited to participate were in fact interrogations, a suspicion that haunted his own postwar writings as he engaged in a restless search for some genre not already contaminated by the culture of conversation and confession, may easily be ascribed to his being an embittered and increasingly paranoid figure. As the "Group Experiment" illustrates, however, social scientists did construct scenes of sociability in the postwar period in order to establish with greater accuracy the concealed psychological profile of the German population. The conversations conducted in the imagined long-distance train compartment were at the same time material to be scrutinized by researchers who wanted to determine the persistence of prejudice under the cover of officially acceptable phrases.[54] Scenes of deliberation were scenes of diagnosis.

Schmitt implied that the reeducational imperative of the postwar period contradicted and undermined the invitation to sociability extended by figures such as Sternberger. But when articulating this critique, he also observed how difficult it had become for him to refuse the culture of conversation and interrogation. It was, he was compelled to concede, far from easy to articulate discursively a rejection of a culture ready to receive and interpret discourse in particular ways. Insofar as it was inseparable from particular modes of speech and self-presentation, or insofar as it was constituted by particular genres made available to or imposed on speakers and writers, the postwar culture of deliberation and examination affected and even shaped Schmitt's own writings. When trying to legitimate his public self-defense, he could not quite identify an adequate name for his texts and remained tied to the forms that he repudiated, the confession and the apology.

Yet this postwar perplexity may be symptomatic of an underlying problem with Schmitt's political philosophy as a whole. A figure known for launching theoretically sophisticated attacks on liberalism, Schmitt created problems for himself by accepting liberalism's own idealized vision of liberal politics as carried out in and through discourse. In a sense, Schmitt ceded language to his political enemy and was left with a curiously impoverished notion of politics without speech. As the political theorist Andreas Kalyvas has noted, Schmitt "incautiously donated to the liberal tradition the public practices (and values) of speech, discussion, and deliberation. In a word, he looked at liberalism through the lens of liberalism and as liberalism wants to be seen: rational, dialogical, consensual, and deliberative. And because these practices were associated with it, he could not incorporate it into his own theory. . . . His vision of liberalism, garnished and mythologized as it was, returned with a vengeance, truncating his own options."[55]

After 1945, there was in fact no type of writing that was safely removed from the postwar culture Schmitt detested, no matter how private, secretive, or set apart from the public conversation it may have seemed.[56] From 1947 to 1951, for instance, Schmitt took notes in what amounts to a kind of diary, although, as we shall see, the genre attribution was again a highly problematic issue. Despite their nonpublic character, these pages of notes now collected in a volume were not quite at a secure distance from the forms of reeducation, the premises of which Schmitt wanted to uncover and criticize. Indeed, the self-inspection that the near-daily jottings performed remained uncomfortably associated with the external examinations to which Schmitt had been subjected. To put it briefly, Schmitt saw private self-interrogations as continuous with interrogations. If he was reluctant about keeping a diary for himself, it was for this reason: he viewed it as a practice through which the individual prospectively makes him- or herself available for a concerned and corrective gaze and thus voluntarily joins diagnostic and therapeutic forms of administration.

Starting his notebook in 1947, Schmitt was troubled by the temptations lurking in the diary. He repeatedly reflected on the diary's potentially dubious character as an expression and generator of self-importance and claimed that diaries are almost unavoidably written in exhibitionist fashion for the gaze of some imagined reader: "Is one allowed to describe one's own life? To keep a diary that others are supposed to read?"[57] Schmitt went through arguments for and against keeping a day-to-day record of one's life, stated that it could breach the Christian obligation to observe humility and was legitimate only if sanctioned by a priest as an instrument of self-correction or for the purpose of self-defense. He was clearly aware of the Christian debates on believers writing diaries to record and assess their own spiritual development. As Puritan diarists anxiously noted, even the most ruthless self-scrutiny often slides back into self-representation, which in turn degenerates into prideful self-assertion, a sin that must be fought by even more ruthlessly honest writing.[58] Schmitt likewise suspected that the diary could easily become an occasion for boundless talk and excessive self-love, a threat captured in the image of the strong attraction that one feels to one's own accomplishments: "Our deeds are our beloved daughters, our all-too beautiful wives, to whom we feel attracted again and again."[59]

In a number of passages in his notebooks, this critique of the diary is conveyed through an engagement with a constellation of notable diarists, such as the German author and contemporary Ernst Jünger, and Samuel Pepys, the seventeenth-century English diarist known for his diligent decade-long notation of his daily life and corporeal enjoyments. These two names appear together when Schmitt claims that Jünger's diaries perpetually threaten to fall into "Pepyism." "Pepyism" is Schmitt's term for the diarist's inclination to mention each and every occurrence or thrill in the world of the senses, no matter how insignificant or fleeting they may be, a charge extended to Jünger's attunement to his private, sensual experiences: "There is too much talk about private things [in Jünger's diaries], too many Burgundy wines, too many orchids, too many professorial dinners, too sybaritic and also too many situation reports. . . . A shot of Pepyism is always floating about."[60] The phrase that keeps recurring is of course "too much." In Schmitt's eyes, Jünger's orientation toward his luxurious comforts made him include every little thrill in his accounts. He portrayed Jünger as a kind of gourmet who ends up tiring the reader with his appetite for the rare and the exquisite. And he leveled this critique at

Jünger in a characterization that mimics the additive structure of the list, which itself may be typical of a genre in which events follow upon one another in an expandable series.

This lack of discrimination, however, cannot be understood as Jünger's personal flaw. It is, rather, a consequence of the journal's constitutive tendency toward all-inclusiveness and its inherent affirmation of quotidian, everyday life. Every diary implicitly demands to be filled up every day with whatever happens, and once it is oriented toward the manifold occurrences in the sensual realm and the diarist's continual appreciation of these occurrences, nothing proves easier than filling it up. A journal requires only that each day be described, and there is no definite end to the exhaustiveness with which each day can be described. The genre has by way of its structure already suspended the decision of how often to write, and by opening up the materials of trivial experience for writing, it has also relieved the diarist of the burden of having to determine what to write about. Although continuous notation may express an obsession with control, the diary nonetheless invokes the fiction of the writer's passivity with regard to events and circumstances.[61] When Schmitt comments on Jünger's inability to omit things, he simply points out that nothing is ever redundant in a diary—that the form itself disposes of criteria by which to prioritize material, erect hierarchies of significance, or impose patterns. Everything that occurs can enter the diary, and nothing that does enter it can really stand out. Instead, the diary opens up a homogeneous temporal continuum as a frame in which one can no longer really say "too much."

The unspoken premise of Schmitt's comments is that writing a diary means surrendering the project of achieving a definite style. The diarist does not pull himself away from the contents of the day to produce a synthetic account in which some things are highlighted and placed in the foreground, whereas other things recede and fade away entirely. The diarist does not elevate himself above the stream of occurrences and encounters; he does not order or distill. And the stretches of writing are held together only by dates under which anything can be entered.[62] In contrast, a style, whatever its specific features, depends on a practice of selection.[63]

Schmitt's critique of the diary is not only conveyed in a scornful, moralizing idiom directed against vanity and sensuality that mutely invoked some stance of dignified asceticism. It also takes place through the very display of concision. Schmitt's often brief and pithy comments are meant to be demonstrations of sharpness delivered against the loquaciousness of the diary that never wants to discard anything or come to a close in a definitive summary or thesis. At one point, Schmitt writes: "Most diarists seem like children to me, who suck on their fingers and who suck on everything that they get their fingers on."[64] The metaphor expresses disgust at the diarist's eager exploitation of his encounters with the perceptible world, but the charge against infantilism is delivered in a statement that seals itself off from further development through its self-enclosed structure. In this way, Schmitt performed his critique of the diary in statements supposed to exemplify control and closure.

The concentrated formulations that Schmitt distributed in his notebook represent a form of resistance to the genre of the diary. Whether or not they are of any quality, his hard, sententious statements are designed to block the emergence of a discursive flow.[65] The maximlike sentence that he preferred closes itself off and refuses to connect with its surroundings. Thematically as well as formally, it is aloof, ready to be detached from the work and carried into other contexts, as illustrated by the astonishing career of such pronouncements as "Sovereign is he who decides on the exception."[66] By inviting extraction,[67] the sententious proposition is indifferent to the date under which it appears and isolates itself from the loose day-to-day narrative of the diarist.

At this juncture, we can suggest a more general characterization of Schmitt's posthumously published notebooks from the immediate postwar period. The editor of the compendium is reluctant to use the term "diary" on the grounds that Schmitt never chronicled any "daily routine" but almost exclusively wrote on legal or political problems, often in conjunction with comments on books that he was reading.[68] However, the structure of the notes, the fact that they are divided into entries marked by dates of inscription, implies at least an affinity with the diary form, and in his preface the editor can hardly neglect the fact that Schmitt had at times been an avid diarist, especially in his younger years. Against the background of these previous stretches of journal writing, *Glossarium,* as Schmitt himself called his notes, does not appear as an absolutely anomalous project in Schmitt's biography, yet it may not seamlessly follow upon earlier records either. On the one hand, the diary is simply the most obvious genre attribution for his textual production, based on both its structure and Schmitt's previous writings. On the other hand, the very choice of the title for the notes from these postwar years—the term "glossary" suggests a principle of alphabetical order rather than diachronic progression—and Schmitt's many reservations about the form complicate the classification. As an examination of the notebooks reveals, the foregrounded but refused resemblance to the diary ultimately points to Schmitt's ambivalence toward this form. His relationship to the diary was similar to his relationship to the questionnaire or the postwar confession: he loathed it but could not quite extricate himself from it.

Schmitt's notes do not constitute a diary, but they are engaged in, and even produced out of, a daily struggle against the diary's formlessness and engrossment in trivialities. Schmitt carried out this struggle on multiple levels, through arguments against the diary, repeated attacks on iconic diarists, conscious and explicitly thematized silence about the events of each day, and repeated performances of sententious concision. He rejected the diary, day by day, by building a glossary of critical definitions within it, by producing thumbnail sketches and epigrammatic rejections that would be out of place in a garrulous, formless form and ultimately challenge its minimalist structuring principle.

Schmitt clearly saw the diary as the generator of vanity and was well aware that every day-to-day record is written for an audience, however much the diarist insists on privacy and secrecy. The narcissism inherent in life writing, Schmitt claimed, is always on its way to the printing press. (In a near-untranslatable quip, Schmitt suggested an alliance between the *Rotationspresse* and the *Ro-Ro-Ro-Pepysm.*)[69] In line with this distaste for eagerly anticipated publicity, Schmitt's critique of the diary took aim not only at its formless form, but also at the way its statements are typically received and interpreted by a readership that is always furtively invited. Ultimately, Schmitt was quarrelling with the curious audience that belongs to or is projected by the genre itself (rather than the empirical crowd that sometime in the future may or may not pick up the book). The notion that the diarist fixes every event and his emotional reaction to it serves to establish reader expectations that cannot be upset by counter-evidence. A diary, no matter what it contains, can always be approached as a window into a more or less turbulent soul. In this sense, postwar journal writing was affiliated with the participation in a "screening" of an apparently opaque personality, to use Schmitt's own term for the questions posed to him after 1945.

Beyond staging a stylistic revolt against the loquaciousness of the journal, Schmitt sought to dislodge a set of stubborn assumptions about the nature of his statements, for no matter what topics he chose to address or how pithy his formulations were, he suspected that they could still be read in an inquisitional vein, as manifestations of a particular person willing to put himself on display in writing. However abstract or sententious the statements deposited in a journal may be, a psychologically interested reader can always frame them as symptoms of a soul.

A brief look at the reception of Schmitt's early journals demonstrates the persistence of such psychologizing readings. One recent reviewer of

Schmitt's diaries announces that "literary psychoanalysts would have a field day with Schmitt's metaphors" and that categorical statements such as "The ideal is the church state" reveal how he oscillates between sexual desire and quasi-religious feelings of guilt.[70] Another commentator claims that the diary discloses how the infamous friend/foe distinction issues from Schmitt's "need for distance," in turn indicative of an unstable psychic life dominated by "disgust and anxiety."[71] In these and countless other readings, the diary is not just one among many possible textual institutions that facilitate the production of a particular kind of statement and generate a particular kind of biography.[72] Instead, alleged expressions of buried anguish and resentment are understood as a privileged source of information about a person, a life, and a corpus of discursive interventions. Once a diary is found, commentators can begin to convert the elements of a political theory into manifestations of a psychological predicament. In other words, the reviewers of Schmitt's diaries participate in the cultural battle that he himself both commented on and fought.

Schmitt knew about the inveterate conventions that govern the interpretation of any diary and harbored no illusions about the possibility of disturbing them. He even sketched out what he thought was the broader cultural context of psychologizing interpretations that rely on exposure and excavation. Postbaroque culture, he contended in a 1947 entry on Thomas Hobbes, posits a split between exteriority and interiority. Once established, this inner/outer division brings with it the valorization of the interior as the domicile of truth, of actual beliefs, real motives, and genuine power, over and above the mere "façade."[73] Schmitt's elliptical analysis of the "whole psychology and sociology of exposure"[74] in the baroque period is familiar enough. As soon as one conceives of a concealed interior as the location of the subject's intentions, one can begin to voice the demand for ever greater degrees of correspondence between inner and outer, avowal and actual belief.[75] To Schmitt, however, this modern craving for transparency and immediacy turned out to be especially corrosive of the process of political representation through which an ideal can become apparent in an embodied, tangible, even awe-inspiring form.[76] For the proponent of perfect sincerity, any exterior is always simply an unnecessary or distorting screen, hence all politically motivated attempts to craft a magnificent myth to capture the fascination and allegiance of a population is an exercise in deception. To Schmitt, the insistence on sincerity and transparency entailed the danger of political destabilization.

The constant drive to go beyond fronts, screens, and surfaces and reveal the always hidden truth seizes upon the diary as a genre that can be enlisted in the process of exposure. What someone writes as a note to herself reveals more about her than what she proclaims to others. The smaller the audience, the more intimate the setting, the greater potential for authenticity. While a diary may of course be replete with deceptions, these can easily be turned back on the author, classed as self-deceptions, and mined for psychological information. By reading Schmitt's diary as the document of a psychodrama, or at least pointing out how it could be read as such, the reviewers quoted above participate in the business of unmasking that Schmitt was himself trying to question through his genealogy of the "façade," namely that the supposedly secret journal is the potential site of truth about a subject, whose statements and commitments can be attributed to a problematic character that exists prior to any polemical engagement.

For Schmitt, however, the mere daily registration of everything one happens to perceive and feel cannot capture a particular individuality. Instead, he thought, genuine selfhood only becomes possible through political conflicts that draw boundaries and give contours to antagonistically related agents.[77] It may be that Schmitt wanted to escape the journal he kept and that his contentious categorical statements were so many attempts to break out of the diary form, not least by calling out opponents. Even so, he suspected that he could scarcely oppose the diary from within, for everything included in a diary can be referred back to the writing self. As soon as a text is labeled a diary, the author will always satisfy a nosy or overly concerned readership.

Even as a reluctant diarist, jotting down notes to himself in a situation of relative isolation and marginalization, Schmitt found himself in an age of discussion and of diagnosis. He implicitly perceived the genre of the private journal as continuous with the genre of the interrogation, for they can both be conceived of as sites of confession where a concealed interiority is being disclosed.[78] If there is a difference between the interrogation and the diary as a form of self-interrogation, it may lie in the boundlessness of the private journal. Once the questioner is removed and the writer has assumed the task of scrutinizing herself, the search for the truth of the self will only be capped by death.[79] In Schmitt's view, the diary genre tends to promote a form of writing that he her-self could take up only grudgingly, because the genre's organizing principles run counter to his valorization of polemics. The diary remains tied to the confession and invites the reader to interpret it as such.

From Schmitt's perspective, then, the ideological culture of the postwar period did not affect his life merely by conferring or withholding publishing rights while leaving everything else untouched. Insofar as this ideological culture was embodied in genres with a particular historical provenance, it extended into the domain of his writing. Postwar ideas about loquacious self-revelation and therapeutically meaningful correction, one could say, followed Schmitt into his private notebook, which struggled against the diary format and what he took to be its ideological premises. Schmitt's writings negotiated the problem of declaring his refusal to speak within the discursive form that was available to him. Expressed more dramatically, the genre of the diary can be said to have haunted his writing, and every one of his performances of concision was an act of exorcism. Schmitt's diary was not a sanctuary from the dominant ideas of postwar Germany and the discursive channels through which they were transmitted, but yet another compromised discursive space.

After 1945, Schmitt was interred and interrogated, pushed to the margins of the forming public discourse—with good reason, given his documented careerist involvement with National Socialism and endorsement and promotion of anti-Semitic policies. He responded to this situation not with penitent reflection but with a mixture of contempt and self-pity. In his writings, some public and some private, he regretted his own predicament and Germany's situation, but seemed not to acknowledge or even understand the duty to pay respect to the victims of German military aggression and genocidal policies. Schmitt himself only felt he had been deprived of ways of speaking not already occupied and inflected by ideas and purposes foreign to him. He thought he had no venue, and perhaps not even a genre, for his nonconversational, nonconfessional, polemical style. In the immediate postwar period, Schmitt felt that he faced only a range of truncated options of writing and thinking.

Nevertheless, Schmitt's often bitter and self-involved comments on the postwar climate of opinion did reveal some of its tensions. He pointed out that the culture of conversation, introduced and modeled by postwar journals such as Sternberger's *Die Wandlung,* existed alongside mass procedures of cross-examination and that the frequent invitations to calm and peaceful deliberations were trailed by the performance of psychological diagnoses that targeted deviant members of the German population. Postwar discourse featured both calls to revive sociability among Germans and attempts to perform social-scientific analyses of them. To Schmitt, the resulting combination or blurring of the genres of conversation and interrogation was deceitful and self-undermining.

Schmitt's writings, however, were far from the only ones that went against the new culture of conciliatory conversation. Writing in the United States but publishing in German journals from very early on, the political philosopher Hannah Arendt put pressure on the idea that postwar Germans would be able to derive any model of a future polity from the traditions of interaction particular to bourgeois society, or the *bürgerliche Gesellschaft*. After years of totalitarianism and genocide, no return to bourgeois society was possible or even desirable. Indeed, Arendt claimed that this particular historical formation had never generated a politically fruitful vision of how people relate to one another, an assertion that clearly ruled out any attempted resurrection of bourgeois sociability. Interestingly, she presented this very repudiation of bourgeois society in the pages of *Die Wandlung*. It is to her critique of bourgeois society that we will now turn.

Chapter Three

✦

The Mob of Bourgeois Society

Hannah Arendt

"The political attitudes of the mob possess a surprisingly strong affinity with the political attitudes of bourgeois society [*bürgerliche Gesellschaft*]."[1] This statement appears in one of Hannah Arendt's articles in the Heidelberg-based postwar journal *Die Wandlung*. The journal often featured her work, and her texts even initiated some of the central debates it housed, as in the case of her early analysis of the notion of collective guilt.[2] Still, *Die Wandlung* was an unlikely venue for reflections on the parallels between the bourgeois society and the mob. Indeed, by associating bourgeois society with the specter of delinquent gangs, Arendt implicitly disqualified the journal's emerging project, namely the promotion of a German *bürgerliche Gesellschaft* animated by practices of sociability.[3] As a closer look at her articles reveals, the early Arendt was one of bourgeois society's most consistent and acerbic opponents.

In its search for a nonauthoritarian principle of social cohesion after 1945, *Die Wandlung*, and specifically its main editor Dolf Sternberger, turned to the notion of the *bürgerliche Gesellschaft* as defined by the social practice of *Geselligkeit*. Carefully or perhaps selectively reconstructed, the concept fulfilled the needs of the postwar period. It corresponded to an available sociotope of the immediate postwar years—the proliferating salons, clubs, and conversational circles—but also seemed reliably nonmilitant after a period of perpetual exhortation and mobilization. The idea of a revived leisurely sociability could even be presented as a reeducation program that would be recognizable to Germans and acceptable to the American administration in Germany. If Germans could only recover a previously aborted but nonetheless available tradition of tempered and voluntary interaction, Sternberger implied, they could perhaps draw nearer more fully civilized Western nations. An immersion into a particular brand of bourgeois sociability would train the German public in the genre of respectful and responsible dialogue and ultimately prepare them for participation in a democratic republic, without itself being explicitly political.

The neatness with which the image of a "Bürger in Gesellschaft und Geselligkeit" satisfied a range of requirements and audiences, however, should not obscure its most fundamental purpose. The *bürgerliche Gesellschaft* was a name for a context of interconnection and cooperation emerging out of the activities of multiple self-managing individuals, without the constant supervision of an external authority. As such, it suggested the presence of an ostensibly weak but resilient self-organizing capacity of societal interaction and could be enlisted as a mode of community formation in a situation of precarious statehood. At a moment when speaking of a German state, a German nation, or a German people had become difficult, the concept of sociability would allow the writers and the thinkers connected to *Die Wandlung* to imagine a certain degree of coherence and unity. And yet, as we shall see, Arendt could not be further from accepting and developing this discourse.

Arendt was in many ways the most prized contributor to *Die Wandlung*, or the one who best fulfilled the ambitions of the editorial board. As a Jewish woman living in the United States but writing in German, Arendt's participation in the project seemed to lend concreteness to the journal's efforts to compose the most diverse community possible—ecumenical, cosmopolitan, open to both men and women. *Die Wandlung* needed Arendt. She did not, however, endorse the quietly introduced editorial program of a revivified sociability, distinctly bourgeois in kind. If anything, her series of articles, dispatched from outside Germany and largely untroubled by efforts to devise reeducational therapies, implicitly (and probably unintentionally) exposed the hollowness of this project.[4]

Arendt's thought was marked by a strong antibourgeois stance, and later commentators even confess to being startled by the "degree of blame [for totalitarianism] Arendt lays at the feet of the Continental bourgeoisie."[5] This undeniable feature in her postwar work also appeared in *Die Wandlung*, most visibly in her account of the fateful consequences of a parochial concept of individual responsibility among the middle class in the article "Organized Guilt." In a review of the central concerns of a range of postwar periodicals, *Die Wandlung* is even said to stand out for having produced "the most detailed psychological profile of the petit bourgeois participant and supporter [*Mitläufer*],"[6] a feat that must be attributed primarily to Arendt.

It may seem that Arendt's deployment of a vocabulary of antibourgeois critique for the purposes of a diagnostic approach to opportunism and conformism under National Socialism cannot be related to Sternberger's ideal of salon sociability. They ultimately spoke about very different things, a split that is most economically displayed in their preference for related but different concepts. Frequently referring to but not completely espousing a Marxist conception of class structure, Arendt used the term *Bourgeoisie* in her German-language texts, a concept that Sternberger avoided in his effort to retrieve a positive image of the *bürgerliche Gesellschaft,* unburdened by any connotations of class antagonism.[7] For Sternberger, the positive resonance of *bürgerliche Gesellschaft* as an association of sociable individuals, but ultimately also of independent-minded citizens, had to be kept apart from the potentially more pejorative *Bourgeoisie,* with its connotations of materialism. Arendt used the concepts *bürgerlich* and *bourgeois* more or less interchangeably and indicated that no positive image of political life could be retrieved from the history of bourgeois society.

Yet there may be less that separates the various conceptions of the *bürgerliche Gesellschaft* than these differences in terminology suggest. Sternberger turned to sociability in order to conjure up some minimal form of social cohesion despite the contemporary uncertainty about Germany's future institutional shape, lack of obvious sources of collective identification, and concomitant risk of fragmentation. For him, the *bürgerliche Gesellschaft* implied that individuals could be relied on to generate manifold voluntary ties without the intervention and shaping force of a preconstituted outside agency. Discrete but gregarious subjects spontaneously build networks of conversation. But it was in fact a version of this idea at which Arendt took aim. She criticized the attempt of liberal thought of bourgeois origin to derive a notion of collective life from the motivations and interests of multiple individuals understood as neatly separable agents. The sphere of politics, she argued, was more than the consequence of usefully confluent individual actions or meshing predispositions. This sphere possessed an integrity of its own, which could not so easily be decomposed into constituent parts. According to her, liberal thought misrepresented the existence of a communal life as the outcome of merely individual pursuits and in so doing expressed "an innate hostility" to all affairs that go under the name "public."[8] Consequently, Arendt did not think it necessary for Germany to pull up alongside other nations such as England that had been the home of a politically vocal bourgeoisie; it was the political outlook of this economically oriented class that was the central problem, in Germany and elsewhere. To some extent, Arendt denationalized the causes of the Nazi disaster, without in any way wanting to relieve the Germans of their collective guilt.

This is a recurrent position in Arendt's early writings. In *The Origins of Totalitarianism,* the book in which the material published in *Die Wandlung* reappeared in modified form, she speaks of the additive conception of bourgeois society and faults it for an inadequate comprehension of the dynamics of human collectivities: "All the so-called liberal concepts of politics . . . such as unlimited competition regulated by a secret balance which comes mysteriously from the sum total of competing activities, the pursuit of 'enlightened self-interest' as an adequate political virtue, unlimited progress inherent in the mere succession of events—have this in common: they simply add up private lives and personal behavior patterns and present the sum of laws of history, or economics, or politics."[9] Arendt's list of theses does come very close to a liberal understanding of the paradoxical constitution of the social whole. According to such a view, individual agents advance the interest of all others precisely when they devote themselves to egoistic projects, making the body politic the unforeseen consequence of private vice.[10]

In the articles published in *Die Wandlung,* Arendt likewise discussed how bourgeois society admits only the most circumscribed and parsimonious approach to the communal dimension of human activity, namely, the coordination of multiple individuals into an assembly of functions and the submission of all under a regime of force. In the *bürgerliche Gesellschaft,* Arendt contended, the community of men is viewed from the perspective of a materially beneficial outcome (wealth for all) or from the perspective of monopolized and augmented power (security for all). In both these cases, the association of human beings only appears in the guise of a process of generation and accumulation, as a matter of enhanced potency. Individuals primarily cluster to boost and render efficient processes of production, and the ongoing aggregation does not modify the notion of the self-contained individual agent as the fundamental unit. In liberal thought, Arendt claimed, the communal, whatever its rewards, remains secondary to the more originary experience of individual isolation.

Arendt's analysis did not, however, remain in the realm of rarefied social theory, as if her objections to liberal views of the *bürgerliche Gesellschaft* sought only to correct a distorted model. Instead, they informed and were elaborated in her analyses of the immediate past. She used the critique of the *bürgerliche Gesellschaft* to trace the descent of modern societies into gang formations galvanized by racism, as well as to explain the societal production of moral indifference that facilitated the implementation of genocidal policies in Germany.[11] To return to the quotation in the beginning, the "mob" does not disturb an otherwise quiet and inherently nonviolent bourgeois society from the outside. The mob is, rather, this society's innermost principle. Needless to say, Arendt's account was completely opposed to Sternberger's vision of revitalized sociability in networks of reemerging German *Bürger* promoted in the very same journal.

A final note on the personal relationship between Arendt and Sternberger. It was friendly, but not quite profound. Judging by Arendt's letters to Jaspers and her husband Heinrich Blücher, she and Sternberger spent time together as acquaintances and colleagues when Arendt visited Germany or Sternberger America, but the intermittent meetings never solidified into an actual sustained exchange of ideas. For Arendt, Sternberger was no more than a "journalistic talent at a high level [*Journalistenbegabung auf hohem Niveau*]," as opposed to an original thinker.[12] Significantly, Arendt's subtly dismissive view of Sternberger's personality resonates with widespread critical views of dispositions affiliated with sociability. Writing to Jaspers, she said that she found Sternberger "a little too clever [*ein wenig zu geschickt*]" and "highly adaptable [*sehr anpassungsfähig*]."[13] This characterization of flexibility and virtuosity fits with standard ideas about sociable interaction meant to be supple, elegant, and inoffensive and hence also necessarily empty of substance. Arendt's quick sketches of Sternberger ascribe to him qualities frequently associated with conversational, sociable attitudes, the political value of which she remained skeptical.

Bourgeois Society and Imperialism

One of the first essays Hannah Arendt published in *Die Wandlung* was "On Imperialism," an article that built on a group of works in which the study of imperialism had served as a vehicle of critique against bourgeois society defined as capitalist. In the writings of Lenin, to mention one of the theorists to whom Arendt referred in her article, imperialism was the most advanced stage of the restless search for fresh possibilities for investment under capitalism, namely the stage during which this search was furthered by the military means of the state.[14] Capitalism was not innately pacific—quite to the contrary, it inevitably gravitated toward militarism and violent conquest.[15] As one could perhaps expect from a discussion of imperialism published in a German-speaking journal in 1946, Arendt's article gauged the possible influence of imperialist projects on landlocked nations with few or no overseas colonies. Theories of imperialism, Arendt suggested, could be relevant to a comprehensive diagnostic history of the aggressive continental warfare of National Socialist Germany.[16] As her first major book would later make clear, Arendt was concerned with the origins and elements of totalitarianism.

But the title "On Imperialism" hardly does justice to the plethora of topics dealt with in the essay's fifteen or so pages. Besides a brief review of Marxist analyses of imperialist expansion in the works of Lenin, J. A. Hobson, and Rudolf Hilferding, Arendt mentioned Jakob Burkhardt's and Oswald Spengler's visions of the rise of despotic mass societies, Balzac's panoramic novels of the Parisian underworld, and the melancholic visions of cultural decline in the works of Friedrich Nietzsche, Charles Baudelaire, and Algernon Swinburne. In addition, she devoted pages to a summary of Hobbes's political philosophy and ranked its importance to bourgeois society in relation to the doctrines of man as a legislative being proposed during the French Revolution. The study of imperialism as a late manifestation of capitalism was, moreover, supplemented with a look at the emergence and consolidation of racist theories through the confrontation of Europeans with native populations, the attraction of anti-Semitic suspicions of an international Jewish network to political movements operating beyond the nation-state, and a basic typology of nihilistic attitudes in their relationship to a society based on private ownership. "On Imperialism" was crammed with the materials of right-wing cultural critics and left-wing historians and theorists and covered the ideologies of imperialism, racism, anti-Semitism, and nihilism. The condensed essay could hardly have pointed to more culprits for the disasters and atrocities of the recent past within its limited space.

Yet for all the historical, philosophical, and literary sources Arendt marshaled to represent a pathological development running up toward the Second World War and the Holocaust, she could not quite combine them into a plausible narrative of how so much destruction could have come about on the European continent. Arendt's own frantic inventory of pernicious historical trends (such as the formation of a mob) and dangerous ideological attitudes (such as nihilism) could not remedy the sense of a disjunction between the nineteenth century as a "Golden Age of Security" and the years of war and genocide. The trends and attitudes appear almost as curious props.

While "On Imperialism" displays an overabundance of narratives, motifs, and references that could help explain the descent into destruction, it also opened with a declaration about the blatant absurdity of all such explanations. It is not that Arendt cannot reconstruct developments in history or locate origins—her article as well as her book endeavored to do just that by considering how bourgeois society became imperialist and how imperialism generated racism that soon roused fanatic political movements. It is that the resulting explanatory narrative cannot fully satisfy the craving for a restored sense of necessity or significance in the experiences. The causes and factors that she listed and analyzed mock the need for a sense of dignity that would mitigate "this element of bloody fool's play" and make the suffering easier to bear.[17] Or, rather, the essay seems to demonstrate precisely how the perceived inadequacy of all available and potentially pertinent accounts leads to, and is exhibited through, a wildly eclectic mixture of materials drawn from several different sources, disciplines, and ideological camps. Arendt did not close the gap between the event of totalitarianism and the available historical explanations for it, but instead sought to highlight the bizarre, nightmare quality of a world swept by destruction.[18] She tried to identify the origins of totalitarianism and thus explain its emergence, but to do so without reducing the incomprehensible scandal of its existence by making it seem like less of a "fool's play."

Almost covered by the cluttered surface of the text is a plainer thesis, one that belongs more to the realm of political philosophy than the numerous references to the socioeconomic factors behind imperialist enterprises would seem to indicate. "On Imperialism" in fact touches on historical events such as the scramble for Africa insofar as they illuminate the underlying principle of cohesion that structures the entity that Arendt labeled the *bürgerliche Gesellschaft.* She did not so much affirm or deny an established schema of interpretation of imperialism—a tradition of Marxist provenance—as she emphasized an additional lesson to be drawn from the unfolding of this particular historical type of domination. As the moment in which different social and economic strata join together to establish ruthless administrative government in overseas colonies, the phase of imperialism is of interest because, according to Arendt, it betrayed a specific conception of society. It is this conception of society that we must recover, to understand better the peculiar combinations of the essay, in which Arendt's discussions of Lenin, Balzac, and Hobbes are packed in without much regard for historical context, bounded traditions, or disciplines of thought. Imperialism is for Arendt not primarily, or at least not only, the most advanced stage of capitalism, but the epoch in which a fatally minimalist understanding of human relatedness becomes most apparent.

Building on the basic conclusions of preceding works on the logic of imperialist expansion, Arendt assumed that the drive to acquire colonies was a response to a set of socioeconomic problems that could not be solved within the borders of the European nation-state. While the agents of capitalist enterprises experienced declining opportunities within their own countries, impoverished sections of the population, whose numbers and degree of destitution exceeded the scope of all welfare schemes, had to find employment. Capitalist firms produced cheap commodities that found no buyers among workers whose reduced wages had made the commodities cheap in the first place. The solution to this dual problem of overproduction and immiseration was to draw previously unconnected areas of the world into the market economy by military means. In other words, the solution entailed the subservience of the state to the economic ends of businesspeople.[19] The overseas enterprises relieved the purely economic pressure of having to find further outlets for production, but it also included shipping crowds of men to newly conquered areas, or even appointing these men with the task of local political administration. The result was, according to Arendt, that a "mob" of adventurers with no firm place in the nation's social order and eager for escape was encouraged to install rule by means of violent subjugation far beyond the nation-state's borders and barely controlled by its institutions. Imperialism was built on an alliance between the "much-too-rich" and the "much-too-poor," the people who wanted to expand production and increase their profits and the people who wanted to escape their nations.[20]

This account of the imperialist project in "On Imperialism," in which expansion is driven by the combined motivation of seeking outlets for superfluous capital and superfluous men, may seem curious but it is not unconventional. In its outlines it reiterated a vision present already in Hegel, for whom the uneven distribution of income in bourgeois society created a situation of underconsumption and excessive production that impelled the conquest of new markets.[21] And this approach to imperialism had also been vigorously contested well before Arendt's intervention—for instance, by the economist Joseph Schumpeter, in his more differentiated analysis of the conditions under which a capitalist nation will become imperialist.[22]

The notion that imperialism is society's means of solving socioeconomic problems was primarily of interest to Arendt because it confirmed her intuition of a more fundamental affinity between the behavior of bourgeois society and the mob. Again, Arendt stated that the mob was the truth of the *bürgerliche Gesellschaft*. Insofar as imperialism represented the phase in which various sections of bourgeois society, its richest members and its scraps, finally became allies in a common project of overseas expansion, it shed light on this society's basic form of integration of individuals into communities. Arendt claimed that the alliance of the *bürgerliche Gesellschaft* with the mob during imperialism revealed that this society had been nothing but a mob from the very beginning. She mobilized the primarily Marxist theories of imperialism as an advanced stage of crisis-ridden capitalism to make a point about the fundamental constitution of bourgeois society.

On what does Arendt base the claim about the affinity between the representatives of bourgeois society and the mob? It is not simply a case of matching material interests between bourgeois capitalists who wanted to open up new markets and the members of the mob who wanted new opportunities or even escapades. Instead, Arendt at various points spoke of the affection (*Zuneigung*) of high society for the mob, or its romantic admiration for the underworld.[23] Such displays of affection did not, she continued, merely betray the escapist longings of those who have become bored of the safe and insulated life in the salons; rather, they should in turn be traced back to an underlying "sense of belonging [*Zugehörigkeitsgefühl*]" or "kinship" that is typically felt only among family members.[24] The mob was connected to other strata of bourgeois society in a relation of "begetting [*Erzeugung*]."[25] In a way that Arendt neglects to describe in any detail, the capitalist system had produced a loose collection of gangsters and adventurers in the urban centers, poverty-stricken and déclassé individuals coming from all classes but without membership in or loyalty to any particular societal group. This mob was not society's waste but, more specifically, its waste *product* (*Abfallprodukt*).[26] As such, it was secretly cherished as offspring by the richer and more respectable bourgeoisie.

Of course, the many metaphors of generation and familial bonds do not in themselves elucidate the imperialist alliance. Arendt's surprising explanation is that in the mob of aggressive but isolated and hence vulnerable individuals, all of whom roam outside the care of the state and the transactions of society but who gang up to form bands, the bourgeoisie could recognize nothing but the image of its own collectivity, its own origins. The "association of déclassé people" in mob groups corresponded, Arendt thought, to the bourgeois conception of state formation as an instrumental aggregation of otherwise isolated and naturally belligerent individuals.[27] In the formation of a mob, bourgeois society could rediscover the narrative of its own beginnings. The mob not only performed vital services to capitalists who drove their nation-states to conquer new lands. The mob also held up a mirror to the bourgeoisie through the way that it was generated and assembled.

In its constitution, the mob even presented the true version of the bourgeoisie's political *Weltanschauung*, purified of concessions to Christian ethics and classical doctrines of virtue, traditions older than the historical bourgeoisie itself and therefore ultimately dispensable to it. Arendt elaborates on this thesis in her highly idiosyncratic explication of Thomas Hobbes's *Leviathan,* who according to her codified the bourgeois values with unparalleled honesty and consistency. Arendt's explication possesses the form of ten enumerated theses but unfolds progressively as interlinked narratives of association. The starting point is the Hobbesian one that each individual is both a danger to and threatened by everyone else and that this equality among potential murderers compels them to contractually delegate their power to a state that can guarantee security for all. With the state's monopoly of violence, Arendt continues in a further thesis, the individual must yield to its authority but is also relieved of any further obligations to others. The form of life guaranteed by the state is thus that of perpetuated atomism,[28] in which peace is preserved only by the submission of all to a state that each individual regards as a foreign center of power. The concentration of power in the sovereign state means that it takes on the mask of a force uncontrolled by any of society's members and eventually comes to be seen as a fate that befalls them from the outside.

Arendt distills out of Hobbes a picture in which the communal dimension of each individual's life is exhausted in the power that controls each member and appears in the guise of fate. The resulting commonwealth is overpowering, since it operates beyond the grasp of any individual, but is also curiously weak, since it conceives of no further bonds between individuals than those absolutely necessary for protection. In Arendt's reading, this polity robs individuals of a measure of control but does not relieve them of isolation.

The perpetuated atomism becomes most visible, she then asserts, among those who drop out of the established system of obedience and protection because of criminal acts or sheer destitution. Outside the bounds of the state and the market relationships of society shielded by this state, these unfortunate individuals find themselves again in a state of nature, forced to cluster anew. They represent a scattered mass of outcasts, of lonely humans who need to join an organization that bundles and directs the otherwise chaotically unleashed forces of people driven by their fear of everyone else. In this way, the starting position of those abandoned by the state and excluded from society recapitulates the conditions that prevailed during the formation phase of that state. By transposing this interpretation of the dynamic of state formation in Hobbes to European history, Arendt then claims that the members of bourgeois society could perceive in the mob, or in the process of formation of criminal gangs among outcasts, a repetition of its own history. It is on the basis of these corresponding narratives—the formation of the Hobbesian state that ruled over all bourgeois individuals and the formation of criminal gangs that ruled over all unfortunate outcasts—that Arendt then speaks of the kinship, the close familial relationship, of the mob to the bourgeoisie. In European nation-states the mob was born much the same way as bourgeois society, and hence the latter could rediscover its almost mythic origin in the former.

According to Arendt, all bourgeois individuals secretly thought of themselves as desperately lonely individuals lost in a state of nature, therefore they came to see their own image in the desperately lonely outcasts living beyond the bounds of respectable society. The alliance between high society and the mob further played out as a story of how the bourgeoisie came into its own by throwing away the "mask of hypocrisy."[29] The peculiar way in which Arendt discusses this moment of revelation suggests a desire to discredit the *bürgerliche Gesellschaft* that overwhelms her care for consistent argumentation. At different points in her essay, she offers contrasting and perhaps even contradictory explanations of why the bourgeoisie decided to declare the mob an ally in the age of developing imperialism. In the German case, it was because the bourgeoisie was weak, could not sustain its rarefied self-image, and hence conceded that it was much like the mob. She wrote: "The less secure a society feels, the more it will be tempted to shed the heavy burden of hypocrisy."[30] In the French case, it was because the bourgeoisie finally understood its strength and could now cast off the virtues it had claimed to represent and emerge as the mob that it was. "After the slaughter of the Communards (1871), the bourgeoisie felt so secure that it could contemplate accepting the Hobbesian philosophy."[31] To accept Hobbesian philosophy here means to end all "hypocrisy."[32] Whether feeling secure or insecure, Arendt proposed, bourgeois society let its mask fall to reveal itself as a mob. Sooner or later, regardless of its level of self-confidence, the fundamental structure of the *bürgerliche Gesellschaft* was exposed in the actions of its members. The alliance of the mob and the leaders of bourgeois society revealed that they always belonged together.

In Arendt's odd combination of theorems of imperialism and Hobbes's political thought, the mobilization of déclassé criminals for the purpose of colonial expansion driven by the need for market opportunities made manifest the fact that bourgeois society was never anything but a mob. But it was a mob in the special sense that it had the barest possible conception of society: its formation was always a matter of exigency. As described by Arendt, the Hobbesian commonwealth does not have the stability or integrity of a community preceding all mere temporary, contractual relationships, but ultimately also lacks the transparency of a limited arrangement subject to revision by its individual members. The mob and bourgeois society can also be seen as analogous or affiliated formations, because the individuals who composed them were cut off from everyone else and only joined groups whose structure and purpose confirmed and solidified this state of affairs. Their parallel communities originated in and were regulated by fear and urgency. In bourgeois society, there were no permanent bonds between individuals understood as coresponsible for something that they all share, and no connections were formed for other reasons than the pressing needs of each person. To the historical bourgeoisie, the life of society was derived solely from the constellation of individual interests.[33]

In "On Imperialism," Arendt summoned the established critique of an imperialist alliance between superfluous capital and superfluous individuals within nation-states to argue that the bourgeois idea of entrance into relationships with others was an issue of controlling and channeling force. The alliance between the bourgeoisie and the mob revealed to the world that, in the bourgeois imagination, individuals are in fact always just vulnerable outcasts, forced to band together to form units capable of greater violence and domination than any single individual. With this conception of the individual agent as an essentially abandoned creature, society either is nonexistent or exhausts itself in the form of a compound of power.

As we can now see, Arendt was hardly a proponent of a return to bourgeois sociability in the postwar period. Instead she used the opportunity to publish in *Die Wandlung* to advance her theory of the *bürgerliche Gesellschaft* as defined by an atomistic and additive conception of communal life. And she also dramatized this model through an account of how respectable society had conducted a love affair with gangster rackets in the imperialist age. The lurid atmosphere that this dramatization generates may seem like a failure to stay within the boundaries of some rigorous school of thought, yet to Arendt, this would be an instructive or even unavoidable failure, for the absurdity that haunts any attempt at explanation of how the catastrophes of the twentieth century came about must be openly demonstrated rather than concealed. Arendt's postwar essays were populated with a repertoire of nearly novelistic figures (such as the déclassé criminal or the capitalist boss), to the point of being garish, yet she presented this deployment of cultural stereotypes as necessary, for unfathomable destruction had improbable sources, and no desire for grandeur or profound meaning in history could or should cover over the disparity between ludicrous-seeming beginnings and absolutely disastrous ends. Indeed, precisely because the enormity of the destruction resisted human comprehension, its sources or origins looked more and more absurd as one tried to explore them.

Bourgeois Society and Organized Guilt

If one of the controversial features of *The Origins of Totalitarianism* was to represent Nazi Germany and Stalin's Soviet Union as two comparable examples of a totalitarian type of government, an idea that disputed the thesis that fascism and communism were entirely distinct movements,[34] Arendt's early postwar articles explicitly built on Marxist theories that were fused with a more general antibourgeois rhetoric against philistines and dull jobholders. In other words, the early Arendt was no supporter of a reinvigorated *bürgerliche Gesellschaft,* a prospect whose value for a future German identity was being explored in *Die Wandlung*. Yet her compressed manner of presentation, the multiplicity and eclecticism of the motifs presented in the essay, may very well have obscured the central thesis despite occasional polemical flashes such as the declaration that the political attitudes of the *bürgerliche Gesellschaft* are identical with the political attitudes of the mob. One of her other essays, however, the article "Organized Guilt," addressed the topic more explicitly.

The text no doubt caused a stir because of its thesis; it considered the validity of the charge that all Germans were collectively guilty of aggressive warfare and genocide. In fact, the editors deemed it necessary to try to mitigate future controversy by adding a prefatory remark to the essay, which contextualized the direct way it addressed German culpability:[35] "It is important to know that the following contribution from Hannah Arendt was written in America in November of 1944 and published in English translation in the journal *Jewish Frontier* in January of 1945."[36]

Arendt was invited to *Die Wandlung,* yet her voice had to be characterized, explained, and embedded in slightly conciliatory remarks. But the resonance of this text, to which Sternberger would refer in his closing statement in the very last issue of the journal, was also due to its directness and comprehensibility. At crucial junctures in her argument, Arendt drew on widely available cultural knowledge. When trying to explain the deployment of great numbers of Germans in a genocidal project, Arendt invoked recognizable, even hackneyed antibourgeois stereotypes, such as the image of the tediously respectable philistine or the parochially status-obsessed members of the lower middle class. She linked administrative mass murder to the conduct and mentality of the *Spießer.*[37] But it is also in the discussion of this figure that one can detect her continued critique of the *bürgerliche Gesellschaft,* for she introduced this customary target of literary ridicule in order to elucidate a broader social theory. Much like in "On Imperialism," she elaborated on the notion that the *bürgerliche Gesellschaft* possesses no concept of human interaction beyond its account of the purely instrumental value of society to the single individual. In the article on organized guilt, the critique of this impoverished understanding of community is installed to do extraordinarily heavy analytical work. It is used to explain central aspects of the implementation of genocide.

In "Organized Guilt," Arendt's aim is not to prove collective guilt, but to analyze the conditions in Germany that form the background for such a claim, namely, the strategically prepared identification of the Nazi Party with the entirety of the German people, and with it the planned erasure of any clear borders between a circle of leading criminals and the large mass of the population.[38] The primary object of analysis is a version of the scorched-earth policy. Increasingly aware of its probable future downfall, the National Socialist regime made sure that the Allies would find no uninvolved group within the German people to which to appeal. The complete identity of party and people was not simply a recurrent propaganda assertion, but was realized in a series of measures by which more and more Germans entered realms previously reserved for smaller terror formations. Arendt lists how all German soldiers officially came under the leadership of the party, how sections outside the SS were enlisted for service in concentration camps, and how strategic information leaks diffused knowledge about genocidal programs into a wider population that could then no longer claim ignorance.

In "Organized Guilt," the question of German guilt is not dealt with in theological or moral terms, nor does guilt become the basis of a novel national identity, two tendencies exemplified by Karl Jaspers's lecture series *Die Schuldfrage.*[39] Instead, Arendt's discussion quickly opens up to the question of the modes of societal integration exploited by the Nazis. As the essay title declares, guilt can be a matter of large-scale organization. If it then finally touches each member of the national community, making it collective, it ultimately shows to what degree society as a whole is conceptualized and structured *as* an organization, as a complex assembly of functions geared to a particular output and little more.

Looking at how the regime set out to absorb the nation into the party, Arendt noted that those who spoke of an ethnological or cultural susceptibility to fascism in the collective of the German people paradoxically demonstrated the success of National Socialist propaganda. In contrast to those who approached the issue of a German national or cultural deformation and even reached back to the age of German tribes fighting the Roman Empire to suggest a narrative of deep-rooted pathologies, Arendt insisted on the modernity of the problem. The fact that one can no longer reliably distinguish between criminals and noncriminals and therefore is led to deal with a people as a single entity, she argued, is the outcome of policies enforced in a very modern society.

When Arendt called organized guilt a modern problem, however, she was not simply saying that it was novel and unprecedented. Rather, she claimed that its conditions of possibility had emerged only in a society shaped by modern methods of production and administration. To organize something is to coordinate a multiplicity of discrete elements into one coherent unit, to recruit individuals and arrange them into a structure designed for enhanced efficiency in the fabrication of commodities, or, as in the German case, the fabrication of corpses. "Organized guilt" is a phrase that captures how more and more Germans were fitted into the vast logistical enterprise or machine assembled for genocide until every member of the population stood in some relation to, and also contributed to, the genocide carried out in the concentration camps.[40]

Faced with the administered mass murder that at least indirectly involved and made use of the entire population, commentators blamed the collective and often cast their accusation in cultural terms: a racially or spiritually homogeneous people carried the responsibility. Within the population organized into total complicity, however, the recognition of guilt by the individual members was reduced by means of the very same organizational structure. In an organizational compound where every member carries out a specific, delimited function, each individual may have a weakened sense of responsibility for the end product of the process as a whole. From the viewpoint of the single individual, the ultimate outcome of his or her actions may seem unintended.[41] Consequently, although outside observers held Germans responsible as one unified, pathological community, few within this community were ready to assume responsibility for the atrocities.[42] The individual may deny culpable involvement in genocide, then, and Arendt did not primarily interpret this denial in psychological terms (as a problem related to individuals' defense mechanisms); instead she saw it as a consequence of the diminished recognition of accountability in complex societies.[43] But this approach did prompt her to reflect on the values and principles of a society that had shrunk to the figure of a differentiated organization for the satisfaction of narrowly conceived individual needs. If guilt can be so easily organized, she maintained, it is because society as a whole is conceived of and exists as an organization, an instrumentally rational arrangement of interlocking functions carried out by isolated individuals, and nothing beyond that. "Organized Guilt" thus treated the same issue as "On Imperialism," namely bourgeois society as an impoverished, tenuous kind of communal formation.

In "Organized Guilt," Arendt also addressed the problem of widespread moral myopia by looking more closely at the mechanisms by which Germans could so easily be absorbed into an organizational structure whose composite effect or output they refused to identify with. However, this part of her analysis was performed in a vocabulary tinted with antibourgeois scorn. In her discussion of the National Socialist effort to mobilize Germany for the purpose of mass murder, she both resurrected and exhausted a nineteenth-century typology of social figures in a way that marked a clear departure from any vision of a renewed *bürgerliche Gesellschaft*. In order to explain the susceptibility of the population to recruitment into the administration of genocide, Arendt even conjured up a common target of antibourgeois criticism, the *Spießer* (the philistine).[44]

Arendt's discussion of the *Spießer* as a social type drew on the traditional portraits of someone primarily preoccupied with the security and comfort of his own family, or "the kind concern and earnest concentration on the welfare of the family, his solemn determination to make life easy for his wife and children."[45] Yet Arendt's narrative was one of changed conditions, or, more precisely, changed economic conditions. What happens to a person preoccupied with issues of (financial) stability ("security [*Sekurität*]," "life insurance," "secured existence for his wife and children") when this very security is threatened by crisis and unemployment and he understands that he can never achieve the desired state?[46] In such a situation, the commitment to a life within the "security . . . of his own private domain [*Schutz der vier Wände*]," a sphere whose future must be economically secured, rapidly turns into a weakness for anyone who promises a regular job, even if this is a job in an apparatus of murder.[47] This was, Arendt claimed, the simple insight of the "organizational genius of murder," namely Heinrich Himmler, who recognized what needs and desires to appeal to only because he was himself a *Spießer*.[48]

Arendt did not directly charge the *Spießer* with a materialistic and hence ethically blind attitude, a disregard for fellow humans for the sake of profit, but she did list what this particular character was prepared to compromise in his desire to safeguard the integrity of his home. An exclusive and increasingly desperate concern with sustained protection, which in Arendt's account is lexically inseparable from a concern with financial safety, made the *Spießer* vulnerable to deployment in administered mass murder if such deployment was presented as work. And when at work, the *Spießer* was shielded from questions of conscience precisely by means of the ideology of the secluded private sphere that he labored to defend. His sole responsibility was that of economic "care [*Sorge*]" for his familial unit: in all other areas, he did not consider himself accountable.[49]

In Arendt's account, the *Spießer* is nothing if not a responsible person who feels deeply obligated to protect his family, in whose constricted circle he thinks his real life takes place.[50] The space beyond the four protective walls is coded as an outside to which his delimited area of accepted obligation is connected only through his work. This narrow view of ethical commitment is both symptomatic of and inadequate to a society that has the division of labor for the satisfaction of material needs as its sole rationale and constitutive principle.[51] It is symptomatic insofar as the wider field of societal and organizational interdependence may exceed the individual's cognitive grasp and emotional attachment. He relates to it in the form of employment, which possesses a purely functional value for him, and a purely functional value for the organization. But it is at the same time inadequate insofar as this individual does draw his sustenance from the social whole, and as the general economic crisis and threat of unemployment showed in Germany, there is no room for illusions of autarchy. The resulting problem is inscribed in the vocabulary of security itself: the *Spießer* is concerned with the security of his family and perceives his home as a secure realm, although the systems that ground such security, namely the insurance schemes that Arendt invoked in her article, come into place only through cooperative arrangements where the economic burden of local damages are distributed over larger populations.[52] The mismatch between levels of actual organizational participation, on the one hand, and perceived and acknowledged emotional and ethical involvement, on the other, then became acute in the age of administered mass murder, when the *Spießer* consoled himself with his commitment to his family but actually carried responsibility for the extermination he participated in as a member of a large-scale organization.[53]

"Organized Guilt" did not add significant new aspects to the semantics of the *Spießer*, and Arendt admitted that it was, at the time of her writing, an old label. But Arendt's article did resituate a familiar cultural stereotype by narrating what happens to a certain figure, the average German, the little man, in the volatile surroundings of economic crisis and, finally, under a regime with a program for genocide.[54] Beneath this extended narrative, however, the figure of the *Spießer* functioned as a widely recognizable personification of an impoverished type of social organization. The problem with bourgeois society, Arendt contended, is that, in the eyes of its members, it exists only to meet basic desires, and any bonds forged for some other purpose than efficient production are dispensable. Bourgeois society is a system of needs. Individuals relate to the social whole in the medium of their focused contribution to its general output and regard it as a means to a defined end, namely, the security and sustenance of their families.

Nevertheless, Arendt did also indicate that this society is visited by the suspicion that its structure of separable cells of domestic life joined together only at the level of production and exchange occluded some significant aspect of human existence. In Arendt's sketch, the opposition to this view of earnest but narrowed responsibility had mostly generated romantic projects of rebellion. The reaction to the shrunken sense of responsibility had always been displays of reckless irresponsibility (typically consumed in novels). The critique of the tediousness of a secure life had been accompanied by some conception of a more exciting life style of risky adventure, overflowing vitality, or provocatively cultivated decadence. Against the dominant life narrative of bourgeois self-preservation, rebels performed spectacles of self-destruction without necessarily shaking off the ideology of the isolated individual.

Yet these extreme reactions to a society of *Spießer* were, Arendt also implied, not without their societal dangers. In "Organized Guilt," Arendt noted that the major ideologues and demagogues of the Nazi movement had all emerged from antibourgeois circles and entered politics with the help of a high society that nurtured a romantic attraction to lawless drifters. She presented the members of the Nazi elite (with the exception of Himmler) as a group of dedicated anti-*Spießer*. She called Joseph Goebbels a bohemian, Herrman Goering an adventurer, Julius Streicher a sexual offender, and Hitler a perverse fanatic. The categories to which the National Socialist elite belonged, Arendt proposed, had their origin in an antibourgeois mythology, and leading Nazi figures embodied social figures that opposed conformism, left the space of the home for foolish trips and projects, and transgressed social and sexual conventions. They were nothing but an assortment of rebels against the "Respectability" of the "jobholder," since their collective image relied on staged violations of ideals of permanent employment, seclusion in the private sphere, and familial reproduction.[55]

In Arendt's narrative, then, the armed bohemians of the National Socialist leadership based a lifestyle and an ideology on the rejection of diligent professional work and quiet family life, but as evidenced by the successful effort to organize guilt, they simultaneously fit the diligent German philistines into a machine for mass murder by manipulating their increasingly frantic efforts to approximate the conditions of steady employment and protected family sphere.[56] In *Die Wandlung,* Arendt presented the Nazi era as characterized by an alliance between opposing factions of the bourgeois world, in which former bohemians came to employ average jobholders to carry out genocide. The Nazi elite consisted of people who first reacted with perversions and recklessness to the tedious parochialism of the *Spießer*, and then set about manipulating precisely that parochialism. As in "On Imperialism," the apparently opposed actors of modern society, the mob and the bourgeoisie, found each other in a drive toward destruction.

This deployment of cultural stereotypes in order to characterize the Nationalist Socialist leadership, and even to analyze the mechanisms behind organized guilt, makes Arendt's analysis look rather like the implosion of a repertoire of bourgeois and antibourgeois attitudes. The analysis of collective guilt culminates in a vision of how bourgeois and antibourgeois types paradoxically connect—one group morally blind and the other recklessly immoral. To risk understatement, Arendt saw no viable resource for a future polity in the ruins of the *bürgerliche Gesellschaft.* For her there was no intact dimension of bourgeois sociability worthy of rehabilitation in the postwar scenario.

Beyond Bourgeois Society

Arendt's articles constituted a serialized critique of what she thought was bourgeois society's fatally reductive conception of collective life, a conception that in turn had fostered a myopic understanding of personal responsibility for the aggregate outcome of everyone's efforts. In her version of the prototypical bourgeois outlook, the human community is nothing more than the outcome of the individual pursuit of sustenance and protection. Arendt's line of attack is summarized in the formulation from *The Origins of Totalitarianism:* "Public life takes on the deceptive aspect of a total of private interests."[57]

Yet despite the many polemical gestures, the critique was not followed by the announcement of an easily recognizable counterproject or a strong positive program, at least not in the pages of *Die Wandlung.* Arendt was, it seems, reluctant to attach herself to a school, and the list of discarded alternatives is long. She drew the satirical profile of the *Spießer* from the archive of bohemian counterculture, but her identification of central Nazi figures as antibourgeois types makes clear that strategies of romantic rebelliousness held no attraction for her. She cited a number of Marxist sources, but remained dissatisfied with their failure to appreciate noneconomic motives and did not envision a constructive political role for the proletariat. Her critique took inspiration from an approach to bourgeois society not uncommon in the history of German political theory, according to which the pursuit of material ends by individuals and groups in society must be supplemented with a further dimension of properly political action, identified with the state as the bearer of a specific ethical or cultural mission. But the affinity is misleading insofar as Arendt's critique did not conclude with an endorsement of a strong state. In her analysis, such a statist vision typically derived from a prior definition of humankind in abstraction from a communal context, as fundamentally egoistic and anarchic and hence in need of stabilizing state governance. Also absent from her articles was any clearly drawn positive picture of a smaller and thicker community held together by infrangible bonds among kin and friends and somehow untouched by the modern developments of industrial production and bureaucratic administration. Despite her frequent borrowing from a large record of critical ideas, Romanticism, Marxism, and Statism are inadequate categories for her portrait of bourgeois society as atomistic, profit-oriented, and subversive to the integrity of the polity. What, then, lies beyond bourgeois society?

In "Organized Guilt," Arendt claimed that the problem with the *Spießer* was his impoverished sense of responsibility. The remedy to this fatal parochialism could include attempts to generate a comprehension of liability that is coterminous with real societal involvement. Arendt's central concern, it seems, would be to make people recognize and admit responsibility for that which in fact represents the outcome of their united efforts. However, the resources for a fundamental social and mental reform in this direction seem rather sparse. The article "On Imperialism" offered words of appreciation for the French Revolution as the moment in which man was first celebrated as a self-legislative being. This emphasis on the dignity of human autonomy would be congruent with her analyses of the denial of guilt and the specter of necessity, or the withdrawal from responsibility and agency. If Arendt's confrontation with the principles of bourgeois society produced a catalogue of figures of self-alienation—the *Spießer*, for instance, retreats into his private sphere, and relates to what is outside it only by identification with the function he performs in a machinelike structure—then her reference to the French Revolution was meant to point to a rediscovery and recuperation of people's capacity for autonomy at the level of the collective. On this reading, Arendt would ultimately advocate an ideal of (collective) self-determination.

Yet Arendt's understanding of how to participate in public affairs as a citizen is not fully captured in a vision of recovered and consolidated autonomy on a societal scale. Even if her articles diagnosed the inclination to disavow any involvement in processes that exceed the family sphere, her response was not to try to facilitate a more extensive, encompassing responsibility or greater political self-confidence. She did not define the need for more participation in political life in terms of each member's realization of what he or she, as a member of a collective, contributes to state power, or how he or she significantly affects the final output of an organization. Such realizations are sufficient and attractive only if the purpose of the society is in fact the efficient production of goods or the generation and exercise of great power. As a recent commentator of Arendt has pointed out, she never thought politics should be the pursuit of sovereignty in the sense of complete mastery over one's conditions and actions—a conception of political activity that might be too closely modeled on the owner's domination of his or her circumscribed sphere of private property.[58]

But even if Arendt did not explicitly outline an alternative to the *bürgerliche Gesellschaft* in the postwar journal, one can glean some requirements for a genuine "public life" from her critiques. First of all, its participants must assume responsibility for something they share, something that lies beyond the bounds of their separated domestic, private spheres—this is what the *Spießer* fails or refuses to do. In addition, the political and discursive engagement of individuals should not be a mere extension of interests that exist for them as isolated agents occupied with their survival, security, or prosperity—the only dimension of existence recognized within bourgeois society.

However, these various elements—collective responsibility for something that is shared and actions and speech that do not merely serve to transcribe and convey preexisting interests—cannot be realized apart. Combined, the requirements are simultaneously fulfilled in the vision of vigorous debate as a process through which responsive individuals distinguish themselves from one another within a bounded space defined by human fabrications, in the form of a polity's norms and laws or even physical, architectural demarcations. This vision, in turn, represents the movement of human culture away from a life dictated solely by natural needs. Arendt's emphasis on dynamic discursivity that unfolds within a common space of human artifice reflects her idea that the bourgeois understanding of society as a union for commerce and production, propelled by individual self-interests and passions, can slip into overtly naturalistic ideologies despite its apparent organizational complexity.

Common life within a defined realm enables discursive interaction that in turn may allow for the realization of a particular kind of human autonomy. In the pages of *Die Wandlung,* this sequence was sketched out in an essay on human rights from 1949. The focus of this article was the problem of safeguarding human rights for people who no longer enjoy citizenship. But in her analysis of everything that refugees were effectively deprived of, one can also discern Arendt's notion of a kind of political life that would transcend the mere aggregation of private interests. Reflecting on the plight of stateless subjects, she confirmed the importance for people to dwell in a "fabricated world [*geschaffene Welt*]."[59] The refugees she spoke about were shut out from all national territories, and in the most basic and concrete sense, they were in need of bounded and shielded areas of habitation. While her discussion of a constructed world spoke to people's need for shelter and sustained protection, it ultimately suggested a principle of cohesion. When people dwell together and attend to and cultivate this space, they do not primarily or only cohere because they all submit to a single power or all contribute to an end product. Instead, they relate to something that they share and that therefore constitutes a common concern and stable point of reference. What unifies people, then, is not what they all surrender or contribute to, or any quality that they all possess and that renders them similar, but a site toward which they all remain turned. With this prior convergence in place, there is room for processes of willed mutual differentiation through speech and action. Within the stabilized confines of a fabricated world, men and women can sustain relationships to each other by virtue of matters that they understand as common to them, and they are able to identify and determine themselves as individuals by arguing and taking positions with regard to these matters. With her discussion of a fabricated world, usually figured in spatial terms, Arendt thus described a condition in which individuals must be judged by what they say and do in their ongoing negotiations with others.[60]

In her analysis of human rights, Arendt showed her interest in a context where the discursive interaction between citizens determines the ascription of features to them, rather than any qualities each of them might possess independent of this process. When she discussed citizens, on the one hand, and stateless persons, on the other, she effectively drew a distinction between having something in common and being alike or unlike. Judged outside the context of a community that coheres by means of shared points of reference, individuals may be alike but have nothing in common. When viewed in abstraction from any specific community, individuals are no longer defined by their articulated approach to whatever things, traditions, ideas, issues, or problems are collectively regarded as shared. Traits emerge that are entirely unaffected by any discursive interaction with others over a common ground. In such a situation, an individual can then be both completely like others and absolutely separate from them, or he or she can both fall under the general category of a species with certain natural properties, or fall under no category, as a unique being with singular qualities. In contrast, human plurality is realized only through the ongoing dynamic differentiation on the level of assertions and claims that are made within a collective.

What one sees in Arendt's articles in *Die Wandlung* are thus the faintly emerging outlines of a theory of the political, defined as explicit contention over the order of things within a bounded, determinate space,[61] a process through which human plurality is realized.[62] Her project was to guard not what people simply are, but what they become by voicing opinions in continual negotiations with each other. And she viewed liberal thought critically, as a consistent effort to reduce the importance and scope of this discursive process. In its attempt to derive society from the spontaneously confluent actions of individuals, as a mere effect of individual interests and defined transactions, Arendt thought bourgeois society disregarded the unpredictable dynamic of voice.[63]

Why did Arendt not, like her editor Sternberger, consider sociability in the medium of conversation as an acceptable mode of discursive integration that had a particular historical place in bourgeois society? Did bourgeois society, in her eyes, truly have no political resources? Arendt would in fact speak directly of conversational sociability in her work *The Human Condition,* published in 1958, but then dispute in rather harsh tones that sociability ever could allow for the crystallization of a plurality of identities. Sociable conversation in the venues of the bourgeoisie, she claims in this later book, is too conciliatory, and conducted by people too anxious to please and gain prestige, to generate anything but a complete homogeneity of views and attitudes. The mutual influence and covert correction at work in sociability serves to minimize frictions and produce a kind of vacuous accord even in the absence of a central authority equipped with means of coercion. In one and the same passage in *The Human Condition,* for instance, Arendt disparages both the norms of high society, convening in exclusive salons, and the modern social sciences for their treatment of people as predictable "behaving particles" interacting in the capitalist market.[64]

For Arendt, the analogy between the salon and the modern market, or between refined sociability and the field of economic transactions, is possible with reference to comparable ideals of uniformity. In *The Human Condition,* she speaks of "the assumed one interest of society as a whole in economics as well as the assumed one opinion of polite society in the salon."[65] The salon and the market are, in this analysis, complementary sites of society, where individuals are seen as, or truly become, more and more alike, as they recycle previously accepted opinions or pursue material ends guided by maxims of instrumental rationality. Commerce and conversation are parallel activities. When everyone adheres to the scripts of sociable interaction and conversation in order to remain inoffensive and pleasing, the potential of speech is betrayed in the medium of language. Whether individuals try their best to observe tacit codes of behavior within delimited circles of sociability or maximize future economic gains, their patterns of behavior smoothly interlock, leading them to collectively forfeit the plurality realized through politics. Sociability may very well possess discursive dimensions, but it precludes the articulation of dissent, and for Arendt, only mutual contestation qualifies as politics.

In the pages of *Die Wandlung,* the editor Sternberger started a quiet campaign for the reintroduction of bourgeois forms of sociable interaction as a therapy for Germans who had emerged from war and totalitarian rule. *Geselligkeit* as practiced by the historical bourgeoisie, he proposed, would soften the rigid attitudes of Germans, train them in the virtues of tolerance and companionship, and ultimately open up the possibility of political argumentation carried out by the citizens of liberal democracies.

Arendt not only saw no such path in the postwar period, but presented a merciless attack on bourgeois society, also in *Die Wandlung*. One of the journal's most important contributors thus leveled a harsh critique at the founding editor's gradually emerging vision of a future Germany, a contrast that was never explicitly discussed in its pages. With the exception of Sternberger's quick references to the antibourgeois tradition embodied in Marxist thought in his article on the aspects of the *bürgerliche* character, the conflicting approaches were never brought into contact. Interestingly, Arendt privately judged Sternberger quite severely after a meeting in Heidelberg in 1952, and even attached one of her critical epithets directly to him. In a letter to Heinrich Blücher, she reported how Sternberger had claimed that "metaphysics are quite superfluous," then she added scathingly: "Sternberger has gone completely bourgeoisie [*ganz verspießert*]."[66]

Yet the debate that never took place nonetheless informed the thought of members of a succeeding intellectual generation. Publishing his account of bourgeois society in the 1950s, the young historian Reinhart Koselleck, trained in Heidelberg (the seat of *Die Wandlung*) and well aware of Karl Jaspers and Dolf Sternberger, professed to have been influenced in important ways by Arendt's early writings. In her *Origins of Totalitarianism,* preliminary parts of which had appeared in *Die Wandlung,* Koselleck found, he later claimed, a convincing representation of the bourgeoisie's systematic blindness to or neglect of political action. Much like Arendt, Koselleck would consider the political costs of the seemingly innocuous bourgeois attachment to commerce and conversation as the twin modes of ostensibly peaceful societal integration.

Yet his was not the last word on bourgeois society and its relationship to an exulted vision of politics as open contestation. In 1962, less than two decades after the end of *Die Wandlung,* Jürgen Habermas would argue against both Koselleck and Arendt. In his review of bourgeois discursive life in coffeehouses, salons, and clubs, he portrayed practices of sociability as foundational for a liberal public sphere in which government decisions could be scrutinized and contested. Going against Arendt, Habermas argued for the virtues and benefits of bourgeois conviviality, disentangling it from mere conformity. It is to Koselleck (chapter 4) and Habermas (chapter 5) that we must now turn.

Chapter Four

✦

Sociability and Hypocrisy

Reinhart Koselleck

The Enlightenment was an age of sociability, civil conversation that typically did not touch on topics so invidious that they would disperse the friendly tone among the interlocutors, or so controversial as to put them in acute danger. This type of interaction required specific localities, spaces set apart from, for instance, churches, courts, barracks, and bureaucracies. A brief list of such new venues, drawn from an influential account of the sociopolitical conditions and intellectual currents of the Enlightenment period, includes coffeehouses, academies, salons, libraries, and library societies. They were the early institutions of bourgeois sociability.

Each one of these spaces possessed its distinct character and its preferred themes. In the academies, people could gather to discuss scientific issues; in the coffeehouses and salons, they could exchange information or engage in witty conversation; and in the library societies, those who came together talked mostly about arts and letters. What these various topics or tonalities of discussion had in common, however, was their apparently nonpolitical or extrapolitical character. The academy, for instance, was not the forum of the state or a religious authority; those who met in libraries to converse on books typically avoided speaking about specific issues and policies; and in the salon, "*l'esprit* could rule without commitment."[1]

According to the author of this book, however, it was in the Masonic lodges that the Enlightenment bourgeoisie "acquired a social form of its own," for they most genuinely constituted spaces where "all distinctions of status were leveled out."[2] While the various "institutions of this novel sociable and social stratum" presupposed an equality of interacting individuals unknown in the feudal world, the Masonic lodges best served the purpose of "intrasocially uniting the bourgeois world."[3] This achievement partly had to do with the lodges' secretive character. As the author of the study puts it, "Joint participation in the same Arcanum guaranteed the equality of the brethren."[4] When male members of the bourgeoisie became initiates in the same Masonic lodge, they shed the status differences attributed to them on the outside.

The book where one can find these reflections on Enlightenment sociability, its constitutive ideals of equality and particular institutional embodiments, is Reinhart Koselleck's *Critique and Crisis.* It was published in West Germany in 1959 but was begun as a dissertation in the early 1950s. In fact, for the young Koselleck, Carl Schmitt, Hannah Arendt, and to some extent even the milieu in which Dolf Sternberger was active, were stations in a postwar education. One can even say that Koselleck's book is the locus of a debate on sociability that never took place directly between the teachers, mentors, and figures of his intellectual socialization after 1945.[5]

Just after the end of the war, Koselleck studied with the sociologist Alfred Weber in Heidelberg, read Karl Jaspers, and also took notice of Dolf Sternberger's efforts in the forming nonacademic sphere of debate. However, Carl Schmitt, who visited Heidelberg on several occasions, exercised an unrivaled influence on his thought and is thanked in the preface to the published version of the dissertation. To borrow a phrase from Koselleck's student friend Nicolaus Sombart, *Critique and Crisis* was written in a landscape between Heidelberg and Plettenberg, the university town that became a center of German reeducation in the immediate postwar years and the village in the Sauerland to which Carl Schmitt retreated after 1945.[6] But Hannah Arendt was also a highly significant reference point in Koselleck's intellectual environment. While Schmitt's presence in the work was acknowledged at the time of its publication and certainly eclipsed any attachment to the Heidelberg spirit in the reception of *Critique and Crisis,* Koselleck himself later pointed to Arendt's early work as a central source of confirmation for him, or as an intellectual project whose main tenets he could recognize as his own.[7]

Given this background, it is perhaps no surprise that the topic of his study is the emergence of a particular kind of bourgeois sociability and its political consequences. More generally, Koselleck was deeply familiar with the intellectual and social life developing within small associations and circles of friends in postwar Germany. As one reader of his work writes, Koselleck's study *Critique and Crisis* must be placed in the communicative context of "esoteric conversational circles, groups of friends, and minor academies" prevalent in the immediate postwar period.[8] Indeed, the period's "typology of talk" seemed to recapitulate the historical formation of semiexclusive salons, clubs, and academic and cultural societies that Koselleck reconstructed in his dissertation and whose corrosive influence on the stability of the state he regretted.[9] *Critique and Crisis* delivers a reflection on the political potentials and flaws of a kind of sociability, a version of which the author himself to some extent had experienced in the postwar period. Koselleck, too, lived in the era of the small discussion circle sketched out in the preceding chapters of this book.

Critique and Crisis possesses the focus and idiom of an academic dissertation. It weaves together political, social, and intellectual history and methodically analyzes and evaluates the rise and character of a species of control that is generated within the *bürgerliche Gesellschaft,* and—this is the central claim—emerges as a potent rival to state authority. Reliant on pressures and principles of interaction inherent to the field of society, this type of control produces and guarantees a measure of societal order and cohesion without the use or threat of explicit compulsion to be applied by a dominating agent. Koselleck's dissertation traces a complex historical process whereby the exercise of authority over individuals is transferred from personal to impersonal sources, from political agents to social interactions, and it assesses the paradoxical effects of this shift.

Yet the multiple influences of Koselleck's work do not flow easily and neatly into a piece of academic research, held together by the structure of a single and internally consistent argument. In light of his close acquaintance with radically different positions on bourgeois society and sociability in the immediate postwar period, it is possible to discern currents and crosscurrents at work under the rhetorically homogeneous surface of a dissertation in history. On closer inspection, *Critique and Crisis* harbors diverging, even contradictory conceptions of the societal field and the norms particular to it.

Koselleck's narration of the rise of the *bürgerliche Gesellschaft* and its forms of control is, to say the least, very critical. He does not view the discovery and support of society's capacity for self-regulation through mechanisms that secure general agreement as an advance over starker relationships of power based on the threat of coercion. On the contrary, he understands the desire of the forming bourgeois society to dismantle structures of obvious political subordination as an unfortunate, even dangerous utopian project, one that eventually results in unforeseen upheavals. What the historical bourgeoisie lacked, he claims, was a specifically political consciousness of unavoidable conflicts and a realization that institutional contrivances and mechanisms of compulsion are needed for the maintenance of stability within any given territory.

However, in his effort to provide a historically concrete account responsive to the philosophies of the emerging bourgeoisie, Koselleck includes statements on the dynamic of sociability from exponents of the *bürgerliche Gesellschaft* that he cannot fully integrate into his argumentative framework. The following reading of Koselleck's study will attend to how his agenda can be read against the grain, by pointing to positions emerging within the work itself. It even remains somewhat unclear how, according to *Critique and Crisis,* one should best interpret society's means of internal self-adjustment or how to evaluate the character and force of social pressures within human collectivities. Is the bourgeois dissolution of explicitly coercive authority into the harmonious and self-adjusting social whole an act of deception that must be exposed, or does it represent an actual draining of combative energies? Is the tendency toward conformity in society a result of subtly imposed hegemonic strategies, or does it in fact indicate the loss of political conflict, a development to be welcomed? Approached in this way, *Critique and Crisis* does not so much state a position as map multiple conceptions of the relationship between the concentrated political rule and the more dispersed and diffuse social enforcement of norms. This makes Koselleck's book an exemplary text of the postwar period.

Origins in Schmitt

In *Critique and Crisis,* Koselleck relates the broad development of what he calls the *bürgerliche Gesellschaft* and its intellectual representatives between the end of the confessional wars and the French Revolution. The study reconstructs the origins of the absolutist state, but also analyzes its demise in relation to the society that grows within it. More specifically, Koselleck's account focuses on the formation of the *bürgerliche Gesellschaft* as an actor in political affairs and its gradual advancement toward the eventual challenge to state power. The resulting work is presented as a study of a pathogenesis. This does not mean that the road to greater political prominence for the bourgeoisie, plotted over two centuries, is understood as the slow spread of an infection. What Koselleck views as pathological is rather the attitude of the new society toward its bid for extended influence. He criticizes the tendency of the Continental bourgeoisie to regard its critique as politically innocent, removed from any interest in actual power, although it culminates in a revolution. The study's elaborate table of contents in effect reads like a thesaurus entry on the word "deception": Koselleck announces that the consecutive sections of the dissertation deal with "Covering [*Verdeckung*]," "Blinding [*Verblendung*]," "Veiling [*Verschleierung*]," and "Concealment [*Verbergung*]."[10]

Koselleck studies the absolutist solution to the urgent problem of religious conflict after the Reformation and the eventual collapse of this absolutist construct. As the historian Anthony La Vopa has pointed out, the narrative Koselleck produces takes its "basic plot line" from the works of Schmitt, most notably from *The Leviathan in the State Theory of Thomas Hobbes: Meaning and Failure of a Political Symbol* from 1938.[11] In this book, based on a series of lectures, Schmitt recounts Hobbes's solution to civil war between religious factions and details how it involves the construction of a strong state that is neutral in all questions of faith. The laws this state decrees are devices by which to secure stability and are not grounded in any notion of truth or revelation. Instead, these laws are simply orders issued by a sovereign who abides only by the requirements of a purely administrative rationality. This disengagement of laws from divine right is a necessary basis for peace: "The assertion of being in the right does not lead to peace, but the compelling decision of a well-functioning legal system of coercion created to end strife."[12]

Yet the erection of the neutral state, a machinelike apparatus that ensures peace and security through means of coercion without reference to divine right, proves vulnerable. According to Schmitt, the problem is that Hobbes's sovereign, while empowered with considerable means of compulsion, does not manage to "exact a conformity of the souls" and hence remains curiously weak.[13] In Schmitt's reading, Hobbes first sets out to unite worldly and religious authority in the figure of an imposing sovereign, and in line with this endeavor, he favors an extension of the authority of the sovereign over religious matters. The sovereign has the right to decide what should count as a miracle or not. At the same time, however, Hobbes still retains a distinction between public reason and private reason and concedes that every person is allowed to follow his own reasoning as long as it does not affect the outward confession of faith. But this, it turns out, makes the state unable to obtain the undivided commitment of its subjects, who more and more come to regard it as a predator without any rightful claim upon their allegiance. The state effectively relinquishes the attempt to mold and control its subjects' inner and hidden beliefs and does not secure the necessary popular acceptance and support; it is unable to satisfy its own "ideological need."[14] Schmitt felt—at least in the book on Hobbes—that the state should not let political and normative authority drift apart and willingly surrender its capacity to manufacture broad consent by means of ideology. The sovereign should not just keep the peace without offering the subjects a myth.

Schmitt views the established dualism of public and private as a deplorable fracture subsequently exploited by the enemies of the state, who proceed to try to enlarge the scope and enhance the perceived value of this inner realm of private discretion. Charged with all the significance that religious conviction had been accorded before its enforced retreat to the private sphere, this inner life beyond the reach of the state is nurtured and developed by secret orders, Freemasons, pietist groups, and literary circles. A plethora of associations, Schmitt indicates, grows in response to people's need for communication and companionship anchored in shared religious and moral beliefs, small "subnational communities of truth," until these associations' claim on the loyalty of their members trumps that of the absolutist state.[15]

In his analysis of Hobbes, Schmitt depicts how small circles of discussion and ritual are able to supply their members with a warm sense of fellowship not provided by the more exclusively technical organ of the state. These associations appeal to subjects that crave solidarity, a human predisposition that is left unexploited by the Hobbesian sovereign, since this figure merely seeks to preside, by force, over a large collection of disconnected individuals. The realm of inner confession, of religious belief and moral conviction, thus solidifies into the site for a plurality of circles, groups, and movements in society. They manage to activate the support of their members by fulfilling their desire for fellowship, yet they cannot provide the state's protection.

Emotional, moral, and religious fellowship but no actual protection—this is, according to Schmitt, the dubious offering of fraternal associations, religious groups, and literary circles in the absolutist state. In a final move described by Schmitt, however, these circles or new forms of association, or some later successors of them, come to regard the administrative machinery of the state—the well-organized executive, the disciplined bureaucracy, the police force—as a means to be deployed to further their own particular interests.[16] In other words, they ultimately begin to seek control over the means of coercion and protection. And when they become successful in their endeavor, the state no longer hovers over a society drained of conflict, a field of quiet contentment and polite interaction, but becomes the medium of conflict between groups and factions that all strive to control the administration of peace for their own purposes. Covertly but unmistakably, however, Schmitt also posits a deceiving agent behind this entire process of decomposition, an agent who may even profit from the fragmentation of the powerful state. In his deeply anti-Semitic account, this agent is the Jewish community.

To Schmitt, generations of Jewish thinkers promoted their influence by struggling for legally protected liberties and rights for individuals against a state that is portrayed as a monstrous being whose power must be checked.[17]

In order to undermine Hobbes's attempted unification of worldly and religious authority in the formidable state and thereby protect the integrity of their own community, Jews had managed to both denigrate Hobbes's positively intended mythological representation of sovereign authority, by painting the Leviathan as a terrible beast, and to champion the consolidation of a constitution that protects their rights from state violation. Schmitt thus attributes to Jews a sense of the attractive or repellent force of mythical symbols that supersedes that of Hobbes, and blames them for the instrumentalization of purportedly universally beneficial laws for the advancement of their particular group interest. In sum, he insinuates that a small religious group unduly exercises influence behind the façade of the neutral state. With this picture of surreptitious strategies employed by a small compact, the reality of which Schmitt claims to have some special knowledge, he joins the ranks of the conspiracy theorists.[18]

Koselleck's study bears a striking resemblance to Schmitt's narrative, and it is no surprise that a reader familiar with both works has called *Critique and Crisis* "a fascinating attempt to fill in historical detail for Schmitt's main thesis [in *Leviathan*]."[19] Indeed, as another commentator observes, "The central argument of Koselleck's *Critique and Crisis* is taken directly from Schmitt's 1938 study on Hobbes."[20] Yet even as commentators have pointed out the striking parallels, they have also emphasized that Koselleck distanced himself from Schmitt's "diluted but still poisonous anti-Semitism."[21] But how exactly does Koselleck remove himself from Schmitt at the level of his argument? How does he devise a replacement for Schmitt's anti-Semitic story?

Koselleck appropriates Schmitt's narrative about the destabilization of absolutist sovereignty, able to offer protection but no satisfying sense of fellowship, but he does not introduce the specter of a deceptive, hidden agent who promotes and even coordinates this process to serve particular ends. Schmitt's anti-Semitism has been removed from the surface of the text. Instead, Koselleck elaborates on the historical account of how people who enjoy and are deeply conditioned by an age of greater security gradually become oblivious to the necessary premises of this security. The very achievements and distinctions introduced under absolutism, Koselleck claims, contribute to the formation of an adversary to absolutist rule that remains in the dark about the political nature and corrosive impact of its own critical project. Koselleck tries to replace Schmitt's paranoid suspicion of a concealed agent with a narrative of the unrecognized agency of an emerging elite in a temporarily pacified society. He moves from an anti-Semitic story of subversive intentions to an account of the unintended consequences of a particular attitude shaped by historical conditions.

From Deception to Self-Deception: Koselleck's Appropriation of Schmitt

Critique and Crisis traces the rise of bourgeois society within the framework of absolutist rule, and it argues that the concentration of power into the hands of the sovereign inadvertently promotes the formation of groups and congregations that absolutism is not able to integrate into its structure. This entails a study of how the beneficiaries of the established stability ironically become unable to appreciate its achievements. The emerging elites of the bourgeois society enjoy a condition of security and can devote themselves fully to the realms of commerce, science, art, and witty sociability in new spaces drained of conflict, but then they gradually lose the sense that their placid environment was made possible by the sovereign's monopolization of the means of coercion.

The development of absolutist rule constitutes an advance over the epoch of murderous religious strife, but it also produces a consciousness that will prove fatal for this very rule. Uninvolved in the maintenance of peace, the members of bourgeois society become progressively forgetful of the conflicts that once determined the political landscape. For them, the eruption of strife is no longer a constant danger, the containment of which necessitates a strict monopoly of power. Their first-order experience is that of people's more or less harmonious interplay, and the perceived self-evidence of this state of affairs leads them to question the distribution of power justified with reference to religious strife. The members of the bourgeoisie can enjoy their pursuits in a realm of sociability segregated from the political decision making, but the eventual effect of this segregation is to deprive them of an understanding of the necessity of politics. The bourgeoisie even comes to believe that the rule of the absolutist state may be rolled back or dissolved, thanks to the socially integrated community's capacity for peaceful self-management. The protocols of interaction in commerce, science, and art should, they begin to think, serve as templates for political behavior. To put it bluntly, bourgeois intellectuals start to believe that peaceful sociability is the best model for the entire polity, and they do not realize that this peaceful sociability can be sustained and protected only when the absolute sovereign is there to keep the peace.

Yet this antiabsolutist attitude forged under absolutism is never actually articulated as a direct challenge to the ruler, a challenge that at least initially would entail open contestation and strife between the power apparatus and the society averse to it. The consciousness of the bourgeois society, its self-understanding, is so deeply formed by its situation that it fails to grasp that it wants to depose a sovereign ruler for the sake of another arrangement and is hence effectively engaged in a quest for greater influence at the expense of another party. Like Arendt, Koselleck indicts the members and exponents of bourgeois society for their lack of a sense of responsibility that is on a par with their actual level of involvement in, and impact on the polity as a whole.

Koselleck elaborates on the bourgeoisie's obliviousness to the nature and the consequences of its actions in his discussion of the rhetoric of criticism. Shielded by the state, the emerging society within it develops standards of behavior and thought particular to the spheres in which it is active, such as science and art. In these fields, people engage in the assessment of the truth-value of statements, the beauty of objects, or the moral status of actions. In short, they become critics. The activity of critical judgment presupposes a certain mind-set, or rather, a certain position. The critic is, in Koselleck's account, a figure at a remove from the objects to be evaluated according to the criteria of truth, beauty, or correctness. This imagined distance between the critic and the matter to be criticized allows for a judicious process of appraisal in which arguments and counterarguments are weighed against each other and a final judgment is made. The critic thus derives his legitimacy from his neutrality and non-involvement, his position above parties, and even imagines himself to be a mere functionary of reason, so distant from the objects of his critique as to have become an impersonal instance raised above conflict. Critique is conceived as an "autonomous process to which individuals may contribute, but which is not defined by their contributions *as* individuals."[22]

For Koselleck, the consciousness of the critic proves to be fatally flawed as soon as the critical judgment is directed at the absolutist rule. The dynamic that Koselleck describes is deeply ironic.[23] It is precisely with reference to its neutrality and impersonality that the critic feels justified in directing his gaze at the measures and the person of the sovereign to appreciate their moral value. Once the critic levels judgments on the moral stature of the absolute ruler, however, he not only erodes the integrity of power, but also articulates a de facto "ruling claim [*Herrschaftsanspruch*]."[24] He seeks to displace the present sovereign and install the rule of the critic. The person who critiques political power enters the field of politics and becomes a political agent, despite any claims to provide neutral assessment, description, commentary, and so on. Political power, one could say, radiates outward or draws people into its force field, politicizing those who engage in reflections on it. Yet the very self-image of neutrality that prompts the critic to launch this campaign also precludes the insight into the unavoidably polemical nature of his claims. The critic does not, Koselleck maintains, quite grasp that the legitimacy on which his attack on the political center is based—neutrality, impartiality—withers away in the course of enunciating criticisms of the state.

The denied or unperceived usurpation of the critic is an occasion for pages of harsh indictments of the "mendacity [*Verlogenheit*]" that characterizes the representatives of the bourgeois intelligentsia.[25] The hypocrisy that Koselleck speaks of does not designate a mere pretense to admirable principles, the falsity of which the subject remains fully aware. The sharp language of denunciation describes a complex relation of the critic to himself—he is a figure who fails to see the truth about his own critical activity and the motivations that drive it.[26] His duplicity is not a self-conscious subterfuge because, in the end, it escapes him. The concealment of his de facto political project remains concealed to him, too, but insofar as he nevertheless does engage in a political battle against the sovereign, he becomes a strangely split agent.

The charge of blindness thus refers to the bourgeoisie's failure to grasp the import of its critique, but it also points to how the commitment to disinterested critique prevents the critic from honestly embracing his own will to power.[27] The critic seems to remain unaware that he harbors desires to grab power and exercise influence not compatible with his professed ethos of neutrality and remove, and also unaware that it is precisely those desires that prompted him to assume this ethos.[28] The bourgeois critic's devaluation of political power as crude violence helps establish his political superiority, but he cannot embrace this superiority over his opponent as a source of energy and pride. The crisis brought on by critique is therefore not simply the crisis of renewed political instability in the age of revolutions, but a crisis of self-division that characterizes the new political subject, whose consciousness as a morally pure being distances him from any open admission of desire for power. It is as if the critic cannot enjoy the thrills of the political revolution that he helps set in motion.

Going further, Koselleck argues that the crisis of a divided bourgeois self also serves to inaugurate a period of endless strife. The specious righteousness of this subject, he implies, makes him unable to "grant moral legitimacy to 'political' alternatives."[29] Hence the critic is quite averse to resolving conflicts in a merely pragmatic manner, by means of negotiation and compromise on the basis of interests and relative strength. Indeed, Koselleck effectively ties the idea of endless political crises—including the Cold War conflict, which he interprets as a clash between two morally charged and therefore irreconcilable utopian visions—to the flawed self-relation of the bourgeois subject. If this subject would overcome his internal split, his dis-integration into a purely moral subject who remains unaware of his actual political engagement, the division of the world could be overcome too. Even the Cold War has its origins in the flawed self-relation of the bourgeois subject, who thinks he remains untouched by and does not even understand the power struggle in which he is involved.

Following his stress on an inadequate perception of responsibility, Koselleck also suggests steps toward correcting the clouded consciousness that arises in the sheltered spaces of society under absolutism. Commentators have proposed that we read *Critique and Crisis*'s severe charges of hypocrisy as a call to make amends for a "lack of self-reflexivity" that would involve actors coming to recognize their "own political potentials."[30] "Koselleck's point," one reader writes, "is that the only way to avoid civil war is to accept the reality of political interests and conflicts and to remain aware that all the players are making a bid for power."[31] On this reading, which puts the emphasis on notions of heightened reflection and enhanced awareness, *Critique and Crisis* constitutes an attempt to restore every party's sense that they are involved in an adversarial situation and that no one either enjoys a position of perfect neutrality or is at leisure to lay exclusive claim to moral righteousness. The problem of the Enlightenment, its conduct of sociability and purely moral ethos, Koselleck indicates, was its peculiar opacity to itself as a movement actually involved in a conflict, and its lack of insight into its genuinely political motivations. Hence its self-proclaimed legatees must undergo a proper education in polemics.

The recurring stylistic devices of *Critique and Crisis* play a role in this simultaneously educational and polemical project, in the way that they seek to rob positively valued terms of their luster and expose their oppositional force. Koselleck continually attaches the negative term "hypocrisy" or *Hypokrisie* to the concept of *Kritik*, to the point where they almost appear to have been permanently yoked together. Critique is always a form of politically fatal hypocrisy. In fact, Koselleck's endeavor never to let the reader forget this central claim, but to craft and reiterate a formula, generates a relentless style whose force seems to exceed the more modest rhetorical needs of scholarly argumentation. In the chapter devoted to the concept of critique, the structure of the opening assertion—"Die *Kritik* . . . wird zu *Hypokrisie*"[32]—is varied again and again and slowly but surely acquires the status of a theme: "Aus der *Kritik* entspringt die *Hypokrisie*";[33] "Die *Kritik* steigerte sich in Gegenkritik zur Superkritik. Schließlich verdummte sie zur *Hypokrisie*";[34] "Die *Kritik* führt sich in ihrer *Hypokrisie* ad absurdum."[35] This rhetoric is indicative of Koselleck's effort to establish new valences, to influence a concept's connotations through the rather propagandistic means of constant repetition.[36] *Critique and Crisis* can be described as a sustained exercise in the politics of style, insofar as it repeatedly inserts the central concepts of the period into sloganlike collocations designed to problematize their status: Enlightenment is persistently linked to the predicament of "blindness [*Verblendung*]."

In a sense, the simple rhetorical operation of embedding Enlightenment or *Aufklärung* in the semantic field of concealment and veiling (*Verdeckung*, *Verschleierung*, and *Verbergung*) performs a rather complex feat. Koselleck rebukes the bourgeois critics of the Enlightenment for their lack of transparency to themselves, or their lack of existential authenticity, and also asserts the need for an acknowledgment of concealed political desires and ambitions. And with his style, Koselleck taps into the polemical resources of figurative language in order to address how the Enlightenment failed to live up to its declared values of transparency and illumination. However, as he seeks to subvert the central concepts of the Enlightenment by tying illumination to obfuscation, he himself also initiates an open struggle in the medium of language, through which polemical positions are made apparent. He both calls for and enacts a political-semantic struggle.

To say that Enlightenment blinds its exponents is, for Koselleck, both to deliver a diagnosis of its failure and to initiate its therapeutic politicization. *Critique and Crisis* transforms the Schmittian anxiety about a deceptive political agent who wants to remain unidentified into an account of the historical conditions that produce a split, deluded, or hypocritical agent. Schmitt tells an anti-Semitic story of Jewish deception; Koselleck appropriates it but recasts it as a narrative of the conditioned self-deception, to be exposed and undone by means of adversarial rhetoric.[37]

The Disavowal of Society in *Critique and Crisis*

The above characterization of Koselleck's argument is incomplete, however, for *Critique and Crisis* registers a problematic that it might not be able to correct with its preferred means, namely, by calling for everyone's greater awareness and acknowledgment of hidden political ambitions. At various points in his study, Koselleck describes the discovery of a specifically social mode of influence. The thinkers he covers conceptualize mechanisms within the social collective that ensure its coherence even in the absence of an explicit and personified authority with the right to penalize the actions of individuals. This power that diffusively resides in the social community itself, rather than with a particular and isolated agent, can exert formidable pressure. One can observe the effects of this social power, but since it is not a power exercised by one actor, it is doubtful whether one can make it confess to its presence, as if it were a person. Koselleck's *Critique and Crisis* thus at least intermittently reflects on an amorphous source of influence on people's behavior, a source that may escape its analysis of the unfortunate self-deception of an at least potentially unitary agent.

Critique and Crisis studies the discovery, in the age of absolutism, of an authority particular to the social realm separate from the state. In his discussion of Locke, Koselleck identifies a conception of society in which its unity is ensured not by the direction of a political center, but through the constant activity of judgment performed by each of its members. Even if society ostensibly possesses no means to prohibit a certain behavior, even if it has no obvious means of coercion, it still retains an effective means of correction, namely, that of its members indicating their approval or disapproval of actions. In Locke's account, people in society offer their moral judgments of each other, and in the process they establish and continually revise their shared standards of virtue and vice. This means that each individual is not only forced to observe the laws of the state but is also subject to a constant scrutiny by all other individuals. The ever-present prospect of attracting the approval or dislike of one's fellows works as a check on individual behavior and, according to Koselleck's analysis of Locke, even supersedes other authorities as a source of guidance. Since individuals are above all concerned with maintaining the good opinion of their peers, they primarily act in conformity with the anticipated societal judgment—"they do that which keeps them in reputation with their company."[38]

The values of the social collective can only be imposed on people through their fear of disapproval, which in turn is rooted in their desire for "company," but this proves to be a means of enforcement that is nearly inescapable. In his summary of Locke, Koselleck states that "not one among tens of thousands can evade the moral judgment of his fellows [Keiner von Zehntausenden sei fähig, sich dem moralischen Urteil seiner Mitmenschen zu entziehen]."[39] Seeking not to jeopardize their reputation among those "they live among and converse with," people orient themselves according to how they may be judged, which in turn produces a certain behavioral consistency.[40] Despite its noncentralized nature, society is in possession of an instrument to fabricate uniformity and cohesion, the mere reputational pressure generated within it. It even seems that the control mechanisms particular to a society can emerge in clear and purified form once the monopoly of violence is in the hands of the state.

Koselleck repeatedly notes the difference in character between the power of the state, on the one hand, and that of society, on the other. It is evident that the more spontaneous self-regulation of society does not depend on the direction of a single mind, but emerges when every member continually gauges the judgment passed on his actions by the community of which he is also a part. Uniformity is thus guaranteed through the constant mutual adjustment of each member to the perceived collective norms that they strengthen through this very process. Koselleck does not dispute the existence of this mechanism in his presentation of Locke's thought and the overview of the formation of secret societies that follows upon it. Rather, he grants it a place next to the exercise of state power and tries to explain its efficacy as an "invisible force [*unsichtbare Kraft*]" with a surprising reach.[41]

Throughout the book, Koselleck even presents a series of thinkers who grasp the prospect of a transfer of authority from the institutions of the state to those of society as an advantageous civilizing reform. Compared with the exercise of state power, society's fluid self-application of norms by means of purely social pressures carries the promise of harmony achieved and sustained without the threat of violence. In addition to its nonviolent nature, the power of social integration is not associated with a single, personal source such as the sovereign. Detached from any determinate subject, it lends itself more easily to suggestions of benevolence and morality. Koselleck himself describes, for instance in his portrait of the French minister Turgot, how the regulatory force of socially enforced norms stripped of all elements of personality and violence can be presented as spontaneous, objective, and benign. Sovereignty possessed by a king can thus be successfully dissolved into the impersonal, less subjective, and less arbitrary forces, in Turgot's account associated with nature, conscience, or the people.

Yet Koselleck's consternation at the arguments in favor of the social world's peculiar force also becomes more and more apparent. In one sense, he judges social authority to be both too weak and too strong. Koselleck's views emerge most clearly in his discussion on Rousseau, whose project he identifies as the attempt of society to occupy the state without compromising its specific mode of maintaining coherence. According to Rousseau, one man's rule over other men should be abolished in favor of the rule of all over all, and such self-legislation of the polity equals freedom. To Koselleck, this solution represents a contamination of the principle of sovereignty, of the determinate and visible single ruler, with the more amorphous social power that does not possess a unitary will, despite its apparent pervasiveness and efficacy. The sovereign will is transposed to a society, without regard for society's inability to form such a unified will.

Koselleck's main concern, however, is not that Rousseau's construction will be haunted by impending anarchy but that the disappearance of the determinate sovereign into the society as a whole, or into the realm of the "invisible [*Unsichtbaren*]," only serves to screen actual rule in order to enforce this rule all the more relentlessly.[42] Assuming that the role of the single leader cannot be done away with if the polity is to retain its direction and cohesiveness, Koselleck argues that Rousseau's attempt to replace the authority of the sovereign with the authority of society amounts to a retreat from view, but hardly a retreat from power.[43] Instead, "genuine power [*wahre Macht*]" is only conveniently elided to produce the appearance of an absence of rule.[44] In other words, there is still a *Chef,* although he might now operate in secrecy and present the collective will as the genuine and spontaneous convergence of all minds: "His greatest achievement lies in his ability to hide his power from the people and direct it so peacefully that the State appears to be in no need of leadership."[45] As the reference to acts of veiling or concealing indicates, the notion that the design of a particular figure is continually being represented as the harmonious confluence of wills is communicated in an ongoing play on the metaphor of Enlightenment: "The Enlightenment as such rules only by veiling its rule [Die Aufklärung als solche herrscht nur, indem sie ihre Herrschaft verdunkelt]."[46]

In his analysis of Rousseau, Koselleck declares his commitment to a particular kind of publicity, the publicity of rule and decision. Koselleck calls for politically clear outlines, and this is achieved once a person emerges as the defined bearer of an action to which one can consent or, for that matter, contest. If a determinate agent announces a decision, it is clearly visible as a decision tied to a particular will rather than something to which everyone has already agreed. Depending on the distribution of power, the dominant decision maker and agent might not permit challenges to his course of action, yet the decision lingers in the space of contestation simply because it cannot fail to point to its contingent character. One alternative has been chosen at the expense of others, but the fact of a prioritization of one alternative over others remains apparent to all.[47]

In Koselleck's account, Rousseau's response to the absolutist paradigm is the attempt to conceal decisions more completely than ever before by letting actual domination disappear behind the mask of unity. The conjuring of a collective will that stems from the community and reflects its natural homogeneity is only a strategy to narrow down the space for possible contestation. Absolutism requires compliance from subjects but pronounces its monopoly of power rather than obscures it, and grants the individual a space of inner reservation. In contrast, Rousseau postulates a spontaneous unity on the level of inner conviction that removes the necessity of any invidious (because admitted) decision making, and yet in fact only requires a greater degree of compliance. According to Koselleck, the postulate of an unproblematic convergence of minds entails a dictatorship more penetrating than absolutism because it must manufacture perfect consent among individuals to substantiate its claims about the unity of the collective will. In a vocabulary that intimates the proximity of Rousseau's vision to the fascist vocabulary of the twentieth century, Koselleck claims that Rousseau in effect argues for the *Gleichschaltung,* the enforced conformity, of all individuals.[48]

Much like Arendt, Koselleck adumbrates a genealogy that links bourgeois society to some notion of pervasive, even totalitarian rule. In *Critique and Crisis,* bourgeois society as a societal formation ideally freed from vertical power relations allows for the conceptualization of a type of control distinct from political rule, a nebulous but still effective social power based on every individual's adjustment to the collective of which they are also members. Koselleck relates how this self-administered control of society by society better approximates the values of spontaneity and benevolence than absolutist rule, yet he also wants to show how it develops into an unprecedented hegemony once it is installed as the principle of the state, prefiguring the totalitarian attempt to achieve the most complete rule possible. The very attempt to dissolve one kind of power relation, the lucidly contoured one of a sovereign ruling over a people, thus ends up in the greater annexation of the human person for the purpose of securing a basis for the pretense to harmony. Given that the existence of power relations is inevitable, power from a "concentrated source" is much better, Koselleck believes, than power from a "diffuse source."[49] Koselleck's response in this situation is to insist on the necessary discrepancy between the state and the society; he does not oppose society as long as it remains a separate realm and even a refuge from power, but speaks of the pernicious effects of society's coincidence with the state.[50]

Yet Koselleck does not quite address the problem of the diffuse social power itself; rather, he deals with its deployment by intellectuals who challenge absolutism. The invocation of the collective's capacity for self-management through other pressures than violent sanctions is, for Koselleck, a matter either of subterfuge or of curious self-deception. He thinks the representatives of the forming bourgeois world relegated to the sphere of social interaction, science, art, and commerce are either launching a concealed attack on the sovereign or descending into delusion. In both cases, they are irresponsible, for they shy away from declaring their bid for power openly, or they fail to grasp the nature of their critique. Koselleck's proposed measure is then to remedy the hypocrisy by locating the faction secretly operating behind the pressure to conform, or to remedy the alienation manifest in all visions of harmony by endowing each agent with a clear sense of his or her own agency and interest.

But even Koselleck's own account of the mechanisms of social control in the chapter on Locke, and throughout the entire book, reveals that these mechanisms may not be directly amenable to the therapy that he proposes. The social pressures that Koselleck speaks of cannot so easily be attributed to a unitary agent. One can observe how a standard of behavior is generated, maintained, and revised within society, but one cannot identify a single, unitary source of authority and change. The answer to the question of who is exercising rule remains unanswered, and this problem cannot be solved by demands for greater honesty.[51] The overt problem is for Koselleck never the peculiar nature of social rule and how to break its spell, but its mobilization for political purposes.

In a telling passage, Koselleck comments on the tendency of the exponents of bourgeois society to argue for the subordination of the sovereign under moral rules; there may be a king, bourgeois critics say, but this king should act in conformity with conscience. Reviewing this argument, Koselleck impatiently notes that the "tangible bearer of this conscience . . . is not named," and hence what he calls the politically relevant question, by which he means the question regarding the actual ruler, "dissolves into an anonymous They."[52] In other words, Koselleck refuses to conceive of a rule by "They" or *das Man,* a kind of rule that is and remains anonymous. Committed to a model according to which integrated and unified agents jostle for power, Koselleck sees the apparent diffusion of power as a disguise or a distortion and never a political problem in and of itself. He disavows the specificity of society, descriptions and analyses of which he nonetheless includes in his book.

This failure to understand the mechanisms of social influence he still brings into his study may set Koselleck apart from Arendt, despite his claims about their shared concern with the irresponsibility fostered in the bourgeois world, because Arendt could in fact imagine situations in which the anonymous rules. In *The Human Condition,* she wrote about how "one-man, monarchical rule . . . is transformed in society . . . into a kind of no-man rule."[53] Arendt observed how conformism can spread to the point where all contestation is smothered and the very possibility of clashes of values and views is forgotten, yet in this process, there is no fully constituted but temporarily self-deceiving agent whom one could identify and whose slumbering self-awareness one could awaken.

The community that tends toward conformity must be ruptured by contestation, but this was, to Arendt, not the same thing as promoting the sincerity of someone already striving for power.

Conclusion: Society and Conspiracy

According to its author, *Critique and Crisis* was inspired by the work of Carl Schmitt and corroborated by the work of Hannah Arendt. The book can also be described as a text stretched out between a conspiracy theory and a conceptualization of the specificity of social power. Schmitt assumes the presence of a unitary enemy agent in situations in which such a presence is no longer obvious. Indeed, if a clearly defined enmity does not take shape, he thinks it advisable to conjure it up in order to relieve the plague of anxiety induced by an amorphous threat. While Koselleck inherits the model of politics as defined by exposed battle lines between fully constituted opponents, his scrutiny of the exponents of the bourgeois society nonetheless produces an account of the self-adjustment of a sociable collective through nonviolent reputational pressures wielded by no agent alone. Yet thinkers who emphasize ostensibly noncoercive associational life are, Koselleck claims, severely deluded if they think they have dissolved all power relations. As Koselleck's rhetoric reveals, then, he very much remains devoted to the project of the "recovery of political visibility."[54]

But in *Critique and Crisis,* the localization of an enemy no longer entails the identification of a particularly sly faction that orchestrates the destruction of the state, as in Schmitt. Koselleck instead opts for a narrative of self-delusion, in which the representatives of the bourgeoisie remain imperfectly aware of their political ambition. Koselleck does away with the anti-Semitic Schmittian conspiracy theory of history and introduces a story of the genesis of an illusion. The firsthand experience of the modes of conduct in the forming society predisposes its members to certain distorted perceptions of their politically consequential claims to moral superiority. Through their familiarity with soft pressures alone, they come to lack an appreciation for the reality of antagonism.

One can, however, just as well summarize *Critique and Crisis* in a way that attributes a distorted perception to its author. Koselleck's understanding of politics as the collision between unitary agents predisposes him to a certain misapprehension of the nature of integrative mechanisms in the social realm—mechanisms that he nonetheless details. Stated more generally, *Critique and Crisis* delineates the principle of overt political rule characterized by crisp decisions taken by visible agents, on the one hand, and the more diffuse social influence flexibly maintained within a collective without the threat of physical compulsion, on the other. Having started his work in a postwar era of sociability, Koselleck clarifies the divergent principles of politics and social life. However, his commitment to political life tempts him to hold on to the principle of defined political agency even in cases where it loses its self-evidence. His analysis of a split and self-delusional political agent can then be seen as an elaborate ploy to superimpose the political upon the social, to somehow extract visibility out of something that cannot generate it.

In other words, Koselleck's narrative of a contamination of the political by the social (how bourgeois members of associations do not understand the inevitability of coercion in politics) can be viewed as an example of the contamination of the social by the political (how the champions of clear battle lines between contending factions do not understand the subtle and hence overtly noncoercive pressures of social situations). This irony is perhaps symptomatic of a work written between salient postwar positions. *Critique and Crisis* was produced in a milieu in which the belief in the legitimacy of a purely social kind of cohesion as a much-needed mechanism to prevent fragmentation (Sternberger) was countered by a concern for the consequent loss of politics as resolute contestation (Schmitt).

Given the intrusion of alternative views within Koselleck's account, one can even read his dissertation as a study of the range of errors that arise from the confusion of various species of authority and control in collectivities. If one believes that the principles of social cohesion can and indeed should replace more direct, austere, or brutal forms of political rule of some over others, one can be accused of naïveté, political immaturity, or even insincerity. The accusation reads: you unwittingly promote the imperceptible smoothing out of differences that should be openly articulated; you do not realize that people—including you—strive to dominate others; or you yourself are not honest about your own ambitions to rule. This is the accusation Koselleck formulates against the Enlightenment intellectuals in the emerging bourgeois society. But if one hopes for or always expects the eruption of political battles, and hence discounts any observations of conformism that emerges out of near-intangible processes of mutual adjustment in society, then one can be charged with having an overly suspicious, cynical, or conspiratorial mind-set. This other accusation then reads: you assume that everyone is always being manipulative, and, above all, you posit a unitary actor where there is none. And this is the accusation Koselleck himself invites.

In his overcommitment to agency, the conspiracy theorist is, in a sense, a champion of politics. The conspiracy theorist does not grant existence to developments that occur because of aggregate effects of multiple actions, effects that may not be intended by any one actor, and he writes off any models that account for the tendency of an entire society toward conformity.[55] Since he insists on the continued presence of a partisan agent supposedly operating in the dark, he also cannot accept any notion of the self-determination of society. The Enlightenment rules by obscuring its rule—this idea from *Critique and Crisis* indicates a certain affinity to conspiracy thinking. Even where everything is illuminated, someone operates behind a screen, and the exponents of Enlightenment do not dissolve power; they just hide its exercise through its apparent dissolution. Or, rather, the conspiracy theorist agrees with the Enlightenment that scrutiny and visibility dissolve power, but also holds that, for this very reason, agents in power are always dishonest and retreating to find cover. Even if the conspiracy theorist does demand more honesty on the part of the hidden rulers, nothing that is shown and acknowledged openly and visibly will ever satisfy his or her suspicions, and no statement can ever be taken for granted. Koselleck may seek to facilitate awareness of partiality and political will against conditioned self-delusions; his mentor Schmitt, on the other hand, descended into an increasingly consuming paranoia.

Koselleck managed to remove Schmitt's anti-Semitic theory of Jewish deception and craft a narrative of the political self-deception of the bourgeoisie, yet in his commitment to the characteristics of lucidly displayed political rule, he still ignored the specificities of the social dynamics that he nonetheless included in his review of bourgeois intellectual history. Soon after the publication of *Critique and Crisis,* Jürgen Habermas, another young scholar familiar with Schmitt and Arendt, pointed to some of the book's peculiarities and problems and even labeled it "a letter from Schmitt," dispatched by one of his students. Finally, in 1962, Habermas published a work that countered Koselleck's vision of a self-deceived (non)-political agent and fitted forms of bourgeois sociability into a redemptive story about an entirely new kind of politics.

Social interaction in particular contexts and venues such as clubs or coffeehouses, and extended through particular channels such as learned journals, Habermas would argue, did not disqualify the bourgeoisie from honest participation in the necessarily adversarial business of politics. Instead, Habermas claimed, the specifically bourgeois way of conducting sociable conversations paved the way for an egalitarian and rational kind of politics. In Habermas's work, Sternberger's postwar vision of noncoercive conversational *Geselligkeit* as a stepping-stone toward a deliberative polity found a new and very influential formulation.

Chapter Five

Saving Bourgeois Sociability

Jürgen Habermas

In 1962, Jürgen Habermas published *The Structural Transformation of the Public Sphere*. In this study, he argued that large-scale economic and social developments of the seventeenth and eighteenth centuries created the conditions for a rational-critical debate with a discernible impact on the political policies of the ruling regimes. After the differentiation of the political system as an organ of control separate from the capitalist market, bourgeois individuals did not just relate to one another as producers and consumers but also gathered in new social venues such as salons, coffeehouses, reading circles, and debating clubs in order to enjoy each other's company, exchange information, ponder literature and discuss manners, and eventually also to scrutinize state legislation pertaining to their spheres of activity.

Habermas told the story of how, during the Enlightenment period, an institutionalized space of deliberation, a "public sphere," formed in the interstices of the free market and the consolidated bureaucratic state. Consisting of private persons in permanent discussion with each other in social venues and through print media, this sphere was situated "above" the realm of manufacture and trade but "below" the state apparatus, the decisions of which it sought to subject to standards of argumentative reason. It held out the promise of dissolving stark state domination and supplementing market laws with discursively grounded rational consensus among deliberating citizens. Habermas thus offered his readers a picture of a social space where individuals realized "their nature as rational beings,"[1] or an actual historical and institutional "location for practical reason."[2]

Habermas's "masterpiece of historical sociology" has inspired, and continues to inspire, a lively discussion in multiple academic disciplines and is even an important reference point in political contexts, at least in the Federal Republic of Germany.[3] Thanks in part to his work on the public sphere, Habermas has been hailed as the key intellectual figure working toward the successful "recivilization of West Germany within the framework of Western liberal institutions."[4] For this achievement, the historian Matthew Specter writes, "we are in his debt."[5] Or, to put it more colloquially, postwar Germany has featured and continues to feature numerous debates on controversial topics, such as the best way to address the Nazi legacy, and "fortunately, Habermas usually wins in the end."[6]

The key terms and narratives of Habermas's early and perhaps most accessible work have also frequently been referred to, supported, or contested in the fields of sociology, political theory, history, literary studies, and media and communications studies,[7] and his vision of the "public sphere" as an essential domain in any healthy liberal-democratic society has risen to the status of a guiding vision for intellectuals and political movements. A virtual magnet for both celebratory and critical responses, few works of modern political theory have had such an impact as *The Structural Transformation of the Public Sphere*.[8]

Yet this immensely influential work may not have offered its early German readers a previously untold story in a completely new idiom. By crafting a redemptive history of European bourgeois society and calling for a regeneration and expansion of its traditions of participatory discussion and debate, the young Habermas was in fact positioning himself within an already existing set of positions. He drew on and modified narratives, picked up and repudiated arguments, and activated attachments and aversions. As the preceding chapters have argued, there were already proponents and critics of bourgeois society and sociable conversations in postwar Germany (and later in West Germany), and by intervening in and reframing their discussion, Habermas could appeal to one constituency while countering another. Therefore, I propose to regard Habermas's work not as the beginning of a discussion on the public sphere, but as an intervention in an already established debate on bourgeois sociability, which his study reformulated or refounded; he provided the debate with more historical detail, but also took it in a new direction.

When excavating the root system of Habermas's work, commentators have of course already shown how he integrated ideas from many of the theorists considered in this book. Peter Uwe Hohendahl, for instance, claims that *The Structural Transformation of the Public Sphere* can be read as a critical response to Reinhart Koselleck's *Critique and Crisis*, which Habermas himself deemed a deeply Schmittian account.[9] Habermas to some extent accepts Koselleck's historical narrative of the growing political role of the bourgeoisie, but supplies a very different assessment of its meaning and import. Yet this observation does not capture the extent of his engagement with the ideas of Arendt and Schmitt. Their images of genuine political life and concomitant critiques of bourgeois society do not just appear in Habermas's work as sources and occasional references; they determine the structure and character of a large part of his argument. *The Transformation of the Public Sphere* is in fact constructed as a systematic rebuttal of those who deny that the bourgeois mode of social integration through *Geselligkeit* and conversational engagement has any constructive political import.

To uncover the organization of this argument, one must look in particular at two of Habermas's overarching claims: first, his notion that bourgeois society does not mean the ruin of dignified political life but rather contains a legitimate vision of societal order that constitutes an advance over previous formations; and second, the idea that institutionalized practices of sociability are the very matrix of this vision. When these two claims and their textual arrangement are examined more closely, *The Structural Transformation of the Public Sphere* emerges in a new light—as a resourceful reappraisal of an already existing debate. Judging by the popularity of his contribution, few attempts at reconceptualizing an already established discussion have been as successful. Habermas's work was at one point an intervention in an ongoing debate, but this is no longer readily apparent, and his book is mostly treated as the original source of a concern with the "public sphere" rather than an attempt to save bourgeois sociability from its contemporary critics. Yet tying Habermas's work to prior analyses of bourgeois society's flaws also serves to recover concerns and counterarguments that he elided rather than addressed. When *The Structural Transformation of the Public Sphere* is analyzed in a way that makes the opposed positions of an extant debate more apparent, both its strengths and weaknesses become more salient.

Habermas on Koselleck, Arendt, and Schmitt

Although it is in a sense ironic that the term "sociability" could provoke any kind of antagonism, its exponents and its enemies made contributions, if not to a debate, then at least to a common context of argumentation. The concept of sociability or *Geselligkeit* was first introduced after 1945 as something of an emergency measure. Responding to the particular challenges of the immediate postwar period, the journal *Die Wandlung* produced a vision of tempered, even conciliatory interactions among men and women, both in the hope that this would appeal to a wide circle of readers and in order to resurrect an embattled but still available native tradition of conduct with potentially beneficial therapeutic effects. The articles of Dolf Sternberger, the editor who most prominently outlined the journal's project, brought out aspects of *Geselligkeit* that could serve to redefine the rigidified identity of the German *Bürger* stripped of secure ownership but also addressed the postwar situation of precarious statehood.

First of all, sociability conjured up the notion of cooperative arrangements not dependent on a government with coercive capacities. Without necessarily making the supposition explicit, Sternberger conceived of individuals as able to associate spontaneously and productively without the direction of state power. While the crucial demonstration of this ability is typically found in the notion of a self-regulating market,[10] *Die Wandlung*'s editor called forth ideas of social but noneconomic modes of integration. In the form of a narrative of a belated Germany having to catch up with other nations, he evoked the scenario of an integrative sociable discourse ultimately animated by sublimated sensual impulses. *Die Wandlung,* for instance, was a site for the "touching spheres [of activity]" seemingly modeled on the mixed-sex setting of the salon. Formulated negatively as a critique of the rigidified comportment of the German *Bürger,* Sternberger derived a fragile vision of associational life from a human propensity toward mutuality with undercurrents of sensuality.[11] The emphasis on the virtues and protocols of sociability practiced in small circles of friendliness would thus work to demilitarize the Germans, provide them with a new sense of civil collectivity (after the end of the *Volksgemeinschaft*), and prepare them for political deliberations by means of sociable exchange. Sociability was in fact a multidimensional form of reeducation or a form of protopolitical interaction suitable to the uncertain period of democratization. But this delineated space of conviviality was quite clearly not a site for pronounced conflicts. Sharp ideological differences threatened and in the end did undermine the "sociable spirit" that Sternberger called for. Sociability hinged on the willingness of its participants to bracket divisive issues and focus on commonalities.

If the postwar plea for sociability met with critique, it was partly because it seemed to deny the very existence of conflict. One of the central charges against the social communication cultivated in the emerging postwar venues of interaction had to do with the inability or unwillingness of its proponents to recognize antagonism and to allow open dissension, whether this alleged flaw was interpreted as a symptom of weakness, a retreat from conflict, or evidence of an uncanny capacity to stifle contestation.

Reinhart Koselleck studied in Heidelberg in the immediate postwar period and was aware of the topics and the tone of the contemporary discourse. To some extent, he also moved in the same conceptual domain, for he chose to examine bourgeois thinkers who sought to explain how discrete individuals, no longer lodged in a stable stratified order, nevertheless came to form relations among themselves and thereby generate coherent collectives. Based on readings in political philosophy, Koselleck presented an account of the formation of a specifically social influence. Given each subject's desire for attention and regard, and fear of approbation and exclusion, the anticipated collective judgment of other individuals can work as a powerful instrument of censure, one that consistently overrides other, more traditional sources of authority. Society coheres by means of its ongoing self-application of noncodified norms, sustained by each individual's approval and disapproval. As soon as the cohesion of the community of sociable agents is seen as the predictable outcome of ongoing exchanges within circles, clubs, and secret societies, the tenor of the critical arguments shifts. In a sense, Kosellek studied the formidable efficacy of social influence in forging acquiescence and noted its tendency to suppress conflict rather than allow for its explicit articulation and resolution. Koselleck's work on the history of political thought and the utopianism of the European bourgeoisie thus pointed to some potentially sinister dimensions of the postwar emphasis on apparently noncoercive and egalitarian forms of interaction in bourgeois society.

Habermas's 1962 work inserts itself into this realm of reflection on the modes of integration available to the bourgeoisie. Its defense of the contested notion of bourgeois sociability is complex. Unmistakable images of bourgeois sociability such as conversations in salons and coffeehouses are integrated into a delineation of the bourgeois "public sphere" as a site of rational communication, a concept with which Habermas counters Schmitt, Koselleck, and Arendt, whose works he had carefully studied. Let us now review his relationships with these three thinkers.

In 1960, two years before the publication of *The Structural Transformation of the Public Sphere,* Habermas published a review Koselleck's *Critique and Crisis.* This review contains a highly condensed version of the argument of Habermas's future book and reveals that the book was at least partially written in response to Koselleck. In a couple of dense paragraphs written in clipped syntax, Habermas summarizes Koselleck's study of the so-called pathogenesis of the bourgeois world. After the absolutist state put an end to civil strife and neutralized the political disruptiveness of irreconcilable religious ideologies, the private individuals who made up the bourgeoisie came together in "the salons, the clubs and the lodges, the coffeehouses and Tischgesellschaften"[12] to constitute a new political agent that subjected the absolutist ruler to critical scrutiny. That this critical project was nothing but a move in a political struggle over power eluded them, however, since they invoked the principles of a purportedly universal morality in their critique.

In his review, which brands Koselleck's narrative as tendentious, Habermas argues that the bourgeois intellectuals did not so much want to dethrone an apparently stronger adversary and seize power as they wanted to change the very nature of power. According to him, the bourgeoisie under absolutist rule did not unwittingly participate in a struggle over influence, but instead tried to alter the conditions and rules of how power is exercised and interests are pursued. Such an attempt to change the political game entirely, Habermas claims, cannot be seen as a particularly poor or particularly sly performance in a game that already exists.

More specifically, the bourgeois project involved putting princely rule to the test of rational critique by means of permanent public discussion. If the grounds and considerations behind policy decisions are made public and assessed in a serious debate where multiple opinions are tested and discarded to allow for the emergence of calm and consensual judgments, then politics can assume a rational form and arbitrary domination is dissolved. This is not to conduct power politics by covert or inadequate means. It is, Habermas asserts, to improve politics. The bourgeoisie was not blind to political practice, but introduced a dimension of rational reflection into political practice.

Interestingly, Habermas explicitly voiced his suspicion that responding to Koselleck meant responding to Carl Schmitt. The polemical overtones in *Critique and Crisis* could, Habermas stated in his 1960 review, be read as symptoms of ideological commitments hidden under the cover of a detailed historical survey of Enlightenment ideas.[13] For Habermas, this agenda was derived from two sources, Carl Schmitt's decisionism and the anthropologist Arnold Gehlen's institutionalism, which converged in a picture of society in need of two elements: strong political authority able to implement direly needed decisions; and institutional frameworks insulated from corrosive scrutiny.[14] In Habermas's view, *Critique and Crisis* was a letter from an older, conservative generation, and his article was part refutation and part unmasking.[15] Koselleck's polemic against the bourgeoisie betrayed an unacknowledged commitment to an authoritarian position, or even a half-conscious fear of destabilizing forces, which led him to argue that political structures must be shielded from irresponsible challenges.

The argument of Habermas's 1960 review of Koselleck is contiguous with *The Structural Transformation of the Public Sphere,* and a few formulations from the review even appear almost unchanged in the book.[16] Yet Koselleck does not occupy the role of the central adversary in the 1962 study; Schmitt and Arendt are more prominently displayed candidates for that position. In the first of the book's seven chapters, Habermas characterizes three sequentially arranged historical sites of political life: the polis of Greek antiquity, the medieval or early modern court, and the bourgeois public sphere. Arendt is the main source for his description of the polis, and Schmitt clearly the most important reference for the political context of the medieval and early modern court. However, the third configuration, the bourgeois public sphere, is Habermas's addition; it does not appear in Arendt's and Schmitt's accounts, and in fact represents a polemical engagement with them.

This, then, is Habermas's mission in the 1962 work: to offer an account of the political life particular to bourgeois society against those who had neglected it or denied its very possibility.[17] His use of Arendt and Schmitt in the historically organized overview of forms of politics and publicness is meant to highlight his own contribution. To Arendt's picture of the Athenian agora and Schmitt's characterization of the ceremonies of royal and religious representation, Habermas adds his narrative of bourgeois subjects who come to interact with one another in new forums of conversation. The opening of Habermas's book is thus structured by his engagement with Schmitt and Arendt, and the resulting narrative in turn constitutes a revision of Koselleck's negative account of the politics of bourgeois society.

Habermas's decision to set up the bourgeois public sphere as a further and essentially modern stage for politics involves a fundamental reevaluation of what constitutes genuine political conduct. This, too, is made explicit by Habermas as he supplies condensed versions of Arendt's and Schmitt's idealized accounts of the Greek polis and the Catholic Church of the Middle Ages, respectively. For Arendt, at least as she appears in Habermas's work, politics is the nonviolent, discursive battle for recognition of excellence among equals. Emerging from the relative darkness of their households and gathering in a common space, free people become visible to each other and disclose who they are in displays of great virtue such as courage. In a space that nobody can claim to own or monopolize, namely the realm beyond the *oikos,* the ground is cleared for a fresh and undecided (rhetorical) struggle. Yet this struggle comes to an end not with the conquest and enslavement of all by one, but with the attribution of the scarce resource of glory to those who prove to be the most formidable. Arendtian political life, then, is agonistic and flares up in demonstrations of virtue and skill to be seen, judged, and remembered.

In Habermas's study, Schmitt's concept of genuine political life likewise centers on displays of grandeur, with the difference that the question of status distribution is not settled through encounters among potential equals in a common space. Instead, a particular preconstituted hierarchy is made visible in the realm of appearance and demeanor, speech and gesture. Employing Schmitt's language, Habermas describes how rulers govern by representation, which means that they rule by making the transcendent present in the realm of humans through carefully designed spectacles of majesty and mystique. The king is not the king without his pomp, the unfolding of awe-inspiring representation. As in Arendt's polis, political life is synonymous with the erection of a hierarchy among people, but Schmitt does not consider this a process that should issue from a vigorous struggle among free citizens.

Habermas both continues and discontinues the tradition he sketches out as an introduction to his own argument. He shares with both Schmitt and Arendt a strong commitment to an exalted idea of politics. When people come together in their special capacity as political beings, they move as if unencumbered by material desires and participate in an elevated collective practice. The community of humans can be more than an aggregate for the satisfaction of needs and exchange of goods, however important these activities are for the maintenance of life or achievement of prosperity. According to Chris Thornhill, this celebration of the political as a distinct dimension in the life of collectivities is a feature peculiar to the German intellectual tradition, which remains informed by a stark division between state and society.[18]

Yet whereas Arendt and Schmitt held that bourgeois society was unable to activate this potential due to its narrow program of efficient production, Habermas claims that it was precisely this denigrated bourgeois society, and perhaps *only* this society, that generated a genuinely political form of interconnection. It did so, moreover, not through the struggle for glory in the nonprivate, nonowned space of the polis or through the glorious representation of the transcendent, but in the continual and collaborative enunciation and assessment of arguments. In fact, public discourse emerges as a "possible mode of coordination of human life" set apart from integration by concentrated power or economic interdependency.[19] The visible differentiation of levels of personal prestige should, Habermas implies, fade away and be replaced by nothing but the ordering of arguments according to their relative validity in discussions. Men should no longer be fierce competitors with one another in the public realm of the polis (Arendt), or worthy embodiments of magnificence with transcendent sources (Schmitt); rather, they should view themselves as contributors to a common pool of arguments to be evaluated by shared yardsticks.

Habermas's redirection of focus, away from the struggle for admiration or the exhibition of privileged contact with the transcendent, demands a new set of attitudes and competences. Political human beings must show a willingness to listen to convincing arguments and be able to contain their impulses of self-assertion. The filtering and ordering of rationally compelling arguments can come to the foreground only when the interlocutors in society relinquish the drive to triumph as persons through force and energy, and limit themselves to argumentative contributions.

Against this backdrop, the burden of Habermas's book is not simply to persuade the audience of the legitimacy of the specifically bourgeois "public sphere" and its special characteristics, but to make the transformation that it recounts seem plausible—namely, the shift from a concern with glory and redemption to a concern with rational argument. Under what sociohistorical conditions were people, and particularly people in power, willing to relinquish their attachment to life-enhancing grandiosity? And under what conditions would a political caste with control over the means of coercion be willing to restrain itself and let a contest between arguments, as opposed to a contest between cohorts with different resources, decide on a course of action, instead of simply continuing and extending dominance? It is clear that Habermas must provide some narrative of how a hierarchy that is determined either in a struggle for reputation (Arendt) or by sacrosanct stratified order (Schmitt) can be dismantled and replaced by a flatter, egalitarian collaboration among purveyors of considered opinions. Yet how could the peaceable and conversational bourgeois conduct of a rationalized politics by argument ever come into being, at least as long as there are differences of power in society, whether they are favorable to the bourgeoisie or not?

We are already familiar with Koselleck's answer to this question. The bourgeois intellectuals during the Enlightenment age did not, Koselleck argues, possess a viable vision for the dissolution of traditional political (and hence necessarily coercive) rule. This class only denied that some kind of political rule involving domination is needed and indeed has great value for everyone who desires peace. And members of the bourgeoisie deny the inevitability of power politics because they are unfamiliar with it, conditioned by their experiences in spheres of sociability removed from conflicts over interest or, on a more suspicious reading, because they seek to conquer political power by surreptitious means. In both cases, the call for the abolition of arbitrary and violent rule in the name of reason and morality comes from people in positions of relative weakness, who imagine that impersonal mechanisms of coherence in society can replace determinate and visible authorities.

Reason and morality are, Koselleck implies, the idioms of people without power. However, these idioms succeeded in corroding the legitimacy of the sovereign and destabilizing political institutions. In its history, the bourgeoisie toppled governments and brought chaos to the world without being inspired by the prospect of seizing power, or without admitting to this inspiration. This new class remains divorced from the particular pleasures of power and rule, but continues its attempts to engineer hegemony and to rule under the cover of nonrule.[20] To Koselleck, the conduct of politics by rational argument and moral consideration is a matter of strategic falsity or, alternatively, of self-deception.

Habermas looks with much less suspicion than Koselleck at the widening sphere of discursive negotiation of collectively binding decisions, yet he never claims that the bourgeoisie entirely dissolves an already established form of political rule by centralized authority. Those who are in power when the bourgeoisie is being formed as a class gradually agree to accept more accountability, and they do it because of a shift in the balance of power that allows for more negotiation. State rule is not abolished entirely, but it is increasingly regulated by means of a principled process of scrutiny in which arguments about policy come to influence decisions and the exercise of power is brought into greater harmony with reason. But how, according to Habermas, does this new situation come about?

In Habermas's account, the bourgeoisie knows one area of society in which the interaction of individuals is apparently exempt from the exercise of direct power, namely the market. Everyone who buys and sells is involved in relationships of mutuality, and no single agent in the market can set the price and hence dictate to others when they should part with or purchase a commodity. Yet this market sphere has to be protected from being constantly disrupted by those who command coercive resources and refuse to play by the rules of the economic game. The threat of expropriation, or at least of political unpredictability, always hangs over the market. The question is, then, how the members of the bourgeoisie can continue to focus on the production and consumption of goods without having to either succumb to political rule or try to assume it by arming themselves, which would require them to abandon market activity and effectively become more like traditional predatory political animals. For the bourgeoisie's members, political authorities must in some way be tamed and taught to respect zones of nonintervention so that the bourgeoisie can remain what it is and continue with its business.

The endeavor to bring political rulers to accountability and bind them by laws is indeed a fierce "struggle [*Kampf*]," and as such it involves some intimation of force and threat of subversion, even if the members of the bourgeoisie are not accustomed to exercising political power and perhaps not even primarily guided by the desire to wield it.[21] Habermas does not give this struggle much attention, nor does he deny that it takes place. Yet this does not mean that one camp emerges as the definite victor; rather, it means that the experts on political power on the one hand (the absolutist rulers, the monarchs), and the experts on production and trade on the other, work out a truce. In the paradigm case, the state regime cannot continue to exercise power over a restive population, nor does the bourgeoisie have sufficient resources, courage, or interest to assume power completely.[22] A complex arrangement is installed whereby legislation and decision making is not simply monopolized by a new class. Instead, the state's exercise of power by coercion is narrowed down and trained to acknowledge and follow considerations that issue from a sphere of deliberation, institutionally anchored in specifically bourgeois social venues and channels of communication.

It is at this juncture that bourgeois sociability is enlisted to fulfill a particular political function. Habermas's bourgeoisie does not merely operate in the market; its members are continuously involved with each other in discursive exchanges too, and this becomes clear once they begin to assemble socially in spaces of diversion and conversation, temporarily pursuing no particular economic purpose. At some point, however, this purely social activity carried on in circles, an activity only weakly associated with any program or ambition beyond social interaction, is repurposed to mediate between politically engaged entities as well as between institutional spheres. As a result, the factions in the conflict (the absolutist regime and the bourgeoisie) effectively become interlocutors who deal with one another in language, and the relationship between the two institutional principles (state authority over subjects in a territory and noncentralized and voluntary market interactions) is continually negotiated and adjusted in discursive negotiations through which justifications are demanded and given. As Habermas writes: "The medium of this political confrontation . . . was peculiar and without historical precedent: people's public use of their reason."[23] In the fissure between the consolidated modern state apparatus and the modern economy of horizontal networks of exchange, there remains a small space for discursive negotiation. The ruler is gradually compelled to adapt to opinions and ideas articulated in a larger population, but the channel by which these ideas are announced, the construct of public opinion, is less a unitary power in itself than an instrument of correction and critique, always operating in a relation to the activity of other, more congealed institutions.[24]

Koselleck claims that the bourgeoisie either assumes power or seeks to assume it yet remains pathologically unaware of the political character of its own speech and actions or hypocritically conceals its desire to rule. Habermas offers a more complicated narrative in which this class does not seize power directly, but instead strives to render the movements of power more predictable by imposing constraints on its exercise over particular areas, primarily the market. It does so by subjecting every announced or impending decision to a standard of reason upheld by a conversing and reasoning public with a home in relatively nonexclusive social venues where argument trumps rank. Critique is then not just a disavowed desire for power, but a form of limited political involvement adopted by a class that wants peace for its world of production, exchange, and augmentation of wealth.[25]

Habermas has no particular admiration for the economic preoccupations of the bourgeoisie, nor does he, like Schmitt or Koselleck, idolize the realities of the exercise of power. Instead, he slips in a sphere between the state and the market, between a regime ultimately leaning on violence and an emergent class tending toward the accumulation of wealth, in which the relationships between them are mediated according to principles and by means of an activity that does not seem to belong to either, namely deliberation, the exchange of articulated reasons. That, then, is the peculiar in-between location of a more dignified, genuinely political life, where the only compulsion exerted over human beings is the gentle force of cogent arguments on their minds.

As noted above, Habermas must confront the challenge of accounting for the supposed shift from direct exercise of power of some over others, to peaceful and orderly deliberation. If the state regime is still vastly more powerful than the bourgeois class, this shift may not take place. And if the bourgeois class could easily dethrone the occupants of the state, what would convince them to install rational debate in which arguments rather than the relative strength of interest groups affect decision making? For Habermas, nobody is completely deceived as to their real interest or real force. The monarchic regime is no longer completely dominant, and the class of producers and traders has an entirely different orientation, toward the market, for which it wants protection from sudden and arbitrary interventions. In this situation of precarious balance, in which those accustomed to the exercise of power by coercion are pushed back without being replaced by identical successors, there is an opportunity for the language of reason to play an important mediating role and for a new political form of life to become visible. It is in this way that the constitution and maintenance of hierarchies as the essence of politics (according to Arendt and Schmitt) is replaced by more egalitarian argumentation. But does this space of deliberation somehow hold an attraction of its own, some sort of staying power, so that it does not collapse with every shift in the balance of forces?

In Habermas's summaries of Arendt and Schmitt, the conduct of politics offers the promise of greatness visible to all. Politics generates stories of heroism, provides models of aspiration or even glimpses of transcendence, all of which could stir affects and ensure commitment to and acceptance of hierarchies. Permanent participation in the exchange of arguments may seem less enticing, and as long as different individuals and groups are stronger than others, it may also seem less feasible. Habermas's account of how the evaluation of arguments superseded spectacles of grandeur in political history therefore invites a discussion of disenchantment. How will the vision of an increasing involvement of the mind come to command the hearts of people, especially given that it does not quite match the core activity of any group, neither the rulers of the state nor the economically active bourgeoisie?

Both supporters and critics of Habermas have expressed worry over how thin and cerebral his vision of politics seems, so that his picture of politics either cannot gather sufficient support or, if realized, will always remain fragile and vulnerable to disintegration. But perhaps the sheer success of his early study addresses this concern. *The Structural Transformation of the Public Sphere* has been immensely influential, even among those who do not consider or even read Habermas's more technical and philosophical work, which could indicate that the story of bourgeois individuals in conversation with one another to some extent does meet the demands of emotional suggestiveness.

In his 1962 text, Habermas welds a normative vision of politics by argumentation with an available range of social experiences in easily imaginable venues. He conjures up images of bourgeois sociability (vivid discussions in coffeehouses and salons, reflected and continued in newspapers and pamphlets) as the surprising foundation of a novel, rational form of politics. Few modern liberal visions have been as stirring as this canny blend of normative ideals and empirical history, or "valorized forms of communicative rationality" and "specific cultural forms."[26] Habermas may rely heavily on idealizations of a particular historical period, but an idealized picture is not the same as an entirely utopian picture. In other words, Habermas *has* succeeded in convincing his readers that his study belongs more to the realm of historical sociology than imaginative fiction.

To use theoretical language, his vision of the specific social conditions of rational discourse may seem "counterfactual" but does not lack "immanence," meaning that it stays sufficiently close to our world to remain familiar and persuasive.[27] In some way, Habermas reenchanted the historical bourgeoisie, and in doing so perhaps he achieved the objective of Dolf Sternberger, who sought to save and enhance the strategic value and appeal of the German *Bürger* by associating this figure more closely with life in *Gesellschaft und Geselligkeit*.

Habermas's vision of a conversational bourgeoisie has, it seems, been able to rival the attractiveness of previous forms of publicness and has come to be accepted as an inspiring vision of political identity. To give reason a home in some recognizable historical-social world—this may be the lasting achievement of *The Structural Transformation of the Public Sphere*. The question remains, however, whether bourgeois sociability can in fact perform the function Habermas wants it to—namely, to serve as the matrix and medium of debates where the most convincing arguments are recognized and espoused by all participants. For Habermas's account to work, he must be able to present an institutional history of talk in which light conversations in bourgeois social sites mutate into rational discussions that can subsequently serve an important mediating function in the relationship between state and society, between those who monopolize the means of coercion and those who develop the means of production. If this transmutation of sociability into rational discussion runs into difficulties, the attempt to embed politics by argument in a particular suggestive historical picture unravels. We must therefore turn to the relationship of bourgeois sociability and rational argument in Habermas's study. We must focus on how Habermas represents the transition from social conversation to political deliberation.

Social Conversations and Rational Deliberations

The Structural Transformation of the Public Sphere is a complex critical reconsideration of a context of political thought. Habermas partly covers the same time period and the same material as Koselleck to counter the negative judgment of the dangerous politics of the supposedly nonpolitical bourgeoisie; furthermore, he presents his idea of a bourgeois public sphere as an advance over previous forms of publicness, at least as they were described and idealized by Arendt and Schmitt, two of Koselleck's main sources of inspiration. The thoroughness of Habermas's refutation testifies to his debt to his predecessors: his work is an intervention.

It could even be argued that Habermas's narrative of bourgeois society, in its basic outline, does not differ very much from Arendt's. The capitalist market and the formation of a bureaucratic state dissolve previous corporative arrangements. In this process, people are drawn into an expanding net of economic interdependencies, but they also become subjects of an enduring, impersonal state administration whose monopoly of violence goes unchallenged within a contoured territory. However, there is one question of dispute, and it relates to how private individuals form discursively encapsulated agreements. For Arendt, the capitalist market erodes traditions and weakens interpersonal bonds, leaving individuals disoriented and vulnerable to integration by race theories or other pseudo-logical belief systems. Paradoxically, it is precisely because bourgeois society disarticulates people and dissolves society into atoms that these people are likely to show such high degrees of attitudinal conformity. For Habermas, however, economically independent bourgeois individuals find each other in new social milieus and can deliberate beyond the realm of status-confirming rituals, theological dogmas, or even negotiations over commodities, all of which would constrain free conversation.

Yet by placing the nonexclusive and rational discussion of policies in the social life of the bourgeoisie, by saying that it takes place in the salons, coffeehouses, and clubs in which bourgeois types congregate for diversion or information, Habermas raises several questions: To what extent can particular kinds of sociability accommodate disputations? How and at what point does conversation turn into critique? How and at what point do "bon mots" transform into political "arguments"?[28] It is at this juncture that we must reconstruct Habermas's account of the difficult transition from sociability to political discourse.

To Habermas, the Enlightenment salons, coffeehouses, and societies that attracted people to a particular location and promoted a special type of interaction deserve the name "institutions," for they coordinated the actions of diverse individuals in ways that remained stable and predictable over time.[29] They offered common thematic orientations, protocols of behavior, and a range of conversational tonalities that facilitated and structured communication. The most prominent or most consequential institutional criterion was, according the Habermas, the suspension of societal rank. The neutralization of status discrepancies among the various participants was, he claims, a constitutive characteristic of bourgeois sociability. The communication across multiple divides could work only if the participants were willing to shed their professional identities and status positions when crossing the threshold into the nonfamilial and nonprofessional social space. Indeed, participants were ideally also required to look away from any economic relationship they may have had to others. In the realm of sociability, people were supposed to greet each other as private individuals rather than as economic agents in relationships of mutual dependence, or as members of a hierarchy entitled to command or obliged to obey.

The temporary and contained suspension of rank for the purpose of fluid social interaction thus opened up a meeting place for different segments of an otherwise divided society, and Habermas notes that the coffeehouses and salons gathered members of both the bourgeoisie and the aristocracy. A community of discourse that disallowed ostentatious displays of status must be inclusive, since the barriers between classes and levels of prestige that were temporarily effaced within it could not in principle be upheld at the entrance.[30] Any given salon or club may of course have been quite exclusive, yet the idea of a suspension of rank for the benefit of free conversation within the salon would at least have disturbed its congealment into a permanent clique.[31]

This vision of a sociable community that could not close itself off with reference to privilege also found its corresponding feature within the interaction. The conversations that took place were based on a principle of reciprocity. In other words, the inclusive character of bourgeois sociability required a balanced distribution of opportunities to speak. And in general, all sociable conversation favors a succession of short, context-sensitive statements rather than long-winded speeches. If one person alone is entitled to speak without interruption, the conversation dies. The suspension of rank and the form of the conversation are interlinked, for the presence of an indisputable authority in a room generally puts an end to easy chats among everyone gathered in it. The protocols of sociability typically prohibit lectures, sermons, exhortations, and non-negotiable imperatives. To speak with Sternberger, poses of fierce struggle and claims to dominance have no place in the venues of sociability.

The bourgeois institutions of sociability that Habermas describes provided venues for interactions that were neither governed by economic pursuits nor constrained by status hierarchies that smother conversation. But did these forms of bourgeois sociability in the Enlightenment period also generate the appropriate climate for rational argumentation? Habermas's claim is not that sociability itself necessarily fostered a critical-rational attitude, but that there are crucial affinities between the institutions of sociability and the basic requirements of genuine argumentation. Most significantly, argumentation can take place only when the importance of status difference has been bracketed and interlocutors are willing to judge reasons on merit without regard for their source.

Insofar as bourgeois sociability instituted the idea of a space where status is inconsequential, it made room for the notion that the relative cogency of arguments should take precedence over status and that opinions' justification should matter more than their origin. Meeting in the spaces of sociability, Habermas's members of the bourgeoisie became able to honor the "content of assertion more than the status of the speaker."[32] To clarify, sociable conversation is not at all the same thing as rational deliberation, but social discourse can nonetheless pass into debate because the two formats share an underlying condition, namely, the temporary elision of hierarchies among persons.

While rigid hierarchies and status obsessions do not necessarily prevent the flow of arguments in all cases—kings have listened to fools—Habermas still assumes that the suspension of rank in the context of bourgeois sociability let the attention of the interlocutors migrate from the power and prestige of the persons making arguments to the validity of the arguments presented. It is not that the ruler should listen to arguments despite his or her otherwise uncontested supremacy, but that forms of domination should ultimately be supplanted by communicative rationality. Once arguments were allowed to exert their nonviolent force over people's minds, all power that went against the prevailing consensus on the most rational policy exposed its brute arbitrariness. Once people have been allowed to embrace reason, they will not be inclined to accept nonargumentative domination; there is a path to reason, but no retreat from it.

Habermas seeks to show how the scene of sociable conversation and the scene of argumentation share central institutional features, but he also needs to clarify how the pleasurable exchange of witty remarks can ever turn into the earnest exchange of arguments. He needs, then, to filter out the potentially disrupting and out-of-place nonrational dimensions of sociability. For him, sociability is not the voluntary participation of many in a kind of elegant discursive dance, in which speakers make entertaining comments on a variety of topics and let the themes evolve and change through witty associations. Historically, this type of light, associative *Geselligkeit* has seemed attractive to a range of thinkers as an example of a purified human interconnection that brings people together through playfulness rather than material need.[33] Insofar as people in conversation occupy symmetrical positions and are unburdened by duties, sociability defined as play can be presented as a miniature picture of an ideal society. In these cases, however, the topics of conversation can never be politically important issues, since all topics are in fact only a means to an end, the end of sustaining the pleasant conversation itself. Needless to say, this is not Habermas's vision of the work performed by sociability.

Habermas does not single out *Geselligkeit* or sociability as an example of ideal human interaction because it is playful. If anything, he implicitly seeks to divest sociability of its playful character and of its sensual dimension. In contrast to Sternberger, who introduced sociability as a subtly sensual practice that would lure the anxiously disciplined German of character into the public arena of negotiation and compromise, Habermas elides the body. More specifically, Sternberger had inscribed sexual difference in the notion of sociability; the German *Bürger* hiding behind an armor of character could not become a political citizen without the mixed-sex setting of sociability as a place for a light "touching of spheres." In *The Structural Transformation of the Public Sphere,* however, sociability appears as a preliminary stage on the path toward politics by rational argument, and for this reason, it must from the very beginning be presented as a more ascetic practice. The fact that the English coffeehouse only permitted men is not a problem for Habermas, since he wants sociability to make room for debate rather than remain tied to flirtation. Statements are supposed to be convincing, not seductive.

To explain how spaces and habits of bourgeois sociability could begin to house rational argumentation during the Enlightenment, Habermas thus needs to do more than refer to the disregard for rank characteristic of both practices. He needs to supply an account of how conversations became more disciplined and rational. He draws this explanation from an overview of the changing conditions of art consumption in the age of the capitalist market. In his story, the commodification of artworks, their circulation on art markets, and the concomitant loss of their sacramental character—their status as outward and visible signs of some transcendent and invisible entity—provide a sort of impulse of disenchantment that initiates the more focused exchange of argument.

The story goes like this: The bourgeoisie encounters art in new institutional settings shaped by the market, such as the concert hall, the art salon, or the book club. In these settings, artworks have been removed from spaces of worship and submission and no longer appear as wonders to which the appropriate response is awe and mute admiration. They are aesthetically appealing, but their relative obscurity—their lack of a clearly articulated "meaning"—has to be discussed and elucidated by members of the audience. As floating commodities on a nascent market, works of art are stripped of their "aura" yet remain opaque as signs or messages to be deciphered, and this process of disenchantment compels the consumers to try to determine what they mean without resorting to old patterns of reception according to which art conveys images of the divine. No longer the extension and glorification of the ecclesiastical or regal power that put them on display, artworks demand a collective hermeneutical effort that proceeds by rational communication. There must be a discussion about their status and meaning, and that discussion must be sober and nonmystical.

Works of art stripped of sacramental force drove the bourgeois audience into a kind of interpersonal communication that tolerated no appeals to revealed truth. Commentators have traced this particular transition in Habermas's study back to Walter Benjamin's concept of the aura or Hegel's thesis on the end of art. "Faced with the autonomy of aesthetic objects, Habermas argues, private people naturally enter into rational-critical debate about such objects."[34] To explain how bon mots could turn into arguments in the contexts of bourgeois sociability, Habermas adduces a story of secularization in the realm of art. It is the introduction of a particular topic that must be dealt with in a sober, rational fashion—namely, artworks extracted from contexts of worship—that helped convert conversations into rational critique.

Yet Habermas's invocation on the secularization of art does not neutralize all possible tensions between sociable intercourse, on the one hand, and rational argumentation, on the other. The point of any sociable conversation is to keep the conversation going and to keep it surprising and amusing. It should be inviting rather than exclusive, egalitarian rather than asymmetrical, and can therefore seem attractive to a champion of rational discourse. But in the end, arguments would be too much of a cumbersome presence in the easy flow of remarks. The person who uses a conversation as an opportunity to present a case for or against particular policy solutions to a problem would quite likely come across as a bore or a pedant. Within the context of sociable interaction, argumentativeness is a form of ponderous assertiveness. At the very least, sociability works, or works best, when invidious issues are removed from the list of possible subject matters, as Sternberger was forced to witness once his journal disintegrated despite appeals to *Geselligkeit*. Sociability tends to collapse when freighted with political discussions. Habermas's idea that bon mots transformed into arguments at a particular point in bourgeois history thus presupposes a conversion of genres that may seem unlikely. A bon mot requires a different discursive milieu from an argument, and a different kind of competence; a speaker good at witty remarks may not be equally skilled at rational analysis.

The problem outlined above is captured in a small phrase that appears in Habermas's work: *geselliges Disputieren*, or "convivial argumentation."[35] It may be true that friends and acquaintances who trust one another can conduct arguments in which they ultimately come to gravitate toward the reasons or solutions that seem best to them. Yet convivial discussion or sociable argumentation may also be something of an oxymoron, for the demands of sociability and the demands of argumentation are different and not always reconcilable. This point is not lost on contemporary political theorists of deliberative democracy. Chatting with acquaintances about some topic that happens to serve well as a conversational theme is not the same as engaging in deliberations and identifying the best response to some shared problem.[36]

Conversations and disputes are partly similar but ultimately separate genres. This is not to say that sociability that does not reach up to rational argumentation can never perform some political function. In *The Structural Transformation of the Public Sphere,* however, bourgeois sociability on its own, an entirely apolitical activity, cannot accomplish very much. It is only when the social venues of the coffeehouse or the salon have become stages for disciplined debate, and arguments have begun to emerge out of conversations, that bourgeois sociability is properly politicized. It is only when sociability has transformed into a critical bourgeois public sphere that it compels state power to harmonize with collective reason. For Habermas, the flow of remarks in conversations that demand mutual deference and bracket antagonisms was simply an institutional forerunner to actual deliberation, a necessary but incomplete phase that prepared the ground for real deliberations by flattening hierarchies.

But this is not the only way to imagine the relationship of sociability to power. Taking one's cue from Koselleck, but without accepting his resentment of the bourgeoisie, one can say that sociable discourse, as the continual performance of politeness, tries to eliminate controversy and remove political issues from the conversation precisely in order to minimize the perceived need for a master of great force whose legitimacy derives from the promise of keeping strife and chaos at bay. The more civil people are with one another, the more they collaboratively diminish the legitimacy of some centralized and disciplining agent.[37] A particular kind of Enlightenment sociability tried to defang power without having made it to the allegedly higher stage of rational argumentation.

Contrary to Habermas's wish, bon mots might not miraculously turn into earnest political arguments, and it is also doubtful whether semi-intimate circles of discussion, whether they are engaged in conversation or argumentation, can serve as ideals for any other form of congregation or for a polity. Small-scale sociable environments tend to promote circumspect and tactful behavior even among strangers and adversaries, and tend to fill up with small talk rather than political discussions.[38] Participants in semi-intimate circles of discussion quickly learn to conceal rather than address divisions, something that may work against seeing them as cells of discussions on controversial issues. Enemies can even behave in a civil manner during the time they spend in the salon, but this does not necessarily eliminate the enmity. The eighteenth-century project was rather to keep enemies in the salon as long as possible, to reduce the palpable need for constant policing by some centralized authority.

When Habermas envisions sociability as the origin of a particular kind of politics, however, he does not consider the specificity of sociable conversations as a genre; rather, he tries to bridge the gap between sociable remarks and arguments and in this way show that a particular political conduct could grow out of the social engagements. Like Sternberger writing in *Die Wandlung* between 1945 and 1949, Habermas must, in his attempt to save bourgeois sociability from its critics, provide a narrative that makes plausible the transition from sociability to political action, which is why the story he presents relies on the natural erosion of borders between conversation and deliberation. On the microlevel of his argument, the relocation of political action into the social settings of bourgeois society, Habermas's rejoinder to Schmitt and Arendt, depends on blending genres of talk.[39] He believes, perhaps disregarding the specificity of both genres, that sociable conversations could evolve into rational deliberations.

Sociability and Conformity

Habermas's account of how a new kind of politics rooted in argumentation became possible in Europe at a particular historical point crucially integrates a picture of bourgeois sociability. The broadly accessible and rationally oriented discussion that he views as the essence of politics, in explicit contrast to Arendt's and Schmitt's ideas of politics, first emerged in the venues of conviviality, of *Geselligkeit,* a practice that set up some important institutional conditions for rational debate, such as the temporary bracketing of rank within a delimited space.[40]

In this way, Habermas's study represents an ingenious attempt to save bourgeois sociability by incorporating it into a large-scale historical reconstruction of the emergence of the bourgeois public sphere, intercalated between the state and the market. In the history of the bourgeoisie, Habermas argues, sociability served as a vital forerunner to the bourgeoisie's discursively mediated involvement in political decision making by the state.

But even if one accepts that the bourgeois sites of sociability did transform into cells of political discussion, one can still argue that they failed to maintain a healthy level of internal dissent. Small circles of interaction can be quite good at generating consensus, but in many cases they do so by eliminating a multiplicity of opinions by means other than rational argumentation. Arendt and to some extent Koselleck both present versions of this suspicion. Demands for loyalty, patterns of mutual confirmation, and the resulting lack of diverse sources of information all conspire to strengthen a narrow set of opinions accepted by friends and acquaintances who gather in a particular place, or write for and read a particular publication. Exploring the importance of coffeehouses as a gathering place for intellectuals during the Enlightenment, the sociologist Lewis Coser writes that these meeting places "helped replace a solidarity based on common styles of life or common descent by one based on like opinion."[41] The bourgeoisie may indeed have dropped rank as a criterion of belonging, only to replace it with conformity at another level: that of opinions.

Deliberating units are capable of stifling dissent or reinforcing already existing patterns of bias within their confines, whether or not this tendency represents any explicit and conscious intention or desire among the members. Participants in group discussions tend to adapt to one another, as each member searches for commonalities with all other members, increases a pool of arguments for his or her already entrenched convictions, and receives and offers continual corroboration of a particular set of opinions. Given time, these deliberating cells soon come to focus on values, intentions, and commitments they can view as components of their shared identity. This may be good for the sense of morale and belonging the individuals enjoy, but it proves less conducive to the group's ability to preserve a repertoire of different approaches or to weigh alternatives according to standards of rationality.[42] In other words, groups that gather in coffeehouses or salons to lead discussions may be quite bad at the very thing that Habermas thinks they are good at. Insofar as they use channels of publication linked to a greater arena, they may of course contribute to the range of arguments and viewpoints at the aggregative level of the entire public sphere, but still fail to maintain this diversity within the confines of their circle.[43]

Sociable conversation does not necessarily turn into critique, and insofar as the bourgeoisie cultivates a critical attitude, it may fail to assume a form of self-critique within smaller groups in which all members share assumptions and opinions. In 1962, the publication year of Habermas's reevaluation of bourgeois society, Arendt had already presented a particularly severe indictment of sociability in *The Human Condition,* the work to which Habermas referred. In fact, Habermas explicitly mentions her negative view of the "rise of the social," understood as the process by which the purely economic networks of interdependence previously confined to the household become the main object of modern public life, so that the preoccupation with the organization and maintenance of material life overshadows the genuinely political desire for recognition and enduring glory.[44]

Yet Habermas does not address the fact that Arendt views bourgeois sociability as yet another manifestation of the "rise of the social." As a self-governing system that reaches optimal efficiency when every participant simply pursues his or her own private interest without regard for any other kind of communication, the market economy dispenses with the politics of the extraordinary deed and word; the sum total of all decisions made by private individuals to further their situation constitutes a pseudo-public life. According to Arendt, however, sociability in the bourgeois era is just another form of collective interaction that minimizes friction and produces an appearance of accord. Arendt claims that mechanisms of imitation and soft mutual influence work smoothly to ensure that each member of a society comes to multiply and prolong "the perspective of his neighbor."[45] To repeat a claim discussed above, in *The Human Condition* Arendt disparages both the norms of high society, convening in salons, and the modern social sciences for their treatment of individuals as predictable behaving particles. She speaks of the "assumed one interest of society as a whole in economics as well as the assumed one opinion of polite society in the salon."[46] For Arendt, both the market and the salon foster antipolitical uniformity, but Habermas does not mention Arendt's critique of salon conversation.[47]

Habermas subscribes to a vision of a lively, deliberative political life in which citizens engage in discussions with one another to generate rational responses to shared problems.[48] To be sure, he sees multiple threats to the model of deliberative democracy within complex societies characterized by unequal distribution of resources and structures of media-transmitted communication. The absence of barriers between media empires and wealthy special interest groups, the imperatives of the market pressuring those who are supposed to evaluate and channel information, the efforts of prominent agenda setters to frame issues in ways that are beneficial to their particular causes—all these features of modern democracies block genuine deliberative, participatory politics.[49] In 1962, Habermas could draw on critics who spoke of the "culture industry," or the "consciousness industry,"[50] and depicted how preschematized mass entertainment paralyzed people's critical capacities, all of which turned them into passive consumers lodged in constricted cells of mindless private enjoyment.[51]

But the three thinkers whom Habermas set out to refute in his book, Arendt, Schmitt, and Koselleck, were actually much more concerned with the character and efficacy of pressures that give shape to attitudes and behaviors within social communities understood as neighborhoods of mutual adjustment, influence, and correction. For these students of the formation and internal dynamic of social contexts, modern media or consumer society was not in itself the most significant or interesting source of political pathologies, nor did it harbor a solution.[52]

In a sense, Arendt and Koselleck accepted that bourgeois sociability stood for the capacity of a collective to organize itself without the constant intervention of any outside authorities, but they also claimed that this was possible because of mechanisms of order internal to the community, or at least to its protocols of interaction. For instance, a smaller sociable community can preserve its integrity and ensure a convergence of commitments because of pressures to conform to extant group norms—pressures that are sensed by each individual member although they may not be overtly expressed and enforced by any particular person. As individuals adapt to prevailing norms, either to reap the benefits of conforming or from fear of isolation, the community that appears to have been constituted from below no longer seems free from all forms of suppression. The absence of explicitly coercive entities can even be regarded as a testimony to the efficiency with which opportunities for dissent and conflict had already been minimized within the forming society. A peaceful collectivity of sociability was entirely possible, its critics maintained, but only at the cost of the eclipse of vigorous contention over values and principles.

Reason and Political Order

To the critics of sociability, the apparent fading of any distinct, personified power in modern society did not necessarily mean the end of stifling forces of integration. Ostensibly noncoercive sociability depends on and continually generates shared understandings of what represents good conduct and acceptable reasoning, although the constituted norms tend to appear as what is normal, or what "is or isn't done."[53] There may be no identifiable agent of power who enunciates injunctions, yet norms are enforced in indirect ways as society coalesces around premises of thinking and behaving that circumscribe what can be said and done. Nobody enforces social norms—or a "nobody" enforces them: overt regulation is replaced with the hegemony of common sense.

Despite many and wide differences among them, Arendt, Schmitt, and Koselleck all derived their critical arguments against bourgeois society from conceptions of "the political"[54] characterized by declared and open conflict over the fundamental principles of communal organization.[55] Their ideal is not quite the autonomous, self-legislative individual, nor the stable and hierarchically ordered community of tradition and religion, but rather something like the performed conflict or the articulated and sustained fracture between groups and individuals, a situation in which differences in interests, beliefs, and norms crystallize and become manifest.

There are many more or less clearly and overtly formulated reasons for this investment in the performance of dissent and conflict, and they range from the pragmatic to the philosophical. Koselleck is a case in point, for he produces rather different arguments against society's tendency to induce unanimity among its members by means of subtle processes of influence. At points, he claims that the presupposition of moral consensus leaves the members of bourgeois society ill equipped to understand and accept those conflicts that do in fact arise between groups with different interests, and he argues that this expectation of agreement blocks the prospect of realistic resolutions necessary for coexistence. This idea ultimately grounds his interpretation of the Cold War conflict, in which two superpowers with utopian self-conceptions were pitted against each other without means to defuse the tension. Convinced of the utter superiority of their paradigm and its eventual historical triumph, they simply did not accept conflict as a state of affairs and therefore could not address it in any sensible way.

Yet one can also discover a more ideological attachment to openly antagonistic relations in *Critique and Crisis,* for instance in the passages in which he claims that the Enlightenment critics failed to grasp and embrace their own desire to attain power and rule over others and hence lacked the integrity and dignity of a self-aware subject. A person, Koselleck implies, should see and honestly acknowledge the fierce energies that truly drive his or her life rather than remain in the dark about motivations and ambitions as a self-alienated, existentially inauthentic subject.

Arendt's thought displays a similarly divided attention to the practical and the existential dimensions of dissent. Having observed how easily Germans could be persuaded to participate in the apparatus of mass murder, drawn by the jobholder's anxiety about maintained social standing and a feeling of unaccountability for decisions made by their leaders, she could understand why societies needed their dissenters to remind people of alternative courses of action.[56] In her picture of a people mobilized for the purpose of genocide, the mass of bourgeois philistines who always work to conform to collective norms, whatever these norms may prescribe, pose a danger when the national infrastructure is programmed for murder.

In her more philosophical texts, however, Arendt also introduced a notion of vigorous and volatile discursive opposition as generative of existential meaning to its participants and delineated the sphere of political engagement as one of "competitive, identity-disclosing action" that forms an internally plural human community.[57] According to Arendt, the practice of politics enables the individual to achieve a unique identity precisely by allowing her to distinguish herself from others through her words and deeds in a fluctuating context of arguments and positions.[58] And as long as the human community is engaged in such political action, as long as its members form and revise their identities in relation to each other through agonistic contestation, it sustains a process of differentiation that prevents it from congealing into a closed, static, and homogeneous unity. Articulated dissent among responsive members of a polity can serve as a safeguard against extremist collective projects, but the ongoing discursive contestation over norms and policies is also the way that the human collective preserves its unpredictability and eccentricity. By continually evolving disagreements, the polity rearranges itself and breaks itself up and in this way escapes attempts to describe it in terms of a set of unchanging, quasi-natural laws. The practice of politics is the realization of human freedom.[59]

Habermas shares a number of commitments with Koselleck and Arendt. All three thinkers exhibit an abiding commitment to the particular dignity and meaning of the political as a collective life-form. And they also think of politics as a peculiarly fragile activity, always in danger of being infected by other spheres of activity, sapped of life and put to rest, whether this happens through social mechanisms of imitation, mutual influence, or covert correction that work to minimize frictions and produce accord; through glaring maldistribution of economic resources that disable egalitarian discourse; or through modern consumerism and media manipulation designed to pacify the populace. For Arendt, Koselleck, and Habermas, politics seems to be the most important but also the most vulnerable of pursuits.

Yet unlike Koselleck and Arendt, Habermas is committed to the idea that a rationally ordered society is possible and desirable. This guiding idea has become manifest in multiple ways over his career, and for philosophers, social theorists, and legal scholars, *The Structural Transformation of the Public Sphere* is hardly his most relevant or lasting work. To be sure, many have criticized Habermas's theories for their alleged aloofness and lack of realism. Todd Hedrick, a sympathetic interpreter of Habermas, concedes that his critics have attributed an otherwordly quality to his thought. In Habermas's universe, "all of the citizens are reasonable, they are engaged in earnest, spirited dialogue about what is equally in the interest of them all, their ethical differences are capable of being overcome or bracketed, and consensus is consistently achievable."[60] Yet Hedrick also maintains that few if any works of modern political philosophers truly rival the scope and ambitiousness of Habermas's ongoing project—namely, to link humanity's capacity for reason with the constitution of the political order.

By exploring the linkage between rational thought and a good and just polity, Habermas has resurrected the reason-based aspirations of political theory in the Western tradition, and has done so without subscribing to a rigid conception of reason as dictating how people ought to live or what specific norms they ought to follow. For Habermas, reason is not substantive or "contentful."[61] Rather than prescribe how to act or paint "too detailed a picture of the good life,"[62] it supports only particular procedures of discursive interaction by which people can come to agree on what course of action to follow. Reason unfolds only through undistorted communication among multiple and diverse individuals and does not demand the submission of all to an already existing and unchanging truth. An Arendtian critique of the threat of reason's tyranny can perhaps only do limited damage to Habermas's political thought, for his rational polity is not a predictable polity; it does not deprive people of the freedom to act.

Let us return, however, to *The Structural Transformation of the Public Sphere* and its account of the sociable bourgeoisie in European history. In his 1962 study, Habermas provided the procedures of rational communication with a particular historical vessel: the institutions of bourgeois sociability. For contemporary commentators looking back at Habermas's evolution, it has often seemed that he first produced a work of historical sociology and then, step by step, began to explore the universal structures of communication as the medium of human rationality. As Habermas progressed in his theoretical work, he could shed the curious but ultimately unnecessary and perhaps even constraining historical material.

From the perspective of this book, though, with its focus on the postwar search for viable templates of a future Germany, other aspects become apparent. Habermas's endeavor to deposit the idea of a rational polity in the social settings of the historical bourgeoisie activated a host of meanings no longer salient to today's readers. As Sternberger's and Arendt's articles and Koselleck's book demonstrate, reflections on the history of bourgeois society and bourgeois sociability in the medium of conversation or "convivial argumentation" were surrounded by hopes and aversions, affirmative and critical arguments.

As the editor of *Die Wandlung,* Sternberger sought to redefine the identity of the German *Bürger* by evoking practices and virtues of a *Geselligkeit* that would serve as a therapeutic and transitional stage on the way to genuine political maturity. Schmitt in turn confronted the apparently calm and inclusive postwar culture of the conversation or *Gespräch* with the discursive situation of the interrogation. Arendt used her space in *Die Wandlung* to present the National Socialist mobilization of Germany as an alliance between antibourgeois and bourgeois subjects, thereby implicitly disqualifying the reformation of the German bourgeoisie through sociability. Koselleck argued that the historical bourgeoisie's world of academies, associations, and clubs in spaces drained of conflict inadvertently helped convert noncoercive interaction into a deeply flawed and unrealistic principle of politics. In other words, Habermas's book entered an already existing context of argumentation and tensions.

What, then, was Habermas's achievement? Sternberger and others regretted the smothered political breakthrough of the bourgeoisie in Germany. By portraying the bourgeoisie as avant-garde practitioners of politics by rational argument, Habermas's book presented the strongest case for why this historical development could be considered regrettable. He thus moved the promotion of bourgeois society beyond mere laments about German backwardness or nostalgic attachments to the peculiarities of a particular class, and supplied a sophisticated picture of the connection between sociability and critical political discourse.

Determined to analyze totalitarianism, Arendt utilized a range of antibourgeois stereotypes such as the philistine to dramatize her critique of the effects of modern political atomism and state subjection, but she also came close to a wholesale condemnation of modernity, with its vast networks of economic interdependency and centralized state structure. In contrast, Habermas located political potentials *in* the modern world by imagining spaces of discursive mediation between the capitalist market and the modern state, spaces explored and occupied by the bourgeoisie.

Inspired by Schmitt, Koselleck denounced the efforts of the bourgeoisie to regulate the sovereign state by means of discourse over values and norms as a deceitful or self-deceptive strategy in an ongoing power game.

Countering this (Schmittian) obsession with the workings of dissimulating agents striving for dominance, Habermas specified under what historical conditions argumentation originating in spaces for nonhierarchical and noncoercive sociable interaction could in fact come to play a constructive role in the resolution of political conflicts.

Chapter Six

✦

Among the Rotarians: Sociability in West Germany

> Men are on the way to themselves when they get together in the evening, drink, talk and express opinions. When they talk without purpose they are on their own tracks, when they express opinions and their opinions rise with the smoke from pipes, cigarettes and cigars and when the world turns to smoke and madness in the village inns, in the private rooms, the back rooms of the big restaurants and in the wine cellars of the big cities.
>
> —Ingeborg Bachmann, *The Thirtieth Year*

The above passage from a 1961 short story by the Austrian author Ingeborg Bachmann lists the places where one can find tables filled with regulars, the so-called *Stammtische* of German-speaking sociability: in the village pubs and inns, and the wine bars and restaurant backrooms of cities. These are the places where people unwind in each other's company, where they drink, smoke, and talk. Bachmann's circles of sociability do not seem particularly inclusive—only men are allowed to join, and the groups that congregate probably exclude strangers and outsiders. Yet the people who meet to talk are not guarded or secretive because they discuss sensitive matters or controversial political issues. The atmosphere seems more light-hearted, and the conversations, Bachmann writes, have no purpose. The interlocutors speak their minds, but this is not a mark of intellectual courage. Rather, their talk roams aimlessly and the opinions are likened to dissolving smoke, as if without any substance. People might be stating their views, but perhaps without real interest in a dialogical exchange of reasons, or even in the reactions of others. The resulting conversations are relaxed yet exclusive, full of opinions yet empty of arguments.

The quotation from Bachmann's story, here taken out of its context, illustrates some of the ambivalence of sociable discourse that this book has explored through accounts of prominent German political writers and theorists active after 1945. Practices of sociability are located in a middle ground between intimacy and publicness, and the talk that belongs to *Geselligkeit* hovers between deliberations on grave matters of political significance and gregariousness bordering on the frivolous.

Is it in these venues that people's values, commitments, and attitudes are formed and consolidated? Do the conventions and habits of sociability somehow help foster responsible and active citizens, willing and able to participate in liberal and democratic political life and to voice considered opinions publicly, evaluate alternative projects and policies argumentatively, or support or criticize candidates for leadership? Can the type of talk that accompanies, or constitutes, sociable interaction prepare its participants for explicitly political and hence potentially conflict-ridden discussions and engagements?

The thinkers treated in this book—Sternberger, Schmitt, Arendt, Koselleck, and Habermas—considered in different ways the relationship between sociable interconnections and political engagements in the context of bourgeois society and its history. This topic has never been the focus of previous studies of postwar thought. As discussed in the introduction, commentators on postwar Germany have often sought to determine to what extent Germans were able to admit responsibility for atrocities perpetrated under National Socialism and to adopt and affirm the institutions and procedures of Western liberal democracies. Concentrating on these intertwined demands, they have emphasized that Germans had to begin to speak openly and honestly of their own guilt as well as involve themselves vigorously in open and public discussions on the future course of the collective. And scholars who have tracked the country's integration into the West and democratization of political institutions over more than five decades have, for the most part, shown how Germans were able to make this transition away from dictatorial or totalitarian rule, belligerent nationalism, and murderous persecution of minorities. The historian Konrad Jarausch, for instance, speaks of the successful "long-term learning processes, both personal and collective, that aimed to prevent a recurrence of oppression, war, and genocide."[1]

With similar ideals and objectives in mind, skeptical observers writing in the more immediate postwar period were concerned that Germans were not willing either to come to terms with the past or to embrace democratic processes of decision making. Speaking of the situation in Germany, they frequently employed a vocabulary of speech versus silence, transparency and openness versus taboos. In 1959, Theodor W. Adorno analyzed the ambiguous notion of "working through the past" and noted how people confronted with explicit references to deportations and mass murder often became evasive and refused to speak openly and frankly about recent German history. It was, he writes, as if "a hollow space formed in the discourse."[2] A few years later, Alexander Mitscherlich asserted that Germans still found it alarmingly difficult to accept the coexistence of multiple different viewpoints and opinions, and as a result, German national discourse was circumscribed by too many dogmas and forbidden topics that ensured a quiet conformity of ideas and attitudes. To the question of whether "taboos inhibit the democratization of German society," Mitscherlich answered in the affirmative.[3]

To Adorno and Mitscherlich, then, Germans were prone to fall silent. All too often, West German citizens refused to speak about their responsibility for events in the past and were too inert and repressed to emerge as fully participating citizens in a democratic discourse. In these critical portraits of a nation, Germany appeared entrapped in a morally culpable and politically sterile muteness. And in many ways, more recent commentators on the early postwar period have taken their cue from these earlier assessments and continued to focus, with significant conceptual variations, on the petrified inarticulateness of Germans after 1945. Thus German intellectual life in the early postwar period was dominated by an "obstinate culture of silence,"[4] in which people passed over crimes. And in the artistic-cultural world one could note an "overall absence of [artistic] work trying to find images, words and narratives to represent the Nazi death machine."[5] The 1950s, finally, were a time of escapist materialism and political quietism; Germans tended to retreat from political activity and effectively handed over the business of governance to trusted paternal figures such as Konrad Adenauer.[6]

This study has not aimed to dispute the importance of the critical interpretations and positions above. Yet the retrieval and elucidation of the postwar language of sociability does move the focus away from the dominant polarities of speech versus silence, genuine openness versus stifling taboos, or democracy versus veiled authoritarianism. In light of the reconstructions and reassessments presented in the chapters above, the question that unites the disparate texts of writers such as Sternberger, Schmitt, Arendt, Koselleck, and Habermas does not simply ask how Germans can be induced to speak and, through speaking, achieve the status of authentic moral and political subjects. Instead, for the writers and thinkers considered in this book, the question was whether a contemporary revival of sociability could promote and shape the future political life of the defeated and broken nation, given the character of sociable interaction and associational life throughout bourgeois history.

Some versions of this previously concealed question would read: Can the sociable interactions among friends and acquaintances in extrafamilial and extraprofessional venues function as a preparatory stage or anticipatory image of processes of political decision making? Do activities in the sites of "organized sociability" lead their participants to understand, or misunderstand, the specific rules and challenges of political activities? How porous are the boundaries between different types of discourse, such as polite and friendly conversations, on the one hand, and argumentative or polemical debates, on the other? To state the matter in the most compressed form possible, one could say that the relevant postwar binary for a series of important thinkers was not simply speech versus silence but rather conversation versus deliberation, or sociability versus politics.

Sociability: Arguments for and Against

The previously neglected but pivotal significance of sociability or *Geselligkeit*—a seemingly trivial theme in an era of profound moral and political challenges—flowed from the search for viable and recognizable modes of cohesion at a time and in a place where traditional supports and names for the collective had been discredited or swept away. As Karl Jaspers declared in his opening words for *Die Wandlung* in 1945, the Germans lacked independent statehood and a functioning economy and could no longer confidently view themselves as members of an intact nation that housed a sovereign people. Needless to say, public invocations of the German *Volksgemeinschaft* were out of the question, both to Jaspers and to the foreign military administration that facilitated the publication of his words.

In this situation of perceived fragmentation, quite a few intellectuals and writers advanced their own makeshift circles of discussion, improvised academies and book-sharing clubs, and gradually repaired and consolidated networks of acquaintances as a paradigm for the reconstitution of the German collective in the medium of spontaneous and civil conversation. After the state had been shattered, the economy ruined, and the claims of aggressive nationalism completely quelled by total defeat, the vision of some lightly organized sociability as a form of nonmilitarized, nonhierarchical, nonpolitical, and nonprofessional interaction filled an empty institutional and conceptual space in a way that salvaged a (traditional upper-middle-class) German identity, all the while being inoffensive to a foreign administration. The claim here, in other words, is not that the plethora of proposed or actual small cells of discussion and mini-institutions such as Friedrich Meinecke's quaint Goethe congregations, the somber group of young authors gathering as Gruppe 47, or numerous other forming circles of discussion or resurrected *Vereine* actually provided a powerful new sense of collective identity.[7] Rather, noneconomic activities in what we would today call civil society temporarily grew in significance in the otherwise sparse institutional landscape and provided writers and intellectuals with glimpses of some imagined future collectivity.

As the editor of *Die Wandlung,* Sternberger formulated a coherent understanding of the meaning of and work accomplished by civil and cultured interaction, and even introduced sociability as a means to nudge the German *Bürger* toward a renewed and politically more constructive identity. If the German *Bürger* were to define himself by performances of polite and tactful behavior rather than secure material assets and rigid sexual self-discipline, this social formation would survive the contemporary economic precariousness and become much more inclusive, but also would finally come to accept the constant negotiations and compromises that make up politics, instead of rejecting them as undignified tactics. Sternberger claimed that Germans could find a path from elegant and affable mingling in the salon to the exercise of collective autonomy, for the pleasures of sociability serve to draw people together, break down the individual's fear of contamination by others, and then sustain interaction without the ordering force of an authority. The salon rather than the market, then, was Sternberger's favored proof of the self-organizing capacity of collectivities.

In this way, Sternberger encouraged his readers to accept a new *Bürgerlichkeit* without a clearly defined *Bürgertum* and begin to share a life through sociability as a first step toward the assumption of responsible citizenship. Yet the hoped-for transition from sociable conversations to political dialogues and debates seemed to come to a halt as the journal's initial editorial collective broke up along ideological lines. Politeness and companionableness could not hold Germans together as the East and the West emerged as congealed blocks in a global conflict.

There were also arguments against the culture of sociable conversation from outside the journal. The Schmittian attack against this vision of beneficial conversations, the release of which was delayed because of Schmitt's marginalized position after 1945, consisted in pointing to unacknowledged power structures in the background of peaceful conversations. Very particular people voiced the need for calm reflection and quiet civility in the postwar situation, Schmitt asserted, namely the ones who had been tested and recruited by foreign administrations and had managed to secure licenses to speak and publish. The absence of sharp polemics and fierce struggle for dominance at the new sites of sociability, Schmitt could then maintain, was not a sign of spontaneously and autonomously achieved pacification. Instead, the language of harmony was a veiled polemical move made by those who enjoyed the support of groups with great means of coercion, and this language was designed to silence opponents and suppress the very idea of opposition.

The climate of continuous conversations among Schmitt's German contemporaries did not prove, he implied, that power had been dissolved, only that power chose to enforce and promulgate agreement and unity in particular ways. Indeed, Schmitt's hypersensitivity to the supposedly real but concealed centers of authority became legible in his apologetic writings, in which he argued that the conversations he was invited to participate in were shadowed by the interrogations to which he was subjected. There were half-hidden asymmetries in the supposedly egalitarian discourse.

This opposition between proponents and critics of sociability as a protopolitical form of life in the postwar moment was to some extent reprised in the idioms of political thought and historical sociology by two young students of bourgeois society's emergence. In his *Critique and Crisis,* Koselleck made the argument that the bourgeois individuals who discovered and developed new modes of discursive interaction in Enlightenment lodges, salons, and academies tended to become oblivious to the need for the absolutist regime that had concentrated the means of coercion and drained society of lethal conflict in the first place. Peaceful and egalitarian forms of interaction among members of small associations and clubs could not supply a template for political order; rather, they depended on a preexisting political order for their very existence and flourishing. It was delusional, Koselleck maintained, to see a path from sociability to an ideal type of politics.

Taking aim at this argument, Habermas reconstructed how the bourgeoisie had come to regulate the exercise of power by subjecting it to a standard of argumentative reason. Power could be tamed and supervised through such rationalization, he thought, if not always completely dissolved. Yet politically efficacious human reason had first taken hold in the institutions of sociability—the coffeehouses, salons, and reading clubs of the Enlightenment period. In essence, sociable conversations in relaxed settings served to bracket hierarchies of rank but also became receptacles of themes such as the meaning of nonsacred art that required rational-critical scrutiny, two factors that meant that good arguments could take precedence over other concerns. In Habermas's account, politically relevant argumentation could evolve out of sociability, thanks to the institutional structure and prevalent themes of convivial exchanges at first deemed nonpolitical.

Both Habermas and Koselleck also referred to Hannah Arendt, a close friend of Jaspers and an acquaintance of Sternberger who became one of the main contributors to *Die Wandlung* between 1945 and 1949. Her early postwar articles for a German-language audience, however—articles on topics such as imperialism or organized guilt —neither confirmed Sternberger's vision of bourgeois sociability as a form of reeducation nor anticipated Habermas's reconstruction of gradual bourgeois politicization. Arendt argued that the bourgeois-liberal faith in the spontaneous formation of a coherent and unified political order out of the happily confluent activities of private and self-managing individuals was representative of an age of dismantled or ruined public institutions and arenas. Bourgeois individuals who did not believe they had anything in common and turned to each other only to secure resources or make economic gains would not, she claimed, be able or willing to assume responsibility for the aggregated outcomes of their actions. The members of the bourgeoisie were resolutely and fatally parochial in their outlook, disavowed life outside the familial or economic spheres, and knew no form of enduring interconnection. Contrary to a widespread misconception, the German bourgeoisie had not even been particularly patriotic.

Arendt leveled this charge at the bourgeois obsession with private life and economic security, moreover, in an acid antibourgeois rhetoric directed at the *Spießer* or philistine. Thus the idea that a bourgeois type of nonhierarchical and civil sociability could slowly move Germans to make a commitment to a more deliberative and democratic collective order seemed ridiculous to Arendt. She granted that bourgeois individuals, who conceived of themselves as lonely and vulnerable creatures, would likely band together, but only to form a mob, a group held together solely by fear.

What happens, then, when the members of the bourgeoisie get together in the village inns and backrooms of restaurants, when they gather for their weekly meetings in clubs and associations, or when they join earnest discussions in literary salons and academies? Are they practicing the art of conducting arguments with one another and even making collective decisions in a way that prepares them for debates and confrontations in a greater democratic arena? Or are they simply relaxing in a sort of artificial and nonexpandable setting, which is ultimately protected and hence made possible by powers located elsewhere? Are the scenes of sociability in a sphere beyond the family, the market, and the state veritable training grounds for politics that allow people to acquire a sense of self-organization and self-governance? Or do these scenes instead represent small exclusive cells of conformity that cause participants to misconstrue rather than comprehend the actual character of political conflicts?

As this review of Sternberger, Schmitt, Koselleck, Habermas, and Arendt indicates, there were arguments for and against sociability among prominent writers and intellectuals of the period, all of whom knew something about the particular postwar sociotope of the discussion circle, friendship network, and revived association. Rather than immediately resolve the questions posed above by somehow picking the most plausible approach among the affirmative and dismissive answers, we can first note how the range of outlined positions cannot easily be subsumed under the rubric of some other, more fundamental polarity. For instance, the proponents and opponents of bourgeois sociability do not perfectly coincide with groups of nationalists and antinationalists, tolerant liberals and authoritarian conservatives. Schmitt is deeply skeptical about the reality of egalitarian sociable conversations, and so is Arendt, but they share few other commitments and convictions.

The question of whether bourgeois society, with its history and in its frayed contemporary form, somehow harbored the potential to regenerate Germany was evidently enough to animate a group of serious publicists and theorists and lead them to articulate attacks on or apologias for specific forms of bourgeois interconnection in the guise of sociability. In a sense, politically interested writers such as Sternberger, Arendt, Schmitt, Koselleck, and Habermas focused on the character of political action in modern society, identified modern society with bourgeois society, and then scrutinized the history of the bourgeoisie for models of interaction that had been or could be advanced as the matrix of a new type of politics. It was against this backdrop that sociability as a preparatory state for politics attracted multiple supporters and detractors.

This overview of voices for and against a particular bourgeois mode of cohesion could prompt one to ask: Did the concept and practice of sociability fulfill important functions in the postwar period? Was the vision of a postwar Germany of sociability translated into reality, however much the vision aroused the approval or disapproval of the thinkers covered in this book? Before we articulate a final judgment on the political value of sociability, we should gauge sociability's actual viability as a mode or practice of cohesion in the landscape of postwar Germany.

The Eclipse of Sociability in West Germany

Did the precarious postwar era turn out to be an epoch of revitalized sociability, as Sternberger, Meinecke, and others had hoped? In the years immediately after the Second World War, writers and intellectuals could imagine a greater role for themselves and their conversations on moral and political matters in an uncertain, not yet settled institutional situation, in which the public was hungry for reading material, commercial mass media were not yet completely dominant, and large-scale hierarchical political organizations were only beginning to emerge after the end of National Socialist rule. But the vision of a new era for bourgeois forms of sociability practiced in circles and extended and made accessible through journals soon dissipated, for a number of reasons. The early Federal Republic of Germany turned out not to be a golden age of sociability. Contexts of light conversation and discussion such as salons, clubs, and reading societies did not make a sustained comeback or come to provide a novel foundation for the nation and its political system as a whole.

If anything, cultural historians have reconstructed how multiple pressures combined to reduce the level of nonfamilial social life in the postwar period. After the currency reform of 1948, long working hours in the buzzing German postwar economy, the increasing availability of mass media to be consumed in private, the rise of a commuter lifestyle in a changing urban environment, the focus on the comforts of a home filled with new types of durable goods, and perhaps also a lingering disillusion with collective life of any kind—all of these trends led to a decline in sociable interactions beyond the minimal circle of the nuclear family and a couple of close friends.

In other words, the German citizen of the late 1940s and 1950s did not have that much time for a beer or a coffee in the company of others. In his 1962 study, Habermas noted, and regretted, this development. Speaking about the twentieth century as a whole, but drawing most of his examples from contemporary Germany, he wrote: "The institutions of social-convivial exchange, which secured the coherence of the public making use of its reason, lost their power or utterly collapsed."[8] Whether or not the bourgeois institutions of conviviality had ever worked as a historically unprecedented medium of rational public debate, they no longer existed in postwar Germany.

There were, as indicated, many reasons sociability was in decline. First of all, one can look at the surging postwar national economy. In 1948, Germans had lived under price controls and rationing for about a decade, the production of basic necessities as well as the industrial output were far below the prewar levels, and the labor force was decimated. High levels of absenteeism at companies and bartering between small producers testified to the impaired functioning of the market. Once rationing was abolished, price controls removed, and the currency reformed in the Allied-occupied areas, the economy experienced an astonishing upswing. Industrial production, guided by a growth-minded government, soon returned to and exceeded the levels of the prewar period.[9] This economic revival shaped the everyday life of Germans and partly accounts for the "notorious homeliness" of the 1950s.[10] With a fifty-hour workweek, one day of rest, and an unemployment rate close to 1 percent in a workforce that also included large numbers of women, few ordinary Germans had the leisure to sustain an extensive social life outside the four walls of the home. Sociability requires ample amounts of free time, a scarce resource in postwar Germany.

The postwar retreat from sociable interaction outside the home also seemed correlated with the affluence in the increasingly wealthy consumer society. A whole range of new appliances, more refined eating habits, and affordable home furnishing—seemingly trivial developments that actually changed the essential features of daily life in fundamental ways—inspired a collective turn toward domesticity.[11] The postwar period saw a slew of new or updated household goods such as Grundig radios, Siemens ovens, and refrigerators and television sets from Neckermann. And perhaps these trends also made society more focused on the new pleasures of the home and the intimate sphere and a little less loquacious.

Socialist intellectuals certainly pointed out how the increasing emphasis on consumption crowded out the pleasures of discursive interaction. The committed socialist writer Franz Fühmann, for instance, offered an amusing image of West German silence and its intimate relationship to an emerging market for consumer goods. In the novella *For the First Time: Germany,* Fühmann's alter ego visits an old acquaintance in the western part of Berlin in 1949, and they begin to debate the advantages and disadvantages of the two competing geopolitical systems.[12] At one point in the conversation, the West German friend ceases to speak and instead simply brings out coveted commodities such as Nescafé, the implication being that the most powerful argument for the West is the abundance of consumer goods.[13] In wealthy and well-stocked West Germany, words were no longer needed to defend the system, and its population could sink into silent satisfaction in the drawing room. The chance to participate in the practice of bourgeois sociability was not as good an argument for the West as the opportunity to consume.

Yet another factor in the decline of conversational sociability may have been the availability of media products to be enjoyed in private.

On average, Germans listened to radio for about three hours a day in the 1950s, a decade that also saw the introduction of successful tabloid newspapers (*Bild-Zeitung* was founded in 1952) as well as the rise of a new kind of news magazine for the more ambitious reader (*Der Spiegel* had been founded in 1946). Television was the very best argument for staying at home, as one could see in the decline of cinema attendance. By the mid-1960s, half of German homes owned a television. If going to the movies had been an at least potentially social activity, families could now turn to television for their daily entertainment.[14] Klaus Nathaus, the historian of German "organized sociability," mentions that widespread ownership of cars and televisions conspired to decrease attendance at local association meetings.[15] While intensified media offerings made people stay at home more, the affordable motor vehicle allowed them to travel more regularly and not spend leisure time in their immediate surroundings; in both cases, the village inns and rifle clubs suffered.

This is all to say that West Germans, should they have had any interest in bowling, may have had to go alone to the alley. Hard-working citizens of the Federal Republic with access to new media for consumption in their refurnished and replenished homes perhaps had little time for, or interest in, conversations with others. Interestingly, sociologists also observed a lack of circles of sociability in the elite strata of West German society. The leadership of various functionally defined sectors of society (such as the business world, the political class, the churches, the media) rarely mingled at sociable events. West Germany lacked a coherent "high society" that could "set the tone" thanks to its widely recognized social prestige.[16]

From the perspective of the 1950s, then, Sternberger's early postwar vision of a revived bourgeois sociability embodied in vivid conversations open to everyone seems unsuited to the postwar period. In light of the precarious economic situation in the immediate postwar years, he proposed to reorient the identity of the German *Bürger* by detaching a more free-floating *Bürgerlichkeit,* to be achieved in performances of sociability, from a particular socioeconomic stratum, the *Bürgertum.* And the West German society that gradually emerged in the 1950s may in fact have become more *bürgerlich,* but then it emphasized a very different catalogue of historically bourgeois virtues and attitudes, such as discipline, diligence, thrift, and family responsibility, as opposed to affability, companionableness, and politeness—the values and behaviors advanced by Sternberger. The bourgeoisie may have risen up after World War II, but not in the way Sternberger had envisaged.

The historian Eckart Conze, among others, makes the case that the Federal Republic of Germany was quietly bourgeois or *bürgerlich,* or rather *kleinbürgerlich*, in the sense that the recent experiences of poverty and need compelled broad segments of the German population to invest their time and resources in consolidating their sense of material comfort and security in the private realm, a development that was sustained by the economic boom of the period.[17] In many ways, Arendt's scathing analysis of the philistine, who dodged responsibility for everything that occurred outside the four walls of the home, seems like a prescient characterization of postwar German society next to Sternberger's evocation of extrafamilial and protopolitical bourgeois sociability. Hard work supplemented by a comfortable but narrow homeliness came to define what constituted *Bürgerlichkeit* after 1945. Whether or not Sternberger's vision of revived sociability was constructive or naive, ideologically appealing or delusional, it gained no traction in the young West Germany.

This mass retreat into the private realm was very visible to observers in early West Germany. Skeptical intellectuals on the left such as the author Martin Walser even viewed the focus on wealth and rapid work pace as a symptom of political apathy, an alarming lack of interest in the prospect of democratically shaping the collective future. Postwar industriousness and the pursuit of prosperity for its own sake drained the population's interest in other spheres of activity and may even have offered it an alternative and acceptable source of national pride.[18]

But right-wing voices, too, took note of similar phenomena, even if they were less disturbed by the impression of stodgy stability. In a 1956 article, the conservative sociologist Arnold Gehlen described how West Germans devoted themselves to amassing goods, viewed politics as the prudent management of economic policy geared toward enhancing the level of industrial output and distributing the generated wealth, and happily accepted expert authorities in clearly demarcated domains of a complex bureaucratized society.[19] In the words of Ludwig Erhard, one of the main architects of the economic miracle, the principal aim of West German politics was to restore people's "earthly happiness."[20] The desire for and enjoyment of affluence eclipsed the pleasures of conversational interaction. West Germany was quite bourgeois, only it lacked precisely the kind of bourgeois sociability Sternberger had envisioned.

Habermas on the Collapse of Conviviality

Interestingly, Jürgen Habermas may have been the sharpest and most systematic theorist of the West German collapse of conviviality, despite or perhaps because of his investment in the historical virtues of bourgeois sociable interaction. Having painted an idealized image of the early bourgeois sites of conversation as the matrix of critical discourse, he proceeded to produce a list of factors behind the disintegration of the institutions of sociability, such as the isolation of the conjugal family from broader social worlds and the rise of commercial mass media.

For Habermas, a lively and discursively oriented bourgeois sociability was not a genuine possibility in West Germany, but rather a deeply buried historical ideal evoked to remind contemporary society of its lost inheritance. When Sternberger introduced and tried to implement and enact the idea of sociability in the journal *Die Wandlung,* the notion that conversations in tender networks of amiable and fluidly interacting individuals could become an important mode of democratic integration in Germany could seem overly optimistic but not altogether unreal. To Habermas, in contrast, the likelihood of some reinvigorated form of bourgeois sociability had been greatly reduced. When *The Structural Transformation of the Public Sphere* dealt with contemporary society, it offered a picture of an increasingly isolated, passive, and mute citizen for whom consumerist habits structured relationships to other people as well as institutional entities. Conversations and debates, which always require the copresence of many active individuals attuned to the demands of reciprocity, had been supplanted by acts of consumption, which could be enjoyed in private and involved no work of assessment and articulation.

The latter part of *The Structural Transformation of the Public Sphere* follows the spread of consumerist attitudes and traces its roots to massive changes in the socioeconomic layout of modern societies. To begin with, Habermas notes how people's contact with the cultural sphere had become desocialized. Everyone goes to the movies, listens to radio, and watches television, but they do so alone or in the company of family and friends, meaning that the encounter with forms of art does not become the object of immediate discussion in a broader social setting. He also looks at the decline in reading, but more importantly describes how books find readers by new, commercially designed paths. Book clubs deliver bestsellers directly to people's homes and thereby circumvent any mediation by lay critics, whose self-appointed task it once was to initiate a debate on literary meaning or aesthetic and moral values.

While art is being consumed in separate cells rather than received into assemblies where people offer their informed judgments, Habermas also argues that the planning and production of standardized cultural objects by branches of the entertainment industry such as big publishers lowers the degree of cognitive engagement demanded of the consumer. Modern books, journals, films, and music are meant to be easily digested by the members of the audience; they all have a schematic structure, each film or piece of music like the other, to relieve the viewer of any serious hermeneutic effort. In short, Habermas argues that there are fewer opportunities for critical debate, and also fewer objects worthy of collective scrutiny.

These converging trends toward smooth consumption in a disassembled public do not, according to Habermas, cancel out all discussion in society. The debating that does go on, however, also assumes commodity form. Habermas claims that discussions take place only in engineered formats such as "professional dialogues from the podium, panel discussions and round table shows" that viewers relate to as consumer items.[21] People who watch a televised debate are not invited to verbalize their own positions but are instead offered arranged events featuring pundits. A division of labor between professional talkers and the rest breaks up the once continuous conversation of the sociable bourgeoisie.

For Habermas, the contemporary erosion of conviviality and top-down organization of discussions are, however, symptoms of underlying changes that combine to weaken individual autonomy. In all spheres of politics and society, expanding and increasingly stratified institutions turn members into dependents. Political parties are governed by leadership cadres that mobilize cohorts of voters by means of psychological and pedagogical techniques. Trade unions and other associations are hierarchically structured and seek to secure benefits in closed negotiations with corporations. Businesses are no longer run by independent individuals but are essentially large-scale bureaucracies that use the media as a platform to enhance the glow of their brands. While parties, special interest associations, and corporations may all represent different interests, they nonetheless form a closed circuit of power that effectively bars broader participation in debates and reduces people to clients.[22]

Indeed, Habermas points out how the intermeshing domains of state and society eliminate the need for a widely accessible and discursive form of mediation between them. Without a space to articulate arguments in public, citizens only approach institutions, including the state, as consumers. People want to be provided for and seek contact with the branches of the social-welfare state that distributes goods, but this "demanding" attitude does not become political in Habermas's sense, for it does not involve a reasoned discussion over the principles of political rule.[23] And by treating its citizens as "needful objects of state power," even the generous welfare state may subtly hollow out ordinary people's experience of democracy in practice.[24]

Looking at the postwar period, then, Habermas claims that mute consumption in a wide array of settings had come to marginalize debate.

And underlying this diagnosis is the idea that contemporary citizens had been deprived of the traditional sources of independence in the bourgeois world. In the early bourgeois epoch, Habermas contends, individuals drew their sense of autonomy from control over private property and their activity as owners of enterprises. Once they emerged as the interlocutors of the state whose arguments had an impact on legislation, they also achieved political autonomy, shaping the conditions under which they lived. However, when nearly all individuals are employees of large businesses without any voice in the conduct of affairs, and are moreover spoken for by political and organizational representatives working out deals behind closed doors, previously autonomous individuals slip into a collective state of heteronomy.

The consumerist attitude toward the outside world—cultural objects, media, associations, and even the state—is thus prepared and continually reinforced by the lack of economic and political stature. If individuals no longer come together in sociable settings to enjoy conversations based on a principle of reciprocity, it is because the idea of everyone's collaborative contribution to discourse is no longer viable and has no institutional support. Conviviality must rely on the activity of multiple participants whose autonomy is materially grounded; it cannot somehow be revived among people who have lost their independence. In 1962, Habermas thus disputed, probably unwittingly, Sternberger's early postwar strategy of refocusing the German bourgeois identity around sociability at a moment when property and economic independence were under threat. The virtues of bourgeois sociability, Habermas implied, could become effective only when they rested on a solid foundation of socioeconomic autonomy. That foundation had eroded in the twentieth century.

In the postwar period, commerce and consumption eclipsed conversation as the premier mode of bourgeois social interaction and integration. Habermas did not shy away from this realization. On the contrary, he presented the most comprehensive diagnosis of the collapse of conviviality, regardless of his enthusiasm about the significance of bourgeois sociability in the historical emergence of the politically potent public sphere. Yet the fact that the most sophisticated proponent of sociability and its political value did not believe in its continued efficacy in postwar German society should warn us against basing our final judgment of sociability on its successful revitalization or atrophy after 1945.

Habermas's picture of attenuated conviviality, or any number of similar cultural-historical analyses, does not conclusively settle the issue of whether sociability once had served or potentially could serve as a preparatory stage toward politics. The question of whether there can be a path from the practice of sociable interaction to the conduct of politics remains, even after one takes a close look at the shrinking pockets of conversation in West Germany. Writing after 1945 and mobilizing a wide range of complex theoretical and historical arguments, Sternberger and Habermas affirmed sociability's positive role, whereas Schmitt, Koselleck, and Arendt repudiated it. Which side was right?

Sociability and Politics: A Final Look

When people enter into contact with one another in spaces reserved for pleasant interaction, they are supposed to avoid invidious topics and sustain a pleasant conversation. Sociability is realized when everyone is willing to speak to all who have assembled, despite any lurking conflicts, mutual irritations, or resentments. The practice of sociability can even be defined as the agreement of all parties to act "as if"—people commit to speak to one another as if they were not divided by irreconcilable allegiances or differences in power and wealth; as if everything that pulled them apart could be ignored, at least for a little while, in a clearly circumscribed space.

Such a performance might seem to come dangerously close to dishonesty or hypocrisy, but these suspicions and accusations miss the point. To be sociable with one another across persistent divides is not to deny the existence of conflict. It is to interact despite the reality of these conflicts, even in the full knowledge of them, yet to hold off articulating them while lingering in a particular, bounded place for conversation. Ideological differences and political disagreements that are relevant elsewhere, or nearly everywhere, might still be contained under very particular circumstances without anyone thinking that those fragile circumstances can or should prevail anywhere else.

One can appreciate sociable interaction understood as a collaborative performance of affability and gregariousness under pressure. Around the coffee table or in the salon, those invited to participate in the sociable occasion silently accept the challenge of overcoming differences and negative affects for as long as that occasion continues. And they are willing to join precisely because they know that there are limits to sociability. Participants are asked to contain their partisan passions for a while, but not to forget them or repress them indefinitely.

In light of this more modest idea of sociability, Sternberger and Habermas may have wanted too much from sociability, while Koselleck, Arendt, and Schmitt may have feared too much. Sociability as a localized collective performance is neither a matrix of political behavior, nor necessarily a threat to the conduct of politics. It involves, rather, a brief neutralization of political conflicts—conflicts that may run very deep and therefore are unlikely to disappear, but nonetheless should not be allowed to control everything that happens in all spaces of society at all times. Neither the proponents nor the critics of sociability were entirely right. There might be no clear path from sociability to politics, but there is no great risk of contamination either. The sociable focus on light interaction exists in tension with politics, as a temporary and delicate containment and postponement of strife, not as a solution to or permanent suppression of conflict.

Sociability involves people's performance of gregariousness under pressure. This also means, however, that it becomes less and less of an achievement as the surrounding polity tends more and more toward homogeneity. The occurrence of sociability is an accomplishment when the people who participate are striving to overcome their many disagreements and mutual dislikes. But when, for whatever reasons, differences are flattened, diversity reduced, and divides effaced in society as a whole, otherwise demanding rituals of friendliness threaten to degenerate into easy celebrations of sameness.

For various reasons, West Germany tended toward a state of sociopolitical stability and harmony in the 1950s.[25] The rapid return to prosperity reduced the likelihood of grievances and fractures along class lines. Companies and trade unions more or less willingly cooperated to ensure that the economy functioned smoothly, and increasing welfare state–type provision of services to the general population prevented the eruption of protest. This was of course the very motivation behind the designing of a more generous social welfare system. And as described above, the production and consumption of goods seemed to crowd out any concern among the citizens of West Germany for vigorous participation in politics. In addition to economic conditions conducive to political peace, potential cultural divisions also seemed to fade. For instance, the leading party of the period, the Christian Democrats, downplayed tensions between Catholics and Protestants and instead presented a picture of a broad unity of values. Finally, after the organized mass murder of Jews and minorities such as the Roma during World War II, and the massive relocations of entire population groups in Europe immediately after it, West Germany was, like quite a few other European nation-states, more ethnically and culturally homogeneous after the war than perhaps ever before. The country would have to wait for the arrival of a new young generation for the clear articulation of dissent.

What positive function could the performance of politeness and companionableness play in the pacified landscape of postwar West Germany? Perhaps no positive function at all. Sociable occasions did not take place in quiet defiance of an otherwise fractured polity, but tended to serve only as yet another forum for an already established consensus. To observe this type of sociability, we can turn to a representation of postwar bourgeois society in an early work by the writer and filmmaker Alexander Kluge, and particularly to a story featuring a West German Rotary Club. Kluge's succinct narrative, meant to capture the flawed associational style that epitomized upper-middle-class social life in 1950s West Germany, will provide us with a final scene of sociability, one that highlights its impoverished character in an all too homogeneous background setting.

Among the Rotarians: Alexander Kluge

Alexander Kluge's early narratives in many ways recapitulate how the postwar search for a viable mode of integration did include a return to bourgeois sociability. *Case Histories* (*Lebensläufe*),[26] his first collection of stories, published in 1962, consists of literary reports from the various niches of the settled, even rigid institutional and associational life of the early Federal Republic. They portray the slightly dull atmosphere and the pedantic adherence to rules and conventions in West Germany at the time, but also describe how a national community that at least partly wanted to define itself as a gregarious society formed and sustained through respectful discourse ultimately performed reconfirmations of indisputably shared sentiments and values. In Kluge's texts, sociability comes across not as a precarious exercise in tolerance, but as a ritual of collective self-congratulation. This is particularly true of the story "The Demise of an Attitude," which follows its protagonist, Chief Detective Scheliha, from the last days of World War II to 1961.

To understand Kluge's portrayal of postwar sociability in this one story, some plot summary is necessary. In November 1944, at the time when the Eastern front is beginning to collapse, a landowner living in the Eastern Elbing region is detained by the police after a brutal murder on his property. Distracted by the unstable circumstances, the local authorities refrain from an indictment, and the perpetrator soon manages to escape in the general turmoil. The files of the neglected murder case end up with Chief Detective Scheliha in Berlin, who is dismayed by the lapses in the administration of justice and decides to follow up on the matter. He is not ignorant of the extraordinary conditions on the crumbling Eastern front, but still regrets the lack of vigilance on the part of the responsible state and party representatives. To make up for the failure, he dispatches an inspector and assistants to the district, and soon thereafter he sets out to join his staff by train. While traveling, Scheliha himself can spot the impact of the approaching Soviet forces—he witnesses the chaos of fleeing citizens and summary executions along the roadside—but none of these scenes persuade him to discontinue the expedition. When the legal system of which he is a part fails to carry out its tasks, he assumes the responsibility of upholding the rule of law.

But Kluge's readers are not offered the spectacle of a difficult manhunt across a landscape of war, ending with the triumph of a heroic loner. Instead, the guilty landowner succeeds in getting out of what will soon be the Soviet occupation zone, survives the war, and is able to avoid further consequences for his actions. In contrast, Chief Detective Scheliha is captured by Soviet soldiers during his investigations and is immediately deported to Siberia, to be released only in 1953. In the final part of the text, set in 1961, the retired Scheliha delivers a lecture at the meeting of a Rotary Club somewhere in the Federal Republic of Germany. The novella ends with a transcript of a debate in which various Rotarians submit their opinions, all rendered in an abbreviated, stenographic style, on the unsettling episode and the legal and moral issues it raises. After a decade of internment in a foreign country, Kluge's protagonist has arrived in a haven of postwar bourgeois society. He has arrived among the sociable Rotarians.

Kluge's novella thus cuts from scenes that depict the crumbling hierarchies of the Third Reich in 1944 to an orderly Rotary meeting in 1961.[27] It connects the moment in which the state apparatus gives way under the pressure of invasion to the image of a reconstituted bourgeois society, in which a local elite of businessmen and professionals voluntarily convenes for the purposes of entertainment and edification. Although the focus is on a specific case, the general critical concern of Kluge's story is to what extent and with what means West German bourgeois society, here exemplified by a club, attends to and resolves the dual problem of a collapsed state formation and a troubling criminal past. In what ways do the values of bourgeois society as codified and performed by Rotary, with its commitment to "reasoned debate," "public service," and "male association," serve as a medium in which the issues of the immediate postwar period could be addressed?[28] What new identity is being forged, and what bonds or relationships sustain the community? By suggesting such questions, Kluge's story reflects, in literary form, on the potentials and limits of postwar bourgeois conviviality.

The Rotary Club is a typical example of a lingering or revived bourgeois sociability in the Federal Republic of Germany. To this day, Rotary gathers professionals and businessmen locally for regular dinners, lectures, and charity events. It is an organization lodged in the sphere of voluntary association beyond the realm of the family, neither managed by the state nor operating in the market.[29] The selection of members depends on criteria such as membership in a profession, social prestige, and economic standing, yet the networking within a group circumscribed by class and position gains legitimacy thanks to obligatory philanthropic activities. "Rotary's aim," a German representative could announce in 1955, "is the willingness to serve others in daily life . . . the cultivation of friendships is one way to be of use to others."[30]

On a cynical view, Rotary only strengthens the cohesion of local elites by facilitating the mutually advantageous exchange of expert services and preparation of business contacts under the cover of civic work. From an internal perspective, however, the weekly assembly forges lateral social bonds that do not deny but definitely transcend patterns of interaction aimed solely at furthering self-interest. Men from various areas of society convene to nurture friendships across professional boundaries through collaborative service. In contemporary German public pronouncements of Rotary principles, members could even introduce the club's effort to draw together members of different occupations as a remedy to the effects of differentiation in modern society. Whereas a complex social organization tends to isolate individuals, reduce them to a function, and limit their field of experiences, German Rotary sought to compensate for segmentation by instituting a venue for face-to-face contact outside strictly purpose-governed professional contexts and the familial sphere of intimacy. According to their self-descriptions, German Rotarians did not duplicate organizations streamlined for the achievement of specific economic or administrative purposes. Instead, Rotary was composed to provide a "cross section of all vocations"[31] that could guarantee a degree of social interconnection.

According to its own contemporary statements, Rotary was designed to remedy the atrophy of communal life in highly differentiated societies, but also to exceed geographical and political boundaries. Each German Rotary member was included in a transregional and even international network of clubs, all of which were open to traveling Rotarians. Given its emphasis on voluntary interaction within an economic and vocational elite dedicated to philanthropic aims, however, Rotary's reach matched the fault lines of the Cold War. The organization, centered in Chicago, was not allowed in the Soviet-controlled area and had also been reintroduced into Germany after being banned by the National Socialist regime. Its exclusion from totalitarian societies, which aimed to give shape to their subjects' entire lives, underlines the particular attraction of Rotary in the Federal Republic of Germany.

While Rotarians in West Germany could present themselves as the legatees of a native culture of humanizing bourgeois sociability forming in a free space between the market and the state, their membership linked them to a greater Western sphere that relieved the resurrected organization of any stuffy small-town connotations.[32] Bourgeois *Geselligkeit* lived on in the era of nuclear stalemate between geopolitical blocks, as a small proof of the welcoming sociability of the Western world. West German Rotarians still marginally participated in a specific postwar culture of sociability that imagined itself to be socially integrative and morally edifying.

It is easy to anticipate the critique, even the ridicule, of an organization such as Rotary. Its constricted character makes it vulnerable to the charge of elitism. In the 1950s, women and members of the working class were excluded, which made the association look like a device to cement societal privilege. The veneer of selfless charity hardly concealed the dominating ambition of the members, namely to create beneficial connections within a societal section narrowly defined by class and gender.

Such objections to fortified social inequality certainly play an implicit role in Kluge's pastiche of a Rotary protocol, but they are not in the foreground. Insofar as Kluge does deliver a critique of the bourgeois conviviality embodied by Rotary, this critique is inseparable from its literary manifestation and depends on his attention to the uses of language. The story "Demise of an Attitude" does in fact convey something of a political critique of Rotary as an exemplar of a certain contemporary associational life, but only in the form of an exposure of the discursive rituals that structure this associational life. Kluge looks at, or imagines, how the Rotarians speak, and indicates the social meaning of this speech.

"Demise of an Attitude" explores the constraints of postwar discourse. What Kluge aims to show with the insertion of a fictive transcript is how unwilling the local professionals and businessmen are to engage in a discussion, and even how their nationalist identity overwhelms their membership in an international philanthropic association. The record of the discussion is the sometimes disturbing, sometimes amusing document of a failure. Symptomatically, the local Rotary president, who has the first word, immediately extends a caution against any probing reflection: "There were some things that one should not think too much about."[33]

The space of bourgeois sociability is, one can glean from this statement, not really a space for earnest self-interrogation.

The initial sequence of contributions to the ensuing deliberations or nondeliberations also indicates how the Rotarians still view themselves as members of a national community defined by common origin, as if the talk of a past incident triggers an aggressive group identity that takes precedence over any other kind of commitment. Provoked by Scheliha's account of his experiences, various Rotary members offer a series of chauvinist statements: "*Rot.*[arian] *Geibel:* He could not imagine that in 1953 the German people had been 'without values,' as the speaker had maintained. German self-control and German values, in the words of the national anthem, did not perish even in 1945. *Rot. Pils:* If there was blood-guilt, it could not attach to the German people, since the crime had been committed in the province of West Prussia. Hence it attached to Poland."[34] In 1961, Kluge suggests, Rotarians are still comfortable with the language of blood and soil.

Kluge's Rotary protocol does not display a felicitous realization of a discursive community that has the strength to absorb and promote a vigorous argumentative revision of collectively binding norms. The recorded replies do not even mirror a subdued debate, only a series of deflections and denials of the notion of unaddressed guilt among Germans, whose cohesion as a people remains beyond question. Kluge's Rotary looks suspiciously like a closed and unreconstructed circle of male comrades.

As the text progresses, however, the contributions grow increasingly banal, and the fictive transcript reads like a jumbled collection of unlinked and often vacuous statements. The record of the conversation features manifestations of stock prejudices against decadence ("*Rot. v. Bergmann:* An inordinate love of justice was reminiscent of perversion, in ancient times there had even been defenders of homosexuality") and formulas out of a repertoire of customary discursive turns, ready to be inserted everywhere ("*Rot. Jacoby:* One must concentrate on the problem itself. *Rot. Schmidthenner:* It was a problem of background and education [*Bildungsproblem*]").[35] As the nationalist sentiments ebb out, the members resort to commonplaces. Now and again, declarations are followed by gestures of collective affirmation captured in phrases such as "(Applause)," "(Loud applause)," "(Lively applause)," or "(Hearty and prolonged applause)."[36] The series of louder and louder applause indicates an escalating sense of group elation.

Kluge recapitulates the reemergence of bourgeois sociability as a practice of integration and socialization in the Federal Republic of Germany, but does so in a satirical manner. The Rotary conversation is not a debate that plays out among a multiplicity of standpoints and not a performance of circumspect gregariousness. It is instead a ceremony that, step by step, generates a mild sort of effervescence. The Rotarians assemble and their attention is fixed on a common theme; they communicate this shared attunement with one another and, through the feedback circuits that are thus set up among them, come to thrive on the mutual encouragement they collectively produce.[37] In the end, the room is filled with "lively applause" for a more or less shared stock of platitudes and prejudices. The open and honest discussion appears to be something like a service through which the group can revalidate itself as a good and moral community.

Judging by Kluge's story, the typical Rotary meeting might be not a medium for the free unfolding of rational argumentation or the collective performance of wary politeness, but an event that rejuvenates group consciousness.[38] To this young author writing in the early 1960s, the debates and conversations of the reconstituted German bourgeois society even possessed a ritualistic quality. They were structured by concatenations of stereotyped miniscripts and served to fortify feelings of accord and mutual support within closed circles of likeminded people.

In times of political divisions, the practice of sociability, of gathering to enjoy human company by engaging in light conversations or some other nonpolitical activity, can offer respite from looming conflicts without in any way annulling them. Bound by conventions of politeness and toleration, the individuals who encounter each other in some delimited space for social interaction precariously maintain a sense of harmony that cannot be presumed in any other public space. When sociability occurs among people from very similar backgrounds committed to a near-identical set of values and convictions, however, it might be less of an accomplishment, less of an exercise in self-imposed restraint and caution out of respect for difference. Often enough, it can turn into an opportunity for those present to extract renewed confirmation of everything they are and everything they believe. In a gathering of already likeminded people conscious of their uniformity, sociability becomes a means to refresh self-satisfaction. Judging by Kluge's 1962 portrait of a generic West German Rotary Club, this might have been a risk in the postwar period.

NOTES

Introduction

1. Stig Dagerman, *German Autumn*, trans. Robin Fulton Macpherson (Minneapolis: University of Minnesota Press, 2011), 12.

2. Ibid., 13.

3. Ibid.

4. Ibid., 36.

5. Ibid.

6. Ibid., 35.

7. Ibid., 37.

8. Ibid., 40.

9. Nina Grunenberg, *Die Wundertäter: Netzwerke der deutschen Wirtschaft 1942 bis 1966* (Munich: Siedler, 2006), 104.

10. Peter Stirk argues that the most important issue for German political theorists after 1945 was the future of the German state: "The unconditional surrender of Germany and Allied assumption of full sovereign power raised the question of whether Germany had ceased to exist as a state." See Stirk, *Twentieth Century German Political Thought* (Edinburgh: Edinburgh University Press, 2006), 135.

11. Paul Nolte, *Die Ordnung der deutschen Gesellschaft: Selbstentwurf und Selbstbeschreibung im 20. Jahrhundert* (Munich: C. H. Beck, 2000), 219.

12. Sternberger relied on but perhaps did not fully acknowledge a tradition of political thought that articulates and evaluates the historical differentiation of political structures of governance from other modes of interaction (such as commerce among economic agents), and the resulting dichotomy between state and society in the modern period. For an overview of how political thinkers came to think of bourgeois or civil society as an area distinct from the state and with its own principles of organization, see Erich Angerman, "Das Auseinandertreten von 'Staat' und 'Gesellschaft' im Denken des 18. Jahrhunderts," in *Staat und Gesellschaft*, ed. Ernst-Wolfgang Böckenförde (Darmstadt: Wissenschaftliche Buchgesellschaft, 1976), 109–30. Hegel is generally viewed as the first German philosopher to conceptualize the emergence of a *bürgerliche Gesellschaft* separate from the state. Familiar with the new economic theories of thinkers such as Adam Smith, Hegel grappled with the simultaneous emergence of a centralized state authority and a context of economic and corporate interconnections among individuals. Hegel viewed this new field, the *bürgerliche Gesellschaft,* as a system of interdependency or a web of relationships between self-interested individuals. See Manfred Riedel, *Studien zur Hegels Rechtsphilosophie* (Frankfurt am Main: Suhrkamp, 1969), 156–58.

13. Charles Taylor offers an overview of the tradition of political thought devoted to civil society and explains its value to thinkers who are trying to imagine communities without state oppression—for instance, groups of intellectuals within the former Soviet Bloc. Civil society, he writes, "includes those dimension of social life which cannot be confounded with, or swallowed up in the state." See Taylor, "Modes of Civil Society," *Public Culture* 3, no. 1 (1990): 95.

14. Jens Hacke relates how Sternberger implicitly rejected the idea that a new Germany must be born in a (belated) democratic revolution—a great foundational act—and instead argued for a cautious but steady reeducational process. See Hacke, *Die Bundesrepublik als Idee: Zur Legitimationsbedürftigkeit politischer Ordnung* (Hamburg: Hamburger Edition, 2009), 24–28.

15. Jeffrey K. Olick, *In the House of the Hangman: The Agonies of German Defeat, 1943–1949* (Chicago: University of Chicago Press, 2005), 141.

16. Commentators on Habermas's entire body of work have claimed that he puts forward an argument for the political potential of civil society and thus upgrades society in a German culture traditionally characterized by veneration for the state as the bearer of a special political and ethical mission. As Matthew G. Specter points out in his intellectual biography of Habermas, his work over four decades in many ways represents "the struggle of German civil society with the state." See Specter, *Habermas: An Intellectual Biography* (Cambridge: Cambridge University Press, 2010), 26. For a critique of how Specter neglects Habermas's significant interests in psychoanalysis, hermeneutics, systems theory, cognitive moral psychology, analytical philosophies of language, and other "influential currents of thought," see Seyla Benhabib's review of *Habermas: An Intellectual Biography* in *Constellations* 18, no. 4 (2011): 589–95.

17. The locus of the society/community distinction is the German sociologist Ferdinand Tönnies's *Community and Civil Society*, ed. Jose Harris, trans. Margaret Hollis (Cambridge: Cambridge University Press, 2001). Tönnies pits a tight-knit community of people joined together by blood relations and traditions against a looser collection of individuals in society, who regard any group attachments as temporary and expedient.

18. Gregg Kvistad reviews the place of the state in modern German political theory and argues that it is typically posited "as a realm of hortatory politics occupied by civil servants who are duty-bound and legally obliged to pursue what is understood as society's general or universal interest." In other words, the activities of men in society were regarded as conflict-laden, divisive, and potentially threatening to public order, and the state was called to define and protect a universalistic common good. See Kvistad, *The Rise and Demise of German Statism: Loyalty and Political Membership* (New York: Berghahn, 1999), 13.

19. Jan-Werner Müller's study on the history and significance of the concept "constitutional patriotism" deals with the relationship between the interventions of Sternberger and Habermas. As Müller shows, Sternberger introduced the expression "constitutional patriotism" in the early 1970s, and Habermas later appropriated it. However, the book's focus on the intellectual history of this particular idea prohibits the author from looking at other points of

connection between the two thinkers. See Müller, *Constitutional Patriotism* (Princeton, N.J.: Princeton University Press, 2007).

20. Of course, Schmitt, Arendt, and Koselleck were not the first to formulate critiques of *bürgerliche Gesellschaft.* On the contrary, German political philosophy as a whole has been characterized by a critical approach to the *bürgerliche Gesellschaft,* starting with the philosopher who first conceptualized its emergence, Hegel (see note 12). Hegel offered a fundamental critique of bourgeois society on the grounds that its members only associate for the purpose of particular ends and thus principally remain agents of their own self-interest; the good of others is, for these agents, an unintended by-product. In contrast, the state is the realm in which individuals explicitly work for and together with others and thus come to promote and ratify an ethical collective existence. See Allen Wood, introduction to *Elements of the Philosophy of Right* by G. W. F. Hegel, trans. H. B. Nisbett (Cambridge: Cambridge University Press, 1991), xxviii. But Hegel is only the first name in a long tradition. In his survey of modern German political thought, Chris Thornhill claims that its defining trait continued to be the emphasis on a particular political form of life, the locus of which is the state: "Legitimate government . . . is [in the German tradition of political thought] not the particular representation of social interests, but rather a political life-form, in which particular interests have a subsidiary position." See Thornhill, *Political Theory in Modern Germany: An Introduction* (Cambridge: Polity, 2000), 16.

21. Malcolm Bull has recently pointed out similarities between Arendt and Schmitt and emphasized their commitment to political life defined by conflict: "Arendt and Schmitt . . . share a conception of the political that is in certain respects very similar, notably in its insistence that the political is the negation of the social." See Bull, "The Social and the Political," *South Atlantic Quarterly* 104, no. 4 (Fall 2005): 678. This book elaborates on the arguments that Bull puts forward in a more schematic fashion and embeds them in their historical context.

22. Friedrich Meinecke, *Die deutsche Katastrophe: Betrachtungen und Erinnerungen* (Wiesbaden: Brockhaus, 1946), 174–75.

23. Olick, *In the House of the Hangman,* 165.

24. Ralf Dahrendorf, *Gesellschaft und Demokratie in Deutschland* (Munich: Piper, 1965), 17.

25. Olick, *In the House of the Hangman*, 162. Lutz Koepnick likewise finds Meinecke's alleged belief that "Goethe's voice had the power to move Germans beyond the ruins of the immediate past" impossibly antiquated. See Koepnick, "Culture in the Shadow of Trauma," in *The Oxford Handbook of Modern German History*, ed. Helmut Walser Smith (Oxford: Oxford University Press, 2011), 718.

26. Meinecke, *Die deutsche Katastrophe,* 169.

27. Thomas Nipperdey, *Gesellschaft, Kultur, Theorie: Gesammelte Aufsätze zu neueren Geschichte* (Göttingen: Vandenhoeck & Ruprecht, 1976), 176. Nipperdey speaks of the interdependence of the association as a form of collectivity and the *bürgerliche Gesellschaft.* The demise of the feudal order, he claims,

entailed the decorporization of individuals previously lodged in cohesive estates, and the elastic form of the association or *Verein* brought individuals together without compromising their freedom to enter and exit social groups. A *bürgerliche* form of life with values, ideals, customs, protocols of interaction, and so on only developed in and with the association.

28. Meinecke, *Die deutsche Katastrophe,* 176.

29. Anson Rabinbach, "Restoring the German Spirit: Humanism and Guilt in Post-War Germany," in *German Ideologies Since 1945: Studies in the Political Thought and Culture of the Bonn Republic,* ed. Jan-Werner Müller (New York: Palgrave Macmillan, 2003), 24.

30. Ibid., 26–27.

31. The discourses that have crystallized around the concepts of mastering the past (*Vergangenheitsbewältigung*) and public sphere (*Öffentlichkeit*) have become increasingly difficult to survey. Arthur Strum has compiled a forty-page bibliography of works that treat the history of the public sphere as well as its relevance to politics, education, law, media, and gender. See Strum, "Bibliography of the Concept Öffentlichkeit," *New German Critique* 61 (Winter 1994): 161–200. The absolute center of this discourse is of course Jürgen Habermas's *The Structural Transformation of the Public Sphere* from 1962. *Vergangenheitsbewältigung* is likewise a concept that anchors an entire debate. For an overview of the discussion of the political, legal, psychological, and pedagogical aspects of the legacy of the Nazi period under the heading *Vergangenheitsbewältigung,* see, for instance, Peter Reichel, *Vergangenheitsbewältigung in Deutschland: Die Auseinandersetzung mit der NS-Diktatur von 1945 bis heute* (Munich: Beck, 2001), or Charles S. Maier, *The Unmasterable Past: History, Holocaust, and German National Identity* (Cambridge, Mass.: Harvard University Press, 1988). For attempts to define the concept and to track its career, see for instance Peter Dudek, "'Vergangenheitsbewältigung': Zur Problematik eines umstrittenen Begriffs," *Aus Politik und Zeitgeschichte* 3, no. 1 (1992): 44–53, or Helmut König, "Von der Diktatur zur Demokratie oder Was ist Vergangenheitsbewältigung," *Leviathan: Zeitschrift für Sozialwissenschaften* 18 (1997): 371–92. For a skeptical or even cynical account of *Vergangenheitsbewältigung* in terms of a cost-benefit analysis, see Helmut Quaritsch, "Theorie der Vergangenheitsbewältigung," *Der Staat* 31, no. 4 (1992): 519–51.

32. Heinz Bude comments on the tendency of psychoanalysts to link the prevention of fascist resurgence to sustained loquaciousness in therapeutic settings. See Bude, *Bilanz der Nachfolge: Die Bundesrepublik und der Nationalsozialismus* (Frankfurt am Main: Suhrkamp, 1992). A title of one of Habermas's articles on politics reads "Discuss—what else? [*Diskutieren—was sonst?*]" Addressing the politically engaged students in 1962, Habermas rejected any form of direct activism and sought to promote a more discursively oriented culture. See Habermas, *Kleine politische Schriften I–IV* (Frankfurt am Main: Suhrkamp, 1981), 203.

33. Alexander and Margarete Mitscherlich asserted that until the Germans had been able to rechannel the libidinal energies previously invested in Hitler, they would remain in a state of moral and political immobility and apathy. For

a concise summary of their project along these lines, see Eric L. Santner, "The Trouble with Hitler: Postwar German Aesthetics and the Legacy of Fascism," *New German Critique* 57 (Winter 1993): 5–24. Peter Uwe Hohendahl claims that Habermas's endeavor to promote the concept of the public sphere can be read as an attempt to work out the features of a healthy democratic culture in order to confront and inspire the still underdeveloped and fragile democracy of the Federal Republic. See Hohendahl, "Recasting the Public Sphere," *October* 73 (Summer 1995): 29.

34. Dirk A. Moses, *German Intellectuals and the Nazi Past* (Cambridge: Cambridge University Press, 2007), 50.

35. Jürgen Habermas, *Strukturwandel der Öffentlichkeit: Untersuchungen zu einer Kategorie der bürgerlichen Gesellschaft* (Neuwied: Hermann Luchterhand, 1962); Alexander and Margarete Mitscherlich, *Die Unfähigkeit zu trauern: Grundlagen kollektiven Verhaltens* (Munich: Piper, 1967).

36. According to a recent intellectual biography of Alexander Mitscherlich written by Tobias Freimüller, the book on the silence of the Germans was greeted enthusiastically and discussed widely in Germany. This response could be viewed as a partial refutation of the book's thesis. Only an audience that was already not repressing the past but was, on the contrary, very willing to discuss it could remain unprovoked by and open to the idea that the Nazi past was not sufficiently discussed in public. See Freimüller, *Alexander Mitscherlich: Gesellschaftsdiagnose und Psychoanalyse nach Hitler* (Göttingen: Wallstein, 2007), 305–7.

37. See Eviatar Zeruvabel, "The Social Sound of Silence: Toward a Sociology of Denial," in *Shadows of War: A Social History of Silence in the Twentieth Century*, ed. Efrat ben-Ze'ev, Ruth Ginio, and Jay Winter (Cambridge: Cambridge University Press, 2010), 32.

38. See Dahrendorf, *Gesellschaft und Demokratie in Deutschland,* 24–25.

39. The title of the book alludes to Karl Popper's indictment of Plato, Hegel, and Marx in *The Open Society and Its Enemies*. According to Popper, the open society is the opposite of the "tribal" or "collectivist" society, in which the rules that regulate individual conduct are protected from change and critique by taboos. See Popper, *The Open Society and Its Enemies* (London: Routledge, 1945), 151–52. The open society has the capacity to respond to critique from individuals: decisions and routines are amenable to critical feedback pertaining to their consequences, hence they possess the character of hypotheses. The open society, then, operates much like a scientific community (in Popper's definition of such a community); it is engaged in a continual process of trial and error, conjecture and refutation, and is ready to admit errors and adjust beliefs or actions. For a summary of Popper's views along these lines, see Steve Fuller's accessible account in *Kuhn vs. Popper: The Struggle for the Soul of Science* (Cambridge: Icon, 2003), 27. The contrast here between the proponents and the critics of sociability does not quite coincide with the opposition between "closed" (irrational, static) and "open" (rational, malleable). While sociability's enemies addressed the tendency of social groups to suppress critique from factions and individuals, they did not value articulated conflict solely as a medium

of rationality and continual adjustment and improvement. Sociability was, moreover, an ambivalent practice or mode of societal integration, coded and evaluated differently by different thinkers. In other words, this study is not a straight indictment of one type of society and an argument for another in the manner of Popper.

40. In his book on civility, Mark Klingwell points out that speakers are typically "cognizant of the particular goals associated with certain dialogic situations—e.g., having an interview, conducting a seminar, trying a case" and therefore see that some things "are routinely and unproblematically unsayable under some conditions." See Klingwell, *A Civil Tongue: Justice, Dialogue, and the Politics of Pluralism* (University Park: Pennsylvania State University Press, 1995), 43.

41. See Clemens Albrecht et al., eds., *Die intellektuelle Gründung der Bundesrepublik: Eine Wirkungsgeschichte der Frankfurter Schule* (Frankfurt am Main: Campus, 1999), 12–20.

42. Ibid., 556. Albrecht and his fellow writers do not consider other competitors at length.

43. The idea that Habermas has multiple sources and extraordinarily wide-ranging interests and therefore cannot simply be understood as a second-generation exponent of Frankfurt School critical theory has made its way into overviews of contemporary thought, for instance Hans Joas's lectures on postwar social theory. See Joas, *Sozialtheorie: Zwanzig einführende Vorlesungen* (Frankfurt am Main: Suhrkamp, 2004), 296.

44. Herfried Münkler has discussed the economic miracle as a West German "myth" or foundational story that endowed social life with shared meaning and secured popular loyalty. See Münkler, *Die Deutschen und ihre Mythen* (Berlin: Rowohlt, 2009), 455–76.

45. In his posthumously published lectures on neoliberalism, Michel Foucault discusses the German school of Ordoliberalism as an example of postwar German endeavors to establish the need for a German state with reference to the requirements of the market economy. According to Ordoliberals such as the economists Walter Eucken and Franz Böhm, Foucault claims, the fragile market was a cultural achievement that needed a minimal and restrained state to protect and guarantee competitive mechanisms. The Ordoliberal objective in the immediate postwar period, or more specifically around 1948, was thus to "found the legitimacy of a state on the basis of a space of freedom for the economic partners." See Foucault, *The Birth of Biopolitics: Lectures at Collège de France 1978–1979*, trans. Graham Burchell (Houndmills: Palgrave Macmillan, 2008), 106. In a critical comment on Foucault, Lars Gertenbach points out that the fundamental premises of German Ordoliberalism were all articulated before the Second World War, although they may of course have received heightened attention in the postwar period. See Gertenbach, *Die Kultivierung des Marktes: Foucault und die Gouvernementalität des Neoliberalismus* (Berlin: Parodos, 2008), 88–89.

46. Moses, *German Intellectuals and the Nazi Past,* 35.

47. Ibid., 32, 37.

48. Ibid., 31. The innovative aspect of Dirk Moses's approach is precisely to link intellectual projects to shared structures of emotion in an effort to connect "individual subjectivity, social psychology, and intellectual life" (ibid., 10). The present study places more emphasis on the features of the various arguments and counterarguments regarding sociability and shows how they do not necessarily correspond to degrees of nationalist sentiment.

49. After the enforced emigration and mass murder of Jews as well as the relocations of Germans in the wake of the Second World War, West Germany was an ethnically homogeneous nation, and the labor immigration from countries such as Italy and Turkey only started in the mid-1950s. For a source of materials on issues of migration and culture in postwar Germany, see Deniz Göktürk, David Gramling, and Anton Kaes, eds., *Germany in Transit: Nation and Migration 1955–2005* (Berkeley: University of California Press, 2007). The gender aspect of sociability will be discussed in chapter 1 and the postscript.

50. Jürgen Habermas, *The Structural Transformation of the Public Sphere: An Inquiry into a Category of Bourgeois Society,* trans. Thomas Burger (Cambridge, Mass.: MIT Press, 1989), 163.

Chapter One

1. Karl Jaspers, "Geleitwort im Auftrag der Herausgeber und des Verlegers," *Die Wandlung* 1, no. 1 (November 1945): 3.

2. To inaugurate a project or open a venue was not an uncommon task for Karl Jaspers in the years after the war. Regardless of where he spoke, he was almost always the first to speak. A selected bibliography from this period makes this clear. For instance, his 1945 contribution to *Die Wandlung* on the renewal of the university was first delivered as an address at the opening of the faculty for medicine at the University of Heidelberg; a text with the title "Volk und Universität," published in *Die Wandlung* in 1947, came out of the first radio lecture in a series organized by the American military authorities and delivered 1946; "Vom lebendigen Geist der Universität," the first publication in *Die Wandlung*'s edition of books, was itself based on the first lecture given in the framework of a series of evening talks by university professors for the benefit of the general public. Finally, one of the most famous books of the immediate postwar era—*Die Schuldfrage*—emerged out of the first lecture series at the University of Heidelberg. Jaspers's status in the immediate postwar period had to do with his consistently uncompromising attitude toward the National Socialist regime. The Allied forces turned to Jaspers for guidance on university matters, identifying him as one of the professors "absolutely opposed to the Nazis." See Suzanne Kirkbright, *Karl Jaspers: A Biography—Navigations in Truth* (New Haven, Conn.: Yale University Press, 2004), 189.

3. Jaspers, "Geleitwort," 3.

4. Ibid.

5. Ibid.

6. Ibid.

7. Monika Waldmüller relates how contacts between the American administration and the future editor Dolf Sternberger led to the founding of the

journal. See Waldmüller, *Die Wandlung: Ein Bericht* (Marbach am Neckar: Deutsche Schillergesellschaft, 1988), 18–25.

8. Wade Jacoby argues that successful institutional transfer from one country to another depends on an alliance between foreign policy makers and an already existing elite. This native elite provides the foreign policy makers with cultural legitimacy and knowledge of the local conditions, whereas the foreign policy makers channel resources to the local elite. Success depends on the connection between a flexible foreign administration that reaches out to some prior organization of civil society in the occupied country. See Jacoby, *Imitation and Politics: Redesigning Modern Germany* (Ithaca, N.Y.: Cornell University Press, 2000). The people behind *Die Wandlung* represented a local academic elite who could further their own causes with support from the American authorities, and Sternberger explicitly proposed a strengthening of the nonstate communal fabric and presented the journal itself as a locus of a voluntary *Geselligkeit.* For a study of the psychological and anthropological theories that underpinned the American reeducation program, and the sociological aspects of its implementation on the ground, see Uta Gerhardt, *Soziologie der Stunde Null: Zur Gesellschaftskonzeption des Amerikanischen Besatzungsregimes in Deutschland 1944–1945/1946* (Frankfurt am Main: Suhrkamp, 2005).

9. Quite a few postwar journals had titles reminiscent of expressionist rhetoric. Apart from *Die Wandlung*, there were *Der Ruf* and *Die Sammlung.* Publishers and intellectuals fell back on an established vocabulary for conveying an atmosphere of earnestness in a state of postwar desolation. See Bernard Fischer and Thomas Dietzel, "Zur Geschichte der deutschsprachigen Literaturzeitschriften 1945–1970," in *Deutsche Literarische Zeitschriften 1945–1970: Ein Repertorium,* ed. Fischer and Dietzel (Munich: K. G. Saur, 1992), 1:1–19.

10. In an interview published in print form in 1999, Sternberger admits that the journal title invited multiple interpretations and goes on to spell out its lofty goal of fundamentally changing the German *Geist.* See Paul Assal, ed., *Erzählte Zeit—erzähltes Leben: Zehn Gespräche mit Zeitgenossen* (Bremen: Demin, 1999), 217.

11. See Robert Wolfe's "Revival of Democratic Culture During the American Occupation of Heidelberg, 1945–1949," in *Heidelberg 1945*, ed. Jürgen C. Heß, Hartmut Lehmann, and Volker Sellin (Stuttgart: Franz Steiner, 1996), 25.

12. Jaspers, "Geleitwort," 3.

13. Ibid.

14. Ibid.

15. Ibid.

16. In letters to Hannah Arendt, Jaspers expressed his reserve toward Sternberger's stance; he seems to have felt that the journal mixed literature and politics at the expense of the formation of political will. See Hannah Arendt and Karl Jaspers, *Briefwechsel 1926–1969*, ed. Lotte Köhler and Hans Saner (Munich: Piper, 1985), 151. For a description of a local Heidelberg tradition of *Geselligkeit* that Sternberger might have been alluding to, see Gesa von Essen,

"Max Weber und die Kunst der Geselligkeit," in *Heidelberg im Schnittpunkt intellektueller Kreise*, ed. Hubert Treiber and Karol Sauerland (Opladen: Westdeutscher Verlag, 1995), 462–84.

17. Dolf Sternberger, "Aspekte des bürgerlichen Charakters," *Die Wandlung* 4, no. 6 (June 1949): 486.

18. Dolf Sternberger, "Versuch zu einem Fazit," *Die Wandlung* 4, no. 8 (December 1949): 706–7.

19. Ibid., 707.

20. Ibid., 708.

21. Ibid., 707.

22. See Dolf Sternberger, "Bürgerlichkeit," *Die Wandlung* 3, no. 3 (April 1948): 199. A recent review of Sternberger's entire career by Claudia Kinkela does claim that the notion of the *Bürger* is the central concept in his work. See Claudia Kinkela, *Die Rehabilitierung des Bürgerlichen im Werk Dolf Sternbergers* (Würzburg: Königshausen & Neumann, 2001).

23. Sternberger, "Versuch zu einem Fazit," 706.

24. For an overview of the debate on Germany's "separate path" or "Sonderweg" as the name for the alleged lag between economic and political modernization, see Maier's *The Unmasterable Past*, specifically the chapter "German History as Case History," 100–120.

25. Dahrendorf, *Gesellschaft und Demokratie in Deutschland,* 63.

26. Sternberger, "Aspekte des bürgerlichen Charakters," 483.

27. Ibid., 477.

28. Building mostly on the sociologist Norbert Elias's work, the theorist Klaus Theweleit's *Männerphantasien* sketches quite a similar history of the German bourgeoisie. In his 1977 publication, he emphasizes the moral identity of the relatively weak German *Bürger* and claims that the defensive bourgeois class became obsessed with sexual purity. See Theweleit, *Männerphantasien* (Frankfurt am Main: Roter Stern, 1977), 444. Leaning on Elias, Theweleit at times uses a similar vocabulary to speak about the corporeal formation of the *Bürger* in the absolutist age—the bourgeois man seeks to gain control over his impulses and affects and even puts a sort of armor [*Panzer*] on. Theweleit, *Männerphantasien,* 381.

29. Sternberger, "Aspekte des bürgerlichen Charakters," 484.

30. Sternberger, "Versuch zu einem Fazit," 704.

31. Stefan Ludwig Hoffmann, *Die Politik der Geselligkeit: Freimaurerlogen in der deutschen Bürgergesellschaft 1840–1918* (Göttingen: Vandenhoeck & Ruprecht, 1999), 213.

32. Sternberger, "Aspekte des bürgerlichen Charakters," 481.

33. For Sternberger, the plea for flexibility has a distinct bodily dimension, as he hoped for a loosening of German ideals of corporeal discipline shaped by the military. See Sternberger's article on a Prussian manual for military exercise, the *Leitfaden für den Turnunterricht in den Preußischen Volksschulen* from 1895, in "Am Leitfaden," reprinted in *Über den Jugendstil und andere Essays* (Hamburg: Claassen, 1956), 107–13. For comments on Sternberger's appreciation of the American habit of relaxed composure, see Gary L. Baker's "German

National Character and the Relaxing American," *Germanic Review* 80, no. 2 (Spring 2005): 124–42.

34. Sternberger, "Versuch zu einem Fazit," 704–5.

35. Sternberger, "Aspekte des bürgerlichen Charakters," 485–86.

36. On the appeal of a calm and comfortable lifestyle after National Socialist rule and war, see Manfred Hettling, "Bürgerlichkeit im Nachkriegsdeutschland," in *Bürgertum nach 1945*, ed. Manfred Hettling and Bernd Ulrich (Hamburg: Hamburger Edition, 2005), 18.

37. Hannes Siegrist shows how appeals to the *Bürgertum* and worries about its demise could be found in numerous early postwar statements in journals for specialized professions as well as in the rhetoric of forming political parties. See Siegrist, "Ende der Bürgerlichkeit? Die Kategorien 'Bürgertum' und 'Bürgerlichkeit' in der westdeutschen Gesellschaft und Geschichstwissenschaft der Nachkriegsperiode," *Geschichte und Gesellschaft* 20, no. 4 (1994): 549–83.

38. Klaus Tenfelde, "Stadt und Bürgertum im 20. Jahrhundert," in *Wege zur Geschichte des Bürgertums*, ed. Klaus Tenfelde and Hans-Ulrich Wehler (Göttingen: Vandenhoek and Ruprecht, 1994), 320–21.

39. "Hat der deutsche Bürger ausgespielt? Eine Neujahrsumfrage der Frankfurter Allgemeine Zeitung," *Frankfurter Allgemeine Zeitung*, December 30, 1950, 10. One of the respondents to the question posed by the newspaper was Carl Schmitt, whose reactions to the postwar situation we will turn to in the next chapter. Prominent West German social historians have since posed versions of this question and sought to ascertain whether one can speak of a decline or resurgence of the German *Bürgertum* in the postwar period. See, for instance, Lutz Niethammer, "War die bürgerliche Gesellschaft in Deutschland 1945 am Ende oder am Anfang?" in *Bürgerliche Gesellschaft in Deutschland: Historische Einblicke, Fragen, Perspektiven*, ed. Lutz Niethammer (Frankfurt am Main: Fischer, 1990), and Hans Ulrich Wehler, "Deutsches Bürgertum nach 1945: Exitus oder Phönix aus der Asche?" *Geschichte und Gesellschaft* 27 (2001): 617–34. For a critical overview of West German research on the *Bürgertum,* especially in the research clusters in Bielefeld and Frankfurt, see Jonathan Sperber, "*Bürger, Bürgertum, Bürgerlichkeit, Bürgerliche Gesellschaft*: Studies of the German (Upper) Middle Class and Its Sociocultural World," *Journal of Modern History* 69, no. 2 (1997): 271–97.

40. "Hat der deutsche Bürger ausgespielt?" 10.

41. The idea that genuine self-determination requires property is developed philosophically by, for instance, Hegel. Alan Patten reconstructs Hegel's justification of private property as a condition that supports free individuals. According to Hegel, individuals can demonstrate their free personality to one another by exercising control over private property in a publicly discernable way. See Patten, *Hegel's Idea of Freedom* (Oxford: Oxford University Press, 1999), 161. Of course, in the article in the *Frankfurter Allgemeine Zeitung*, the editors refer to a more basic notion of how property relates to independence. If you rely on others to give you a wage, you are dependent on their goodwill.

42. Sternberger, "Bürgerlichkeit," 196.

43. Ibid., 199. Sternberger's rhetorical question "Why should *Bürgerlichkeit* not survive the *Bürgertum*?" anticipates numerous recent discussions of how the mentality and values of the historical *Bürgertum* (cultural interests and virtues such as civic engagement) may have survived the disappearance of a clearly defined social class. See, for instance, Heinz Bude, Joachim Fischer, and Bernd Kauffmann, eds., *Bürgerlichkeit ohne Bürgertum: In welchem Land leben wir?* (Munich: Wilhelm Fink, 2010), or Paul Kaiser, "Bürgerlichkeit ohne Bürgertum?" *Aus Politik und Zeitgeschichte* 9–10 (2008): 26–32.

44. See Hettling, "Bürgerlichkeit im Nachkriegsdeutschland," 18.

45. Hans-Ulrich Wehler, *Deutsche Gesellschaftsgeschichte 1949–1990* (Munich: C. H. Beck, 2008), 142.

46. Taylor, "Modes of Civil Society," 95.

47. This is a standard if contested definition of civil society. See, for instance, Frank Adloff's *Zivilgesellschaft: Theorie und politische Praxis* (Frankfurt am Main: Campus, 2005), 8.

48. For an account of political crisis as the backdrop to theories of civil society, see Adam B. Seligman's "The Fragile Ethical Vision of Civil Society," in *Citizenship and Social Theory*, ed. Bryan S. Turner (London: Sage, 1993), 139–61.

49. Sheldon S. Wolin, *Politics and Vision: Continuity and Innovation in Western Political Thought* (Princeton, N.J.: Princeton University Press, 2004), 262.

50. See Dirk van Laak, *Gespräche in der Sicherheit des Schweigens: Carl Schmitt in der politischen Geistesgeschichte der frühen Bundesrepublik* (Berlin: Akademie, 1993), 43.

51. This congregation of authors stylized itself as a site of reasoned discursive exchange among friends and colleagues, and a good embodiment of a genuine literary public sphere. For an interpretation of Gruppe 47 along these lines, see Jörg Lau, *Hans Magnus Enzensberger: Ein öffentliches Leben* (Berlin: Alexander Fest, 1999), 148. Yet Gruppe 47 was at the same time a very important agency for authors trying to make it on the literary market. In an interview with the author F. C. Delius, the literary critic Jürgen Schutte speaks about the market aspect of Gruppe 47 and calls it a "literary stock exchange." See Sabine Cofalla, Friedrich Christian Delius, and Jürgen Schutte, "Gespräch über die Gruppe 47," in *Die Gruppe 47 in Bildern und Texten*, ed. Toni Richter (Cologne: Kipenheuer & Witsch, 1997), 196.

52. Alexander Kluge, "Die Gruppe 47: Glücksfall einer nicht-öffentlichen Öffentlichkeit," in Richter, *Die Gruppe 47 in Bildern und Texten*, 14.

53. Ibid.

54. Klaus Nathaus, *Organisierte Geselligkeit: Deutsche und britische Vereine im 19. und 20. Jahrhundert* (Göttingen: Vandenhoeck & Ruprecht, 2009), 14.

55. Ibid., 252.

56. See Lewis Coser, *Greedy Institutions: Patterns of Undivided Commitment* (New York: Free Press, 1974), 4.

57. For an overview of the complex postwar history of Rotary, see S. Jonathan Wiesen, "Service Above Self? Rotary Clubs, National Socialism, and

Transnational Memory in the 1960s and 1970s," *Holocaust and Genocide Studies* 23, no. 1 (2009): 1–25.

58. For an important early statement on this process of devolution of responsibility for order and peace in the practice of sociability, see the philosopher Friedrich Schleiermacher, "Versuch einer Theorie des geselligen Betragens," in *Schriften aus der Berliner Zeit 1796–1799*, vol. 2 of *Kritische Gesamtausgabe*, ed. Günter Meckenstock (Berlin: Walter de Gruyter, 1984), 166.

59. Georg Simmel, "Soziologie der Geselligkeit," in *Aufsätze und Abhandlungen 1909–1918*, vol. 12 of *Gesamtausgabe*, ed. Rüdiger Kramme and Angela Rammstedt (Frankfurt: Suhrkamp, 2001), 180.

60. Niklas Luhmann, *Gesellschaftsstruktur und Semantik: Studien zur Wissensoziologie der modernen Gesellschaft*, vol. 1 (Frankfurt am Main: Suhrkamp, 1993), 137.

61. Ulrich Schulz-Buschhaus, *Moralistik und Poetik* (Hamburg: LIT, 1997), 236.

62. Manfred Hettling views the National Socialist ideas of *Volk* and racial unity as attempts to avoid the burden of actively constituting a coherent community in an increasingly differentiated modern bourgeois society. See Hettling, "'Bürgerlichkeit' und Zivilgesellschaft: Die Aktualität einer Tradition," in *Zivilgesellschaft als Geschichte: Studien zum 19. und 20. Jahrhundert*, ed. Ralph Jessen, Sven Reichardt, and Ansgar Klein (Wiesbaden: VS Verlag, 2004), 57.

63. Niklas Luhmann defines the problem of politics as the problem of producing collectively binding decisions in *Gesellschaftsstruktur und Semantik: Studien zur Wissenssoziologie*, vol. 4 (Frankfurt am Main: Suhrkamp, 1999), 101–37.

64. Monika Waldmüller tells the story of the conflict among the editors chronologically, describing the specific issues that prompted it, such as the debate on elections procedures in Germany. See Waldmüller, *Die Wandlung: Ein Bericht*, 91–94.

65. The line is quoted from a letter by Werner Krauss to Dolf Sternberger on October 24, 1946. Werner Krauss, *Briefe 1922 bis 1976*, ed. Peter Jehle (Frankfurt am Main: Klostermann, 2002), 288. Sternberger himself appears to use the word *solidarisch* here, which is a term generally claimed by the left. When addressing the Marxist Krauss, Sternberger may have modified his vocabulary and chosen to talk of solidarity rather than sociability.

66. Sternberger, "Versuch zu einem Fazit," 707. Sternberger would later speak of the composition of the editorial board as an outcome of the American delusion of a great anti-Fascist coalition in Germany. See *Erzählte Zeit—erzähltes Leben*, 214.

67. Karl Jaspers, "Unsere Zukunft und Goethe," *Die Wandlung* 2, nos. 7–8 (October 1947): 574.

68. For an overview of the Goethe's importance as an interpretive key, see Barbro Eberan's *Die Debatte um die Schuldfrage 1945–1949* (Munich: Minerva, 1983), 89. C. G. Jung is one prominent example of a public figure who presented the Faustian character as an encapsulation of the German trajectory.

"For Jung," the Germanist Stephen Brockmann writes, "the legendary literary figure Faust is the epitome of the psychopathology of the Germany soul, with his split personality, limitless arrogance, satanic pact, and inability to come to terms with fundamental realities." See Brockmann, *German Literary Culture at the Zero Hour* (Rochester, N.Y.: Camden House, 2004), 34.

69. Jaspers, "Unsere Zukunft und Goethe," 563.

70. Ibid., 574.

71. For a discussion on the notion of destruction as capital, see Niklas Luhmann's brief statement "Immer noch Bundesrepublik? Das Erbe und die Zukunft," in *BRD ade! Vierzig Jahre in Rück-Ansichten von Sozial- und Kulturwissenschaftlern*, ed. Otthein Rammstedt and Gert Schmidt (Frankfurt am Main: Suhrkamp, 1992), 95–100. Luhmann writes that West Germany profited immensely from the compulsion to cast aside discredited traditions, which allowed for a fresh intellectual start.

72. Helmut Fuhrmann, *Sechs Studien zur Goethe-Rezeption* (Würzburg: Königshausen & Neumann, 2002), 111.

73. See Ernst Robert Curtius, "Goethe oder Jaspers?" in *Goethe im Urteil seiner Kritiker: Dokumente zur Wirkungsgeschichte Goethes in Deutschland*, ed. Karl Robert Mandelkow, vol. 4 (Munich: C. H. Beck, 1984), 307.

74. For a discussion of Goethe's use of the label "philistine" as an invective against members of the bourgeoisie, especially civil servants in the bureaucratic order, see Dieter Arendt's "Das Philistertum des 19. Jahrhunderts," *Der Monat* 21, no. 248 (1969): 33–49. For a more sustained theoretical discussion of the philistine as a figure of indifference to art, see Dave Beech and John Roberts, eds., *The Philistine Controversy* (London: Verso, 2002).

75. See Curtius, "Goethe oder Jaspers?" 305.

76. Ibid., 307. This debate on Goethe seems perhaps a matter of personal irritation regarding a perceived affront against an icon, but as a struggle over a central source of cultural validity in a state of moral bankruptcy, it can be read as a displaced reaction to the notion of a collective guilt, an idea with which Jaspers's name was associated in an often undifferentiated way. Jaspers's attack on Goethe, which was more of an attack on the instrumentalization of Goethe's currency as a protective device, implied that nothing German was uncontaminated.

77. It should be noted that Curtius was not in any straightforward way a cultural nationalist. The overall aim of Curtius's scholarly work *Europäische Literatur und Lateinische Mittelalter* was to put forth evidence for the unity of European literature, a unity that resisted dissolution into unconnected national literatures and complicated standard segmentations of literary history. See Curtius, *Europäische Literatur und Lateinische Mittelalter* (Bern: A. Francke, 1948). This postulate of cultural oneness in Europe shifted attention from the cultures of separate peoples or nation-states, which was clearly a significant move after a period of aggressive national chauvinism. See Anselm Haverkamp, *Latenzzeit: Wissen im Nachkrieg* (Berlin: Kadmos, 2004), 16.

78. Curtius, "Goethe oder Jaspers?" 306.

79. Ibid., 307.

80. Curtius's attacks were motivated less by ideological disagreement, as in the case of Werner Krauss, than by disapproval of the premises of the discourse itself. The conversations that Jaspers and Sternberger wanted to initiate were geared toward facilitating and maintaining communication. Sternberger's images of friendship and Jaspers's repudiation of prophecy or cultish Goethe expertise can be read as attempts to eliminate unequal distributions of authority that would hamper dialogue—to shut out any final verdicts. The participants would ideally occupy interchangeable positions, no one above the other, which would also make each contribution a potential occasion for further contributions. Curtius's attacks were meant to unsettle precisely this symmetrical situation, not only by pointing to Jaspers's illegitimate role as a teacher, his arrogating authority to himself, but also by shifting to another discourse in which reciprocity is no longer a requirement. More specifically, Curtius turned to literature, and of course to Goethe, to mobilize the means to close down the conversation. Rather than continuing the back-and-forth of an academic exchange tied to Jaspers's name, he privileged "a forceful word." The model for this fantasy of the "forceful word" that definitely ends debate is the right of dismissal that issues from the rhetorical power of (Goethe's) poetry, the sheer force of his successful phrase-making, coded as expressive of youthful vitality. Against Jaspers's *Zurechtweisung* Curtius presented Goethe's own practice of *Zurückweisung* and pointed to pithy, self-enclosed polemical verses where the ridicule of the opponent is supported and sealed by formal concision. Against a discourse that sought to diminish asymmetries and hence remove the means to unilaterally terminating conversations from any position on its inside, Curtius delivered a message whose form alone would demonstratively repudiate further statements.

81. Quoted from Fuhrmann, *Sechs Studien*, 114.

82. In *Die Wandlung: Ein Bericht*, Monika Waldmüller briefly goes through the mainly economic reasons for its termination: e.g., a paper shortage; the financial difficulties of the publisher, Lambert Schneider; and the increasing consumer power of the Germans after the 1948 currency reform in combination with the emergence of lighter publications on the forming press market.

83. Sternberger, "Versuch zu einem Fazit," 699. The phrase "Ende selbständiger deutscher Staatlichkeit" is a quotation from Jaspers.

84. Ibid., 700.

85. Ibid., 699.

86. Waldmüller describes *Die Wandlung* as located on the threshold between the loss of state sovereignty at the end of the war and the recovery of a qualified independence. See *Die Wandlung: Ein Bericht*, 39.

Chapter Two

1. Rüdiger Safranski, *Ein Meister aus Deutschland: Heidegger und seine Zeit* (Munich: Carl Hanser, 1994), 449.

2. This is according to the official self-description of the still-active Club zu Bremen itself. See http://www.dczb.de/club_zu_bremen.php.

3. Safranski, *Ein Meister aus Deutschland*, 450.

4. "Organized sociability" is the historian Klaus Nathaus's term for stable and regularized noneconomic and nonpolitical associational life in *Organisierte Geselligkeit.*

5. Between September 1945 and October 1946, Schmitt was detained by U.S. forces. In March 1947, he was arrested again and brought to Nuremberg, but released in less than two months. For information on Schmitt's experiences in detention and his answers to the questions posed by U.S. authorities, see Helmut Quaritsch, ed., *Carl Schmitt: Antworten in Nürnberg* (Berlin: Duncker & Humblot, 2000).

6. Van Laak, *Gespräche in der Sicherheit des Schweigens,* 52–56.

7. Carl Schmitt, *Glossarium: Aufzeichnungen der Jahre 1947–1951*, ed. Eberhard Freiherr von Medem (Berlin: Duncker & Humblot, 1991).

8. Ibid., 226.

9. Ibid., 93.

10. Ibid., 168.

11. Ibid., 256.

12. For an overview of forms of sociability in small circles in postwar West Germany, see van Laak, *Gespräche in der Sicherheit des Schweigens,* 63–64.

13. On Schmitt's contempt for the major trends of the postwar period, such as humanism, liberalism, Christianity, and Europeanism, see Jan-Werner Müller, *A Dangerous Mind: Carl Schmitt in Post-War European Thought* (New Haven, Conn.: Yale University Press, 2003).

14. Schmitt, *Glossarium*, 3. The phrases *edle Einfalt* and *stille Grösse* allude to the German archeologist and art historian Johann Joachim Winckelmann's (1717–68) characterization of masterpieces of art.

15. There were many champions of smooth social virtues as a form of spiritual disarmament strategy in Germany and elsewhere. See, for instance, F. A. Hayek's diagnosis of the Germans in *The Road to Serfdom*, ed. Bruce Caldwell (Chicago: University of Chicago Press, 2007), 167–68.

16. In liberalism, Schmitt claims, political struggle dissolves into economic competition and sociable or spiritual discussion. See Schmitt, *Begriff des Politischen: Text von 1932 mit einem Vorwort und drei Corollarien* (Berlin: Duncker & Humblot, 1963), 70–71.

17. Schmitt, *Glossarium*, 215. Chris Thornhill writes that Schmitt "saw the liberal belief in 'social harmony' as a metaphysical belief, which jeopardized the most reliable factual precondition of social peace—that is, the will of the sovereign state itself." Thornhill, "Carl Schmitt and Early Western Marxism," in *The History of Continental Philosophy*, ed. David Ingram, vol. 5 (Chicago: University of Chicago Press, 2010), 27–28.

18. On Schmitt's assessment of the metaphor of the beehive, see Teresa M. Vilarós, "The Spirit of the Beehive: On Carl Schmitt's 'The New *Nomos* of the Earth,' " *South Atlantic Quarterly* 104, no. 2 (Spring 2005): 359–70.

19. Famous in this regard is Schmitt's polemic against the rhetoric of humanism in his tract on the concept of the political in *Der Begriff des Politischen*, 55.

20. Many commentators on Schmitt's work, regardless of their very different final judgments on his character and his contribution to legal or political

philosophy, come to a similar conclusion: Schmitt had few novel ideas after 1945. Raphael Gross, who studies the anti-Semitic center of gravity in Schmitt's work, claims that the postwar corpus assumes the form of a project of self-stylization. See *Carl Schmitt und die Juden: Eine deutsche Rechtslehre* (Frankfurt am Main: Suhrkamp, 2000). In a similar fashion, Dirk van Laak writes of the self-absorbed character of the postwar writings. See *Gespräche in der Sicherheit des Schweigens*, 71.

21. Speaking of the increasing communist influence in Prague in March 1948, for instance, Schmitt feels he can refer to his prewar publication *Legalität und Legitimität*, a study that according to him had already captured the features of the historical situation. See Schmitt, *Glossarium*, 107.

22. A typical example of this practice is found in Schmitt's one-page remark at the beginning of the republished *Gesetz und Urteil*, his study on the autonomous status of judges' decisions from 1912. In this short note added in 1968, Schmitt above all deplores all the supposedly confused debates around his concepts and claims that the postwar republication could bring calm to the agitated discussion. *Gesetz und Urteil: Eine Untersuchung zum Problem der Rechtspraxis* (Munich: C. H. Beck, 1969), v.

23. John Frow argues that genres present "a relatively bounded and schematic domain of meanings" whose principles of organization often "reflect unspoken ideological premises." See Frow, "Genre Worlds: The Discursive Shaping of Knowledge," *Arena Journal* 23 (2005): 134, 140.

24. As Frow formulates it, "Genres give schematic guidance . . . to the users of texts"; to recognize the generic membership of a text is, among other things, to understand how it can or should be read and understood, an act of classification that limits the number of interpretations. See Frow, "'Reproducibles, Rubrics, and Everything You Need': Genre Theory Today," *PMLA* 122, no. 5 (October 2007): 1633.

25. Detained in Nuremberg, Schmitt was questioned three times by Robert W. Kempner, a jurist working for the American administration. He also produced four written statements in his own defense. One of the questions he had to answer in written form concerned whether his theoretical writings had supported and supplied arguments to Hitler's aggressive politics of German expansion. See Quaritsch, *Carl Schmitt: Antworten in Nürnberg*, 68.

26. Seeking to explain the lingering interest of Schmitt's work, Friedrich Balke notes how his sensitivity to the conditions of the time has a tendency to overrule or complicate his declared agenda. Ideas and doctrines that Schmitt officially negated, Balke asserts, frequently seeped into his work. See Friedrich Balke, *Der Staat nach seinem Ende: Die Versuchung Carl Schmitts* (Munich: Wilhelm Fink, 1996), 8.

27. In an article on Schmitt and Michel Foucault, Astrid Deuber-Mankowsky criticizes Schmitt for failing to reflect on the political dimension of governing and policing subjects *within* the modern state. Against the backdrop of Schmitt's comments on the interrogation and the diary as diverse forms of enforced confession continuous with a whole host of modern diagnostic and disciplining procedures, this characterization may not be entirely fair. See

Deuber-Mankowsky, "Nothing Is Political, Everything Can Be Politicized: On the Concept of the Political in Michel Foucault and Carl Schmitt," trans. Jennifer Bierich and David Pan, *Telos* 148 (Spring 2008): 135–61.

28. See, for instance, Carl Schmitt, *Politische Theologie: Vier Kapitel zur Lehre von der Souveränität* (Berlin: Duncker & Humblot, 2004), 59.

29. See Steve Fuller, *Thomas Kuhn: A Philosophical History for Our Times* (Chicago: University of Chicago Press, 2000), 95.

30. Carl Schmitt, *Ex Captivitate Salus: Erfahrungen der Zeit 1945/47* (Cologne: Greven, 1950), 9.

31. Dirk van Laak mentions the meeting in June 1945 (*Gespräche in der Sicherheit des Schweigens,* 31) and presents it as Schmitt's first brief encounter with the processes of postwar legal and moral reform. As Klaus Himmelstein has shown, Eduard Spranger was a deeply conservative professor, concerned with the education of a vital German nation throughout his career and not averse to the rise and rule of National Socialism. Never a party member, however, he was much less compromised than Schmitt and could continue working as a professor after the war. See Himmelstein, "Eduard Sprangers deutsches Bildungsideal auf den Trümmern von 1945," in *Die Schärfung des Blicks: Pädagogik nach dem Holocaust*, ed. Klaus Himmelstein and Wolfgang Keim (Frankfurt am Main: Campus, 1996), 61–75.

32. Schmitt, *Ex Captivitate Salus,* 12.

33. Ibid.

34. Ibid., 11.

35. Ibid., 9–10.

36. Ibid., 9.

37. A typical feature of the interrogation, as it is practiced within modern institutions, is precisely that the one conducting it must pay particular attention to what the subject unconsciously betrays about him- or herself. See Michael Niehaus, *Das Verhör: Geschichte—Theorie—Fiktion* (Munich: Wilhelm Fink, 2003). Given this focus on unwillingly emitted signs, the interrogation cannot be understood as a conversation in any traditional sense: the interlocutors do not really speak to each other. And yet for the observation of the interrogated subject to take place at all, he or she must be continually motivated to produce statements, *as if* he or she were conversing.

38. Michael Niehaus argues that modern interrogations are frequently represented as pedagogic situations—the person who is interrogated carries the truth, but must be led to reveal it. See Niehaus, *Das Verhör*, 14. In line with this half-concealed analytical task, the person posing questions should in no way be overtaken by personal vindictiveness, and in Schmitt's eyes, Spranger does appear more as a concerned and analytical pedagogue than as a judge or an opponent. See Schmitt, *Ex Captivitate Salus*, 11.

39. Schmitt, *Ex Captivitate Salus,* 9.

40. In her analysis of the discourse of tolerance, the political theorist Wendy Brown has looked at how the question of tolerance has shifted from the domain of beliefs and ideas to the domain of identities, although tolerance of "dissident beliefs is—or ought to be—on a different ontological chessboard

from tolerance of sexual or ethnic 'difference.'" See Brown, *Regulating Aversion: Tolerance in the Age of Identity and Empire* (Princeton, N.J.: Princeton University Press, 2006), 35. She follows Michel Foucault in arguing that the disciplinary institutions and practices of the modern period tend to equate specific beliefs and practices with the essential truth about a given subject (homosexual acts, for instance, are now seen not as contingent events but as the true expression of a homosexual subject).

41. For an analysis of the modern conception of the criminal as a psychiatric case, see Michel Foucault's "The Dangerous Individual," in *Politics, Philosophy, Culture: Interviews and Other Writings 1977–1984*, ed. Lawrence D. Kritzman, trans. Alain Baudot and Jane Couchman (New York: Routledge, 1988), 125–51. Foucault analyzes how a crime is, in the modern period, not simply an isolated action or random event but an expression of a core personality, a manifestation of a criminal subject, who is the real target of the punishment.

42. Friedrich Balke, "Gesetz und Urteil: Zur Aktualität einer Problemstellung bei Carl Schmitt," in *Gesetz und Urteil: Beiträge zu einer Theorie des Politischen*, ed. Joseph Vogl (Weimar: Verlag und Datenbank für Geisteswissenschaften, 2003), 52.

43. Schmitt, *Ex Captivitate Salus*, 9.

44. In a review of literature on interrogation techniques and the use of negotiation theory, Loch K. Johnson treats the relationship between the two parties in an interrogation: "Perhaps the most appealing and relevant aspect of negotiation theory is the principle that one should try to learn as much as possible about an opponent's strengths, weaknesses, fears, needs, and aspirations. This is exactly what good interrogators try to do as well. It is an approach that can lead to the development of a human connection between two sides." See Johnson, "Educing Information: Interrogation: Science and Art," *Studies in Intelligence* 51, no. 4 (December 2007): 4.

45. Schmitt, *Ex Captitivate Salus*, 77. Dirk van Laak notes how the hallowed concept of silence in the circles around Schmitt constituted a very questionable and all too convenient repudiation of any human court to sit in judgments over other humans. In this context, piety served as a shield against accusations. See van Laak, *Gespräche in der Sicherheit des Schweigens*, 127.

46. Schmitt, *Ex Captivitate Salus*, 76–77.

47. Andrew J. Perrin and Jeffrey K. Olick, introduction to Theodor W. Adorno, *Guilt and Defense: On the Legacies of National Socialism in Postwar Germany*, ed. and trans. Perrin and Olick (Cambridge, Mass.: Harvard University Press, 2010), 17.

48. See Andrew J. Perrin and Jeffrey K. Olick, "Translators' Introduction: Before the Public Sphere," in Friedrick Pollock, Theodor W. Adorno, et al., *Group Experiment and Other Writings: The Frankfurt School on Public Opinion in Postwar Germany*, ed. and trans. Perrin and Olick (Cambridge, Mass.: Harvard University Press, 2011), xxiii.

49. See Perrin and Olick, introduction, 17.

50. Perrin and Olick, "Translators' Introduction," xxiv.

51. Ibid., xxviii.
52. Ibid., ix.
53. Ibid., xxiii.
54. It should be added that Adorno himself argued for a principled resistance to light sociable interaction, but for entirely different reasons than Schmitt. Speaking of the carefree conversation with a stranger in a train, he cast participation in polite and easy companionableness as a betrayal of suffering. See Theodor W. Adorno, *Minima Moralia: Reflexionen aus dem beschädigten Leben*, vol. 4 of *Gesammelte Schriften*, ed. Rolf Tiedemann (Frankfurt am Main: Suhrkamp, 2003), 26.
55. Andreas Kalyvas, *Democracy and the Politics of the Extraordinary: Max Weber, Carl Schmitt, and Hannah Arendt* (Cambridge: Cambridge University Press, 2008), 124–25.
56. The following discussion draws from Jakob Norberg, "Day-to-Day Politics: Carl Schmitt on the Diary," *Telos* 157 (Winter 2011): 26–37.
57. Schmitt, *Glossarium*, 13. The editor of *Glossarium* claims that the notes were intended for some eventual publication and cites among other things Schmitt's own concern with the legibility of his jottings as well as his corrections of them.
58. On the dangers of spiritual diaries as viewed by Puritans, see Jennifer A. Herdt, *Putting on Virtue: The Legacy of Splendid Vices* (Chicago: University of Chicago Press, 2008), 197–218.
59. Schmitt, *Glossarium*, 13.
60. Ibid., 130. Schmitt is reading Ernst Jünger, *Strahlungen* (Tübingen: Heliopolis, 1949). If Sternberger hoped for a greater acceptance of some light or low-intensity sensuality as a means of demilitarization in his articles in *Die Wandlung*, Schmitt staunchly invoked renunciation and asceticism. The literary scholar Helmut Lethen has called Schmitt's 1947–51 diary a late document of the so-called cold personality cultivated in the interwar period. See Lethen, *Verhaltenslehren der Kälte: Lebensversuche zwischen den Kriegen* (Frankfurt am Main: Suhrkamp, 1994), 218.
61. See Louis Menand, "Woke Up This Morning: Why Do We Read Diaries?" *New Yorker*, December 10, 2007, 106–12.
62. For a study of the diary as formlessness framed by a purely temporal formality, see Elke Siegel, "Remains of the Day: Rainald Goetz's Internet Diary *Abfall für alle*," *Germanic Review* 81, no. 3 (Summer 2006): 235–54.
63. See Willy Sanders, *Gutes Deutsch—besseres Deutsch: Praktische Stillehre der deutschen Gegenwartssprache* (Darmstadt: Wissenschaftliche Buchgesellschaft, 1996), 23.
64. Schmitt, *Glossarium*, 96.
65. On sententiousness in the works of Carl Schmitt, see Arnd Wedemeyer, "Herrschaftszeiten!: Theopolitical Profanities in the Face of Secularization," *New German Critique* 35, no. 3 (Fall 2008): 121–41.
66. For a list of gnomic and eminently quotable statements, see ibid., 133.
67. I borrow this formulation from Geoffrey Bennington, *Sententiousness and the Novel: Laying Down the Law in Eighteenth-Century French Fiction*

(Cambridge: Cambridge University Press, 1985), 8. On the self-sufficiency of sententious statements and the difficulty of their integration in the larger cloth of the text, see ibid., 44–45.

68. See the editor's preface in *Glossarium*, v.

69. Schmitt, *Glossarium*, 225. It should perhaps be added that Pepys himself wrote his diary in cipher and may not have contemplated inviting an audience. However, Schmitt always suspects that the diarist longs for a larger readership. Schmitt even seems to have difficulties conceiving of a kind of writing that is not supposed to have a public impact. Utterance for him is always rhetoric, and the diary might just be bad rhetoric.

70. See Christian J. Emden, "The Brilliant Fascist: Carl Schmitt and the Limits of Liberalism," *H-German Net Reviews*, June 2005, http://www.h-net.org/reviews/showrev.php?id=10599.

71. See Patrick Bahners, "Der Unterschichtenkerl," *Frankfurter Allgemeine Zeitung*, December 29, 2006.

72. On the diary, the memoir, and the psychoanalytic therapy session as historically contingent social institutions that work as "biography-generators," see Alois Hahn, "Identität und Selbstthematisierung," in *Selbstthematisierung und Selbstzeugnis: Bekenntnis und Geständnis*, ed. Alois Hahn and Volker Kapp (Frankfurt am Main: Suhrkamp, 1987), 9–25.

73. Schmitt, *Glossarium*, 40.

74. Ibid.

75. See Lionel Trilling, *Sincerity and Authenticity* (Cambridge, Mass.: Harvard University Press, 1972).

76. For an interpretation of Schmitt's theory of representation, see John McCormick, *Carl Schmitt's Critique of Liberalism* (Cambridge: Cambridge University Press, 1999), 157–205.

77. For an analysis of political struggle as generative of political selfhood, see Sarah Pourciau, "Bodily Negation: Carl Schmitt on the Meaning of Meaning," *MLN* 120 (2005): 1066–90.

78. For a recent discussion of Foucault's analysis of the confession and its intimate link to subjection and obedience, see Jean-Michel Landry, "Confession, Obedience, and Subjectivity: Michel Foucault's Unpublished Lectures *On the Government of the Living*," *Telos* 146 (Spring 2009): 111–23. For a consideration of the important link between inwardness and confessional practices as well as the diary as the successor of the Christian confession, see Alois Hahn's outline of the sociology of confessions, "Zur Soziologie der Beichte und anderer Formen institutionalisierter Bekenntnisse: Selbstthematisierung und Zivilisationsprozess," *Kölner Zeitschrift für Soziologie und Sozialpsychologie* 3, no. 34 (1982): 407–34.

79. Hannah Arendt writes on Jean-Jacques Rousseau: "With the loss of the priest and his judgment, the solitude of the would-be confessor had become boundless." Arendt, *Rahel Varnhagen: The Life of a Jewish Woman*, trans. Richard and Clara Wilson (New York: Harcourt & Brace, 1974), 20. As noted above, Schmitt singles out Rousseau and August Strindberg as miserable confessors in *Ex Captivitate Salus*.

Chapter Three

1. Hannah Arendt, "Über den Imperialismus," *Die Wandlung* 1, no. 8 (August 1946): 656. My translations of quotations from Arendt's articles are informed by her formulations in *The Origins of Totalitarianism*, in which most of the material that appeared in *Die Wandlung* was later published.

2. In his concluding article in the last issue of the journal, Sternberger singled out "Organized Guilt" as a daring article that generated much discussion among the readers. See Sternberger's comment in "Versuch zu einem Fazit," 701.

3. As Roy T. Tsao points out in his reappraisal of *The Origins of Totalitarianism*, Arendt uses the term "mob" not in the word's "older sense of the merely uncouth and disorderly poor, but with the slang connotation of a specifically criminal underworld." See Tsao, "The Three Phases of Arendt's Theory of Totalitarianism," *Social Research* 69, no. 2 (2002): 584.

4. Arendt's letters to her husband Heinrich Blücher reveal that she met with and ran into Sternberger during some of her postwar trips to Germany and even attended his seminars, but they hardly bear witness to some substantial and lasting intellectual engagement between the two. See Arendt and Blücher, *Within Four Walls: The Correspondence Between Hannah Arendt and Heinrich Blücher 1936–1968*, ed. Lotte Kohler, trans. Peter Constantine (New York: Harcourt, 1996), 212.

5. Dana Villa, "Genealogies of Total Domination: Arendt, Adorno, and Auschwitz," *New German Critique* 34, no. 1 (2007): 35.

6. See Eberan, *Die Debatte um die Schuldfrage 1945–1949*, 96. With time, Arendt's contributions to *Die Wandlung*, and especially "Organized Guilt," would prevail over Sternberger's as the dominant or the most memorable set of articles published in the journal. According to Eberan, this focus on the psychology of the petit bourgeoisie was in fact what set the journal apart from the discourses of other intellectual groups, which, when addressing National Socialism and the war, often spoke of the deeply flawed German national character, the long Prussian tradition of militarism, or the West's fatal turn away from Christianity.

7. Arendt, "Über den Imperialismus," 661.

8. Hannah Arendt, *The Origins of Totalitarianism* (New York: Meridian, 1958), 146.

9. Ibid., 145–46.

10. For a recent overview of models that present the political community as the unplanned outcome of private vices as well as an assessment of their continuing relevance for contemporary theory, see Malcolm Bull's "The Limits of Multitude," *New Left Review* 35 (September–October 2005): 34–36.

11. The phrase social production of moral indifference is drawn from Heinz Bude's *Bilanz der Nachfolge*, 18. He uses it to summarize the sociologist Zygmunt Baumann's work on the modernity of the Holocaust.

12. Arendt and Jaspers, *Briefwechsel 1926–1969*, 605.

13. Ibid., 152–53, 605.

14. The title of Lenin's study is *Imperialism, the Highest Stage of Capitalism* (Moscow: Progress, 1978).

15. For an overview and assessment of contrasting theories of capitalism and militarism, see Michael Mann, *States, War, and Capitalism* (Oxford: Blackwell, 1988), 124–45.

16. In Arendt's articles between 1942 and 1946, she represented Nazism as the "immediate heir to the racist, expansionist politics that emerged in the last decades of the nineteenth century. . . . Hitler's genocidal dictatorship is treated simply as the horrific consummation of the malignant tendencies of imperialism's older forms." See Tsao, "The Three Phases of Arendt's Theory of Totalitarianism," 582. After the war, however, she would not so much modify or revise this thesis as she would simply change focus and write exclusively on the internal logic of totalitarianism as an unprecedented type of human government. The latter is the dominant theme of the third section of *The Origins of Totalitarianism*, and Arendt does not make much of an effort to link it to the earlier parts on anti-Semitism and imperialism. In an attempt to work out the separate features of imperialism and totalitarianism in Arendt, Tsao points out that she sees the rapacious hunger for expansion, profit, and power as typical of imperialism, while totalitarianism stands out for its suicidal tendencies.

17. Hannah Arendt, "Über den Imperialismus," 650.

18. Peter Baehr stresses how Arendt sought to bring out and represent the near-incomprehensible, surreal quality of totalitarianism, an effort that gave her account a sometimes literary quality. See Baehr, *Hannah Arendt, Totalitarianism, and the Social Sciences* (Palo Alto, Calif.: Stanford University Press, 2010), 87–91.

19. This is a conventional Marxist interpretation of imperialism: in the imperialist age, the state becomes an instrument of capitalist business ventures. Even left-wing critics have noted, however, that capitalism is the economic system in which the dominant mechanism of extraction is precisely not dependent on direct violence or coercion. See Gopal Balakrishnan, "States of War," *New Left Review* 36 (November–December 2005): 23.

20. Hannah Arendt, "Über den Imperialismus," 651.

21. For a succinct discussion of Hegel as the first thinker to delineate an economic theory of imperialism, see Albert O. Hirschman, *Essays in Trespassing: Economics to Politics and Beyond* (Cambridge: Cambridge University Press, 1981), 167–76. For the relevant passages on civil society in Hegel, see G. W. F. Hegel, *Grundlinien der Philosophie des Rechts oder Naturrecht und Staatswissenschaft im Grundrisse*, vol. 7 of *Werke*, ed. Eva Moldenhauer and Karl Markus Michel (Frankfurt am Main: Suhrkamp, 1986), §244–48.

22. Joseph Schumpeter published his sociological reflections on imperialism in 1919, arguing that the reckless enterprise of imperialism, involving high costs and uncertain gains, was anathema to the more calculating approach of capitalists as well as the inherent cosmopolitanism of the market-oriented bourgeoisie and should rather be ascribed to the lingering hold of old power elites and the atavistic glorification of military conquest. See Joseph Schumpeter, *Aufsätze zur Soziologie* (Tübingen: J. C. B. Mohr, 1953), 72–146.

23. Hannah Arendt, "Über den Imperialismus," 655. The close connection between high society and gangsters is a recurrent theme in *The Origins of*

Totalitarianism. Writing on imperialism, Arendt recapitulates: "We have seen the behavior of high society during the Dreyfus Affair and watched Disraeli discover the social relationship between vice and crime; here too, we have essentially the same story of high society falling in love with its underworld, and of the criminal feeling elevated when by civilized coldness, the avoidance of 'unnecessary exertion,' and good manners he is allowed to create a vicious, refined atmosphere around his crimes." Arendt, *The Origins of Totalitarianism,* 190.

24. Hannah Arendt, "Über den Imperialismus," 655–56.

25. Ibid., 654.

26. Ibid., 655.

27. Ibid., 656.

28. In his article "The Right to Have Rights," Werner Hamacher shows that Karl Marx critiqued bourgeois society as an association of dissociated egotisms and viewed it as the institutionalized form of the Hobbesian vision of the state of nature. Like Marx, Arendt argued that bourgeois society, as described by Hobbes, does not take man out of the supposedly natural condition of perpetual antagonism between opposed individuals so much as it elevates it to the dominant principle of politics. See Hamacher, "The Right to Have Rights (Four-and-a-Half Remarks)," trans. Kirk Wetters, *South Atlantic Quarterly* 102, no. 3 (2004): 348.

29. Hannah Arendt, "Über den Imperialismus," 655.

30. Ibid.

31. Ibid., 661.

32. Ibid., 656.

33. Confronted with this bleak account of the *bürgerliche Gesellschaft,* one may ask why this particular societal formation pictures men as isolated agents driven by pure self-interest. In *The Origins of Totalitarianism*, Arendt does offer a rather conventional explanation for this development. Arendt claims that, historically, the bourgeoisie was shut out from and never aspired to government; instead the bourgeoisie focused on commerce and viewed the state as subservient to its economic ends—a necessary well-organized police force with the task of enforcing property rights. The members of the bourgeoisie thus remained essentially private persons: "This privateness and primary concern with money-making had developed a set of behavior patterns which are expressed in all those proverbs—'nothing succeeds like success,' 'might is right,' 'right is expediency,' etc.—that necessarily spring from a society of competitors." See *The Origins of Totalitarianism*, 138. As the bourgeoisie later turned from business to the conduct of national and international politics, however, they reconceptualized the political life of human communities according to principles and concepts developed in the realm of private commerce, something that amounted to a "radical refoundation of the political association." See Villa, "Genealogies of Total Domination," 35. This included launching an imperialist project of expansion in which the state secures new markets and recasting the state as the mere outcome of individual actions. The development of (1) a purely economic life form in the absence of political participation and

(2) the subsequent projection of economic categories and modes of operation on the polity can be described in terms of a sequence of *compensation effect* and *spill-over effect*. See Jon Elster's "Patterns of Causal Analysis in Tocqueville's *Democracy in America*," *Rationality and Society* 3, no. 3 (1991): 277–97.

34. For a discussion of Arendt and liberal anticommunism, see Anson Rabinbach's "Eichmann in New York: The New York Intellectuals and the Hannah Arendt Controversy," *October* 108 (Spring 2004): 107. See also François Furet, *Das Ende der Illusion: Der Kommunismus im 20. Jahrhundert*, trans. Karla Bartsch et al. (Munich: Piper, 1996), 542–43.

35. For a brief discussion of Arendt's essay as a provocation that the editors felt they had to couch in explanations, see Norbert Frei's *1945 und wir: Das Dritte Reich im Bewußtsein der Deutschen* (Munich: C. H. Beck, 2005), 150.

36. Sternberger, "Vorbemerkung der Redaktion," *Die Wandlung* 1, no. 4 (April 1946): 333.

37. The idea that National Socialism was an ideology and a government suited to the *Spießer* or the *Kleinbürger* has long been a left-wing commonplace. In 1945, the poet and cultural icon of the GDR Johannes Becher stated that the Nazi ideology fitted the psychological needs of the *Spießer.* See Thomas Ahbe's "Der Kleinbürger als Froschkönig," in *Unsere Feinde: Konstruktionen des Anderen im Sozialismus*, ed. Silke Satjukow and Rainer Gries (Leipzig: Universitätsverlag, 2005), 180.

38. Hannah Arendt, "Organisierte Schuld," *Die Wandlung* 1, no. 4 (April 1946): 336.

39. Karl Jaspers distinguished between moral, criminal, political, and metaphysical guilt, distinctions that did not appear in Arendt's article. He was also, as in his "Geleitwort" for *Die Wandlung* and other texts, concerned with possible principles of cohesion for postwar Germans and linked the consciousness of guilt to the formation of a new political community.

40. Hannah Arendt, "Organisierte Schuld," 338.

41. Arendt pictured the postwar choir of Germans exclaiming, with one voice, "this we have not done [*dies haben wir nicht getan*]" ("Organisierte Schuld," 340).

42. In postwar Germany, the previous members of the "machine" administering mass murder seemed unaware of their personal guilt although they were able to recall exactly what kind of work they had performed. According to Arendt, they moreover pointed to the deadly consequences for themselves if they had not carried out their delimited function, ultimately suggesting that they could not be held responsible for acts they carried out under the threat of severe sanctions. In light of such claims, organized guilt can in fact constitute a type of *collective* guilt, insofar as the individual may not be responsible for mass murder as an individual, yet remains guilty and must be punished as a member of an organization. Collective guilt is, in such a situation, not merely the collective of individually guilty subjects, but a description of the paradoxical condition in which the collective is unequivocally guilty although all individuals composing it may not always be.

43. A very common approach to the reaction of Germans to the thesis of collective guilt has been to speak of multiple defense mechanisms. Thomas Koebner, for instance, lists a number of strategies through which Germans tried to avoid the attribution of blame and guilt. See Koebner's "Die Schuldfrage: Vergangenheitsbewältigung und Lebenslügen in der Diskussion 1945–1949," in *Deutschland nach Hitler: Zukunftspläne im Exil und aus der Besatzungszeit 1939–1949*, ed. Thomas Koebner, Gert Sautermeister, and Sigrid Schneider (Opladen: Westdeutscher, 1987), 303. Arendt was likewise sensitive to the ways in which Germans sought to minimize their own responsibility, but her approach to the problem stayed sociological rather than psychological. If a certain society allows for a certain crime, then the problem has to be solved at the level of society. Thus, rather than proposing therapeutic measures for individuals in denial, she called for the reconstitution of the human community.

44. Hannah Arendt, "Organisierte Schuld," 340.

45. Ibid., 341–42.

46. Ibid., 341.

47. Ibid., 340–41.

48. Ibid., 340.

49. Ibid.

50. Arendt's discussion echoes the critique of the *bürgerliche Gesellschaft* formulated by the early Marx in "Zur Judenfrage." Marx calls security or *Sicherheit* the supreme concept of bourgeois society and claims that, insofar as this society grants its members freedom, it is the freedom of a monad. See Karl Marx and Friedrich Engels, *Werke* (Berlin: Dietz, 1972), 1:364–65.

51. Joachim Ritter explicates Hegel's conceptualization of the *bürgerliche Gesellschaft,* according to which it has division of labor as its only principle of constitution and therefore must be called a system of needs. See Ritter, *Hegel und die französische Revolution* (Frankfurt am Main: Suhrkamp, 1965), 56.

52. For a discussion of the rise, significance, and mechanisms of the insurance society, see François Ewald's "Die Versicherungs-Gesellschaft," in *Politik in der Risikogesellschaft*, ed. Ulrich Beck, trans. Mechthild and Thomas Blanke (Frankfurt am Main: Suhrkamp, 1991), 288–301.

53. Joseph Vogl characterizes the *Spießer* as a figure who remains insensitive or unaware of social and cultural complexity and clings to a small set of basic values and attitudes fitted for smaller, noncomplex environments. See Joseph Vogl and Alexander Kluge, *Soll und Haben: Fernsehgespräche* (Zürich: Diaphanes, 2009), 70.

54. Hannah Arendt, "Organisierte Schuld," 341–42.

55. Ibid. Arendt's use of anglicisms in her German text indicates that the *Spießer* is an international phenomenon and not particular to German national history. For an overview of *bürgerliche* values and *antibürgerliche* styles of attack, see Hannes Siegrist, "Bürgerlichkeit und Antibürgerlichkeit in historischer Perspektive," in *Der Aufstand gegen den Bürger: Antibürgerliches Denken im 20. Jahrhundert*, ed. Günter Meuter and Henrique Ricardo Otten (Würzburg: Königshausen & Neumann, 1999), 35–50.

56. Robert Paxton describes the career of the Nazi movement, its trajectory from a conglomeration of antibourgeois figures on the margins to a mass party in charge of the state apparatus and reaching out to larger, traditional sections of society. See Paxton, *The Anatomy of Fascism* (New York: Knopf, 2004).

57. Hannah Arendt, *The Origins of Totalitarianism*, 145.

58. Commenting on *The Human Condition*, the political theorist Patchen Markell explores how Arendt wants to preserve what she calls the "nonsovereign" character of human action. See Markell, *Bound by Recognition* (Princeton, N.J.: Princeton University Press, 2003), 5.

59. Hannah Arendt, "Es gibt nur ein einziges Menschenrecht," *Die Wandlung* 4, no. 8 (December 1949): 764.

60. Michael Bösch discusses the importance of a world of things for the ongoing realization of human plurality and argues that, in Arendt's work, the identity of objects over time becomes the guarantor of plurality. The fluctuating and perennially shifting communicative interactions of humans, through which they achieve a plurality of articulated identities, require a stable space to appear. See Bösch, "Pluralität und Identität bei Hannah Arendt," *Zeitschrift für philosophische Forschung* 53, no. 4 (1999): 577–78.

61. Sheldon Wolin claims that Arendt identifies the political neither with the state nor with society: "It [the political] signified not a state or a society but a determinate public space, a forum, an agora, set aside, jealously defended so that those men who wished to test themselves by the highest standards of excellence might compete, by speech and action, in the presence of their peers." See Wolin, "Hannah Arendt: Democracy and the Political," in *Hannah Arendt: Critical Essays*, ed. Lewis P. Hinchman and Sandra K. Hinchman (Buffalo: SUNY Press, 1994), 292–93.

62. With her negative attitude toward modern developments and insistence on a more bounded life, it may seem that Arendt thinks in an essentially nostalgic vein, whether the object of nostalgia is the Greek polis or the stable nation-state. Nevertheless, with her stress on never-ending and unpredictable contestation, through which individuals display themselves to each other, she does not quite fit the image of a nostalgic communitarian. In fact, contestation may depend on the loosening of collective norms and dissolution of stabilizing prejudices that might only become possible when communities that rely on common traditions are thinned out and even endangered through increasing intellectual, social, and geographic mobility. The political erupts, so to speak, at a critical moment. For a description of Arendt as something of an anticommunitarian, see Dana Villa, "Hannah Arendt: Modernity, Alienation, and Critique," in *Hannah Arendt and the Meaning of Politics*, ed. Craig Calhoun and John McGowan (Minneapolis: University of Minnesota Press, 1997), 179–206.

63. For a conception of the employment of the "voice" option in the political domain, as opposed to the silent character of market-oriented choices, see Albert O. Hirschman's *Exit, Voice, and Loyalty: Responses to Decline in Firms, Organizations, and States* (Cambridge, Mass.: Harvard University Press, 1970).

64. Hannah Pitkin analyzes the surface inconsistencies of Arendt's notion of the social and points out that she groups the salon and the market under the

same heading in *The Human Condition.* See Pitkin, *The Attack of the Blob: Hannah Arendt's Concept of the Social* (Chicago: University of Chicago Press, 1998), 191.

65. Hannah Arendt, *The Human Condition* (Chicago: University of Chicago Press, 1958), 40.

66. Arendt and Blücher, *Within Four Walls*, 205.

Chapter Four

1. Reinhart Koselleck, *Critique and Crisis: Enlightenment and the Pathogenesis of Modern Society*, trans. Anon. (Cambridge, Mass.: MIT Press, 1998), 66.

2. Ibid., 72.

3. Ibid., 67, 75.

4. Ibid., 77.

5. As an editor, Sternberger obviously read Arendt and even singled her out as the journal's most exemplary contributor; her essays underscored the journal's open, cosmopolitan character. Schmitt in turn reacted, with venom, to *Die Wandlung* as an American-supported publication and to Karl Jaspers's visible role in publicly addressing German guilt, but he was intellectually active only in cautious, nonpublic ways, and started publishing as late as 1950. Finally, in *The Origins of Totalitarianism*, Arendt included several references to Schmitt's prewar work, which she called arresting reading, but she displayed no particular interest in determining his continued influence or engaging with his position in a more systematic way. Jaspers, Sternberger, Arendt, and Schmitt were thus in some cases aware of each other, but did not make interventions in a single, unified debate.

6. Nicolaus Sombart, *Rendezvous mit dem Weltgeist: Heidelberger Reminiszenzen 1945–1951* (Frankfurt am Main: S. Fischer, 2000), 264.

7. See Manfred Hettling and Bernd Ulrich, "Formen der Bürgerlichkeit: Ein Gespräch mit Reinhart Koselleck," in Hettling and Ulrich, *Bürgertum nach 1945*, 54.

8. Jan-Friedrich Missfelder, "Die Gegenkraft und ihre Geschichte: Carl Schmitt, Reinhart Koselleck und der Bürgerkrieg," *Zeitschrift für Religion und Geistesgeschichte* 58, no. 4 (2006): 334.

9. Van Laak, *Gespräche in der Sicherheit des Schweigens,* 33–34.

10. Koselleck, *Kritik und Krise: Ein Beitrag zur Pathogenese der bürgerlichen Welt* (Freiburg: Karl Alber, 1959), iv.

11. Anthony J. La Vopa, "Conceiving a Public: Ideas and Society in Eighteenth-Century Europe," *Journal of Modern History* 64, no. 1 (1992): 85.

12. The passage reads: "Nicht die Behauptung, Recht zu haben, führt zum Frieden, sondern nur die unwiderstehliche Entscheidung eines sicher funktionierenden, gesetzlichen Zwangssystems, das dem Streit ein Ende macht." Carl Schmitt, *Der Leviathan in der Staatslehre des Thomas Hobbes: Sinn und Fehlschlag eines politischen Symbols* (Hamburg: Hanseatische Verlagsanstalt, 1938), 69.

13. Wolin, *Politics and Vision,* 245.

14. Tamsin Shaw argues that the rise of the state and the breakdown of traditional authorities such as the Catholic Church present an intractable problem

for modern political philosophy. On the one hand, the modern state requires normative consensus in order to rule. On the other, the process of secularization and the fracturing of religious communities make uncoerced consensus nearly impossible, which leaves the state vulnerable. While liberals hope that normative validity and political authority can coincide when the scope of the state's power has been narrowed and only rests on a few rational principles that everyone can agree on, Schmitt felt otherwise. See Shaw, *Nietzsche's Political Skepticism* (Princeton, N.J.: Princeton University Press, 2007).

15. Brown, *Regulating Aversion,* 39.

16. Andreas Kalyvas notes that for Schmitt, liberalism's core project is dismantling the power of a sovereign and hence it stands in opposition to democracy defined as popular sovereignty: "Liberalism, according to Schmitt, emerged as a theory that aimed at the fragmentation of political power." See Kalyvas, *Democracy and the Politics of the Extraordinary,* 130.

17. Raphael Gross writes that Schmitt points to a number of "'Jewish' authors, from Spinoza to Mendelssohn to Marx, as bearing primary responsibility for the state's destruction and as having destroyed it in a conspirative manner." Gross, *Carl Schmitt and the Jews: The "Jewish Question," the Holocaust, and German Legal Theory*, trans. Joel Golb (Madison: University of Wisconsin Press, 2007), 157.

18. For a reading of Schmitt's *Leviathan* along these lines, see Gopal Balakrishnan, *The Enemy: An Intellectual Portrait of Carl Schmitt* (London: Verso, 2000), 220.

19. David Dyzenhaus, *Legality and Legitimacy: Carl Schmitt, Hans Kelsen and Hermann Heller in Weimar* (Oxford: Clarendon, 1997), 89.

20. William E. Scheuerman, "Unsolved Paradoxes: Conservative Political Thought in Adenauer's Germany," in *Confronting Mass Democracy and Industrial Technology: Political and Social Theory from Nietzsche to Habermas*, ed. John P. McCormick (Durham, N.C.: Duke University Press, 2002), 234.

21. La Vopa, "Conceiving a Public," 85.

22. Kirk Wetters, *The Opinion System: Impasses of the Public Sphere from Hobbes to Habermas* (New York: Fordham University Press, 2008), 82.

23. La Vopa speaks of Koselleck's "ironic narrative" in *Critique and Crisis* as a whole. See La Vopa, "Conceiving a Public," 83.

24. Koselleck, *Kritik und Krise*, 81.

25. Ibid., 98.

26. David Runciman notes that Hobbes defines hypocrisy as the endeavor to conceal "the vice of sedition behind the language of godliness, piety, and other supposed virtues." Yet hypocrisy tends to fall into self-deception, Hobbes believes, as the hypocrites soon start believing their false presentation of their own virtue. With time, the perpetrators of sedition come to believe that they are acting out of piety. See Runciman, *Political Hypocrisy: The Mask of Power from Hobbes to Orwell and Beyond* (Princeton, N.J.: Princeton University Press, 2008), 34–35.

27. Koselleck's account of how the prospering bourgeoisie remains blind to its own ambitions, however, turns on the notion that this class does in fact

want to translate its burgeoning social and economic prominence into political influence and, deep down, views itself as the bearer of political power, but formulates its relationship to the sovereign in the morally guided and disinterested critique of the exercise of power. This means it condemns that which it in reality strives for, namely the opportunity and capacity to rule over others, and remains removed from the insight into the existential rewards of power. Koselleck, *Kritik und Krise*, 99, 102.

28. For an affiliated interpretation of ressentiment in Friedrich Nietzsche's work, see Bernard Reginster, "Nietzsche on Ressentiment and Valuation," *Philosophy and Phenomenological Research* 57, no. 2 (1997): 281–305. The man of ressentiment is weak but preaches meekness as a value to enslave stronger and more dominant men. Yet if he succeeds in this enterprise, he may not fully enjoy his victory, for he comes to dominate others by preaching values contrary to domination.

29. La Vopa, "Conceiving a Public," 83. Kari Palonen writes that Koselleck faults Enlightenment thinkers for not understanding that the "competitive pluralism" of purposes is the very "mark of politics." See Palonen, "The History of Concepts as a Style of Political Theorizing: Quentin Skinner and Reinhart Koselleck's Subversion of Normative Political Theory," *European Journal of Political Theory* 1 (2002): 94.

30. Missfelder, "Die Gegenkraft und ihre Geschichte," 335.

31. La Vopa, "Conceiving a Public," 85.

32. Koselleck, *Kritik und Krise,* 81–82.

33. Ibid., 98.

34. Ibid., 102.

35. Ibid., 103.

36. Koselleck assumes that every political conflict is both reflected in and carried out by means of a semantic struggle, in which factions fight over designations. In later theoretical reflections on conceptual history, he asserts that political units of collective action define and sustain their distinct identities by coining neologisms and slogans that give shape to their projects and serve as rallying points. Given the deceptively unpolitical political agent he studies in *Critique and Crisis*, Koselleck does not so much analyze such a struggle as he tries to resume the fight. See Koselleck, *Vergangene Zukunft: Zur Semantik geschichtlicher Zeiten* (Frankfurt am Main: Suhrkamp, 1979), 112.

37. Koselleck does not lose sight of the historical and structural conditions that shape the critical project. He explains how the absolutist state, because of its rigorous separation of spheres, conjures up an adversary that cannot fail to misrecognize its challenge to the established rule. Yet the blame, accompanied by expressions of something close to contempt, falls exclusively on the intellectual members of the *bürgerliche Gesellschaft.* The study, it seems, does display polemical symptoms, because it lashes out against one figure in a drama that it simultaneously describes in terms of a historical process characterized by unwanted and unanticipated consequences.

38. Koselleck, *Kritik und Krise,* 47. Koselleck here supplies a quotation from John Locke.

39. Ibid.
40. Ibid., 42.
41. Ibid., 48.
42. Ibid., 136.
43. Ibid., 139.
44. Ibid.
45. Ibid.
46. Ibid.
47. Niklas Luhmann discusses political decisions and the paradoxical, even self-undermining nature of their communication. Every collectively binding decision must be communicated and presented *as binding* and, moreover, anchored in something that renders it legitimate (such as references to authority or collective will). Yet precisely because the decision must be communicated, it draws attention to itself as a recent decision and thus, however faintly, invokes the possibility of alternative routes. See Luhmann, *Gesellschaftsstruktur und Semantik: Studien zur Wissensoziologie,* 4:106.
48. Koselleck, *Kritik und Krise*, 138.
49. Steve Fuller, *The New Sociological Imagination* (London: Sage, 2006), 115.
50. Hannah Arendt, *Essays in Understanding 1930–1954: Formation, Exile, and Totalitarianism,* ed. Jerome Kohn (New York: Schocken, 1994), 423–27.
51. Koselleck seems to have trouble understanding an era no longer characterized by the primacy of politics. See Klaus von Beyme, *Theorie der Politik im 20. Jahrhundert: Von der Moderne zur Postmoderne,* expanded ed. (Frankfurt am Main: Suhrkamp, 2007), 91.
52. Koselleck, *Kritik und Krise*, 124.
53. Hannah Arendt, *The Human Condition*, 40.
54. Friedrich Balke, "Kreuzzug und Kartei: Carl Schmitt und die Juden," *Neue Rundschau* 111, no. 3 (2000): 171.
55. Karl Popper famously makes a distinction between social science and conspiracy theory: "The characteristic problems of the social science arise only out of our wish to know the *unintended consequences*, and more especially the *unwanted consequences* which may arise if we do certain things." See Popper, *Conjectures and Refutations: The Growth of Scientific Knowledge* (New York: Basic Books, 1962), 124–25.

Chapter Five

1. J. M. Bernstein, *Recovering Ethical Life: Jürgen Habermas and the Future of Critical Theory* (New York: Columbia University Press, 1995), 40.
2. Pieter Duvenage, *Habermas and Aesthetics: The Limits of Communicative Reason* (Cambridge: Polity, 2003), 12.
3. Gopal Balakrishnan, "Overcoming Emancipation," *New Left Review* 19 (January–February 2003): 117. To indicate Habermas's singular position in West German intellectual life, based on his entire oeuvre, Stefan Müller-Doom gathers a number of appreciative epithets given to Habermas, such as the

"Hegel of the Federal Republic." See Müller-Doom, *Jürgen Habermas* (Frankfurt am Main: Suhrkamp, 2008), 121.

4. Specter, *Habermas*, 203. Specter shows that Habermas's achievement involved not only bringing an intellectually conservative Germany closer to Western traditions of liberalism and democracy, but also persuading German left-wing intellectuals of the values of a liberal constitutional order.

5. Ibid., 207.

6. Georg Stanitzek, *Essay—BRD* (Berlin: Vorwerk 8, 2011), 21.

7. See Strum, "Bibliography of the Concept Öffentlichkeit."

8. Nancy Fraser, a persistent but very sympathetic critic of Habermas, summarizes the critical responses to Habermas in her entry in a recent Habermas handbook. In the German-speaking and Anglophone academic world, historians and political theorists have criticized Habermas's idealized notion of the bourgeois public sphere for its inherently exclusive, discriminatory, homogeneous, or (nationally bound) unitary character. See Fraser, "Theorie der Öffentlichkeit," in *Habermas Handbuch*, ed. Hauke Brunkhorst et al., trans. Nikolaus Gramm (Stuttgart: J. B. Metzler, 2009), 148–55. For a comment on the more recent "agonistic" left-wing critiques of Habermas, see John S. Brady, "No Contest? Assessing the Agonistic Critiques of Jürgen Habermas's Theory of the Public Sphere," *Philosophy and Social Criticism* 30, no. 3 (2004): 331–54.

9. See Hohendahl, "Recasting the Public Sphere," 30.

10. See Craig Calhoun, "Civil Society and the Public Sphere," *Public Culture* 5, no. 2 (1993): 271.

11. Seligman, "The Fragile Ethical Vision of Civil Society," 144.

12. Jürgen Habermas, "Verrufener Fortschritt—verkanntes Jahrhundert," *Merkur* 147 (1960): 470.

13. See ibid., 477.

14. Habermas repeatedly returned to the pernicious influence of Carl Schmitt and Arnold Gehlen. Max Pensky writes that Heidegger, Schmitt, Jünger, and Gehlen "appear again and again in his [Habermas's] political writings with such frequency and regularity that one is tempted to speak in terms of a response to a trauma." See Pensky, "Jürgen Habermas and the Antinomies of the Intellectual," in *Habermas: A Critical Reader*, ed. Peter Dews (Oxford: Blackwell, 1999), 221.

15. When he examined the situation in the postwar Federal Republic of Germany in an effort to see how modern liberal nations measured up to this inheritance, Habermas could also draw on the work of Carl Schmitt. Habermas described a contemporary Germany run by rival interest groups that made compromises behind closed doors, unavailable to any transparent, public, and rational discussion of policies. This was a description culled from Schmitt's diagnosis of parliamentary democracy, but here again, Habermas granted the description not to discredit the ideal but to call for its restoration as a guiding principle. See Ellen Kennedy, "Carl Schmitt und die 'Frankfurter Schule': Deutsche Liberalismuskritik im 20. Jahrhundert," *Geschichte und Gesellschaft: Zeitschrift für historische Sozialwissenschaft* 12, no. 3 (1986): 402.

16. In the *Merkur* review of Koselleck, Habermas writes about the bourgeois "Idee, daß politische Autorität im Medium einer solchen Öffentlichkeit in rationale sich auflösen, Herrschaft in ihrem Aggregatzustand sich wandeln würde" ("Verrufener Fortschritt," 472). In *The Structural Transformation of the Public Sphere*, one finds a very similar formulation: "Die 'Herrschaft' der Öffentlichkeit ist ihrer eigenen Idee zufolge eine Ordnung, in der sich Herrschaft überhaupt auflöst" (*Strukturwandel,* 153).

17. In their overview of the notion of civil society in modern political theory, Andrew Arato and Jean Cohen points to Habermas's relocation of political action to modern bourgeois society as the gist of his contribution. Contrary to Arendt and others, Habermas inserts the emergence and decline of a new type of public sphere into the history of modern society. See Arato and Cohen, *Civil Society and Political Theory* (Cambridge, Mass.: MIT Press, 1992), 211.

18. Thornhill, *Political Theory in Modern Germany,* 16.

19. Craig Calhoun, "Introduction: Habermas and the Public Sphere," in *Habermas and the Public Sphere*, ed. Craig Calhoun (Cambridge, Mass.: MIT Press, 1992), 6.

20. Interestingly, left-wing authors who criticize Habermas's conception of the bourgeois public sphere come quite close to Koselleck's conception of covert rule. Claiming that the public sphere is in fact very exclusive and prohibits nonbourgeois themes and approaches to societal problems, they view it as a medium of hegemony. Nancy Fraser sums up and endorses this view of the bourgeoisie effecting a "shift from a repressive mode of domination to a hegemonic one, from rule based primarily on acquiescence to superior force to rule based primarily on consent supplemented with some measure of repression." See Fraser, "Rethinking the Public Sphere: A Contribution to the Critique of Actually Existing Democracy," in *Habermas and the Public Sphere,* ed. Craig Calhoun (Cambridge, Mass.: MIT Press, 1991), 117.

21. Habermas, *Strukturwandel*, 152.

22. The notion that the bourgeoisie generally does not want to assume political power is widespread. Joseph Schumpeter writes: "We have seen that the industrialists and merchants, as far as they are entrepreneurs, also fill a function of leadership. But economic leadership of this type does not really expand, like the medieval lord's military leadership, into the leadership of nations." See Joseph Schumpeter, *Capitalism, Socialism, and Democracy* (New York: Harper & Brothers, 1942), 137.

23. Habermas, *Public Sphere*, 27.

24. As Jens Greve notes in his introduction to Habermas's thought, power in society does not have one defined and stable location but is generated in the dispersed interactions between institutional entities such as the state and the public sphere. See Greve, *Jürgen Habermas: Eine Einführung* (Konstanz: UTB, 2009), 152.

25. Andrew Arato and Jean Cohen write that for Habermas, bourgeois society aims not at the destruction of the existing state (which is Koselleck's suspicion) but at a "new form of political dualism in which a political public

sphere would control the public authority of the modern state." See Arato and Cohen, *Civil Society*, 216.

26. Amanda Anderson, *The Way We Argue Now: A Study in the Cultures of Theory* (Princeton, N.J.: Princeton University Press, 2006), 151.

27. Bernstein, *Recovering Ethical Life*, 48.

28. Habermas, *Strukturwandel*, 91.

29. Ibid., 97.

30. Nancy Fraser's criticism of Habermas, which builds on and includes the critical argument of several historians, takes aim at precisely this point in Habermas. Fraser claims that the bracketing rather than elimination of social status in special discursive arenas is never quite sufficient and that relations of subordination continue to infect formally inclusive and egalitarian discourse. See Fraser, "Rethinking the Public Sphere," 120.

31. Walter Reese-Schäfer points out that any group gathering in a salon or a coffeehouse may have been quite exclusive but that the bourgeois public as a whole could not be, given that the general themes, pieces of news, and artworks that people talked about could not be protected from discussion by others. No authority could contain the unbound circulation of commodified artworks and news to be discussed. Every small group thus knew that it found itself in a much larger context of conversation, something that prevented the illusion of total exclusivity. See Reese-Schäfer, *Jürgen Habermas* (Frankfurt am Main: Campus, 2001), 40.

32. Ernest Gellner, *Plough, Sword and Book: The Structure of Human History* (Chicago: University of Chicago Press, 1988), 85.

33. Werner Jung notes that the sociologist Georg Simmel viewed the practice of *Geselligkeit* as a miniature image of an ideal society. See Jung, *Georg Simmel zur Einführung* (Hamburg: Junius, 1990), 91–93.

34. Jonathan Hess, *Reconstituting the Body Politic: Enlightenment, Public Culture, and the Invention of Aesthetic Autonomy* (Detroit: Wayne State University Press, 1999), 115.

35. Habermas, *Strukturwandel*, 109.

36. For a distinction between conversation and deliberation, see Simone Chambers, "Rhetoric and the Public Sphere: Has Deliberative Democracy Abandoned Mass Democracy?" *Political Theory* 37, no. 3 (2009): 323–50.

37. The literary scholar Fritz Breithaupt offers an amusing take on the conventional image of the weak and pallid bourgeoisie as a fitting candidate for political rule. Breithaupt claims that in each story of the rise of the bourgeoisie, including Habermas's central treatment of the bourgeois public sphere, a weak man appears—the middle-class man—and makes an argument for why his weakness is in fact an advantage. See Breithaupt, "The Invention of Trauma in German Romanticism," *Critical Inquiry* 32, no. 1 (2005): 81.

38. In an article from 1970, Niklas Luhmann argued that the problem with the small circles of conversation of which Habermas wrote was precisely that they blunted or did not allow for the distinction between friends and enemies. See Luhmann, "Öffentliche Meinung," *Politische Vierteljahresschrift* 11 (1970): 4–5.

39. Arato and Cohen write that Habermas "quite deliberately constructed his model of the public sphere in the structural position that Arendt considered the very negation of public life, the intermediary or mixed realm between the private sphere and state, which she called 'society' " (*Civil Society*, 221).

40. Habermas, *Strukturwandel*, 65.

41. Lewis Coser, *Men of Ideas: A Sociologist's View* (New York: Free Press, 1965), 20–21.

42. In a consideration of recent debates on the relative merits of deliberative processes versus aggregative techniques, Deborah Perron Tollefsen writes: "High social cohesion . . . provides psychological benefits to group members. But it is this unified agency that often contributes to the suppression of dissent within the context of group deliberation and hence to poor decision making." See Tollefsen, "Group Deliberation, Social Cohesion, and Scientific Teamwork: Is There Room for Dissent?" *Episteme: A Journal of Social Epistemology* 3, no. 1 (2006): 42.

43. To use a term suggested by the legal scholar Heather K. Gerken, one can choose to promote second-order diversity (diversity of opinions at the level of the entire public sphere) rather than first-order diversity (diversity within every small-scale group): "Second-order diversity involves variation among decision-making bodies, not within them. It favors *inter*organizational heterogeneity, not *intra*organizational heterogeneity." See Gerken, "Second-Order Diversity," *Harvard Law Review* 118, no. 4 (2005): 1102–3.

44. Hannah Arendt, *The Human Condition,* 38.

45. Ibid., 58.

46. Ibid., 40.

47. Arendt would also be quite skeptical of the idea of "public opinion" as the syncretism of individual voices that takes shape when multiple arguments from various sources are all subjected to the same standard of rationality. For her, the formation of one unified "public opinon" puts an end to the plurality of opinions, without which there is no politics. If anything, the notion of a "public opinion" reflects the unity of state sovereignty and thus does not represent a real advance over state coercion.

48. In a recent article on mass communication, Habermas speaks of "the co-operative search of deliberating citizens for solutions to political problems" and accords an "epistemic dimension" to such discourse. See Habermas, "Political Communication in Media Society: Does Democracy Still Enjoy an Epistemic Dimension?" *Communication Theory* 16, no. 4 (2006): 413.

49. In conclusion to his list of deficiencies in the contemporary public sphere, Habermas writes: "The kind of political communication we know from our so-called media society goes against the grain of the normative requirements of deliberative politics" (ibid., 420).

50. The concept "culture industry" was coined by Theodor W. Adorno and Max Horkheimer in their work *Dialektik der Aufklärung: Philosophische Fragmente,* vol. 3 of *Gesammelte Schriften*, ed. Rolf Tiedemann (Frankfurt am Main: Suhrkamp, 1981). Building on this work, the essayist Hans-Magnus

Enzensberger coined the term "consciousness industry" in the introduction to his book *Einzelheiten I* (Frankfurt am Main: Suhrkamp, 1962). Enzensberger's collection of essays featured analyses of television news, the language of news magazines, the pocketbook phenomenon, etc.

51. This evolution was largely inspired by the interwar writings of Walter Benjamin and Bertolt Brecht on film and radio. Again, Hans-Magnus Enzensberger figured as a facilitator of this debate with his "Baukasten zu einer Theorie der Medien," *Kursbuch* 20 (1970): 159–86.

52. Later interventions have stressed the emancipatory potential of innovative media use, while retaining and refining the notion that the particular possibilities and constraints of channels of communication determine the limits of what can be said, thought, and conceived. The focus of many left-wing intellectuals in the Federal Republic is encapsulated in the following title of an article by the sociologist Oskar Negt: "Mass Media: Tools of Domination or Instruments of Liberation?" trans. Leslie Adelson, *New German Critique* 14 (Spring 1978): 61–80.

53. Jon Elster writes that "It *isn't done*" is "a revealing phrase that often accompanies social norms." See Elster, "Social Norms and Economic Theory," *Journal of Economic Perspectives* 3, no. 4 (1989): 110. A German equivalent would be "Das gehört sich nicht."

54. In recent academic debates, theorists have tended to distinguish between politics (as usual) and a more elusive category, "the political." In a dense essay that reviews the thought of Jacques Rancière and Giorgio Agamben, Joseph Vogl distinguishes politics as the game played within an already established frame of relationships from the political as the disruptive moment in which (or the subversive activities through which) this frame is interrogated and undermined. See Vogl, "Asyl des Politischen: Zur Topologie politischer Gelegenheiten," in *Das Politische: Figurenlehren des sozialen Körpers nach der Romantik*, ed. Uwe Hebekus, Ethel Matala de Mazza, and Albrecht Koschorke (Munich: Wilhelm Fink, 2003), 38. In her analysis of the use of the noun "the political" in Arendt-inspired circles of political theorists in American postwar academia, Emily Hauptmann suggests that those who employed the neologism wanted to distinguish political theory as a sustained reflection on a distinct kind of human potential from an increasingly technocratic political science geared toward research that could support and evaluate specific government policies. See Hauptmann, "A Local History of 'the Political,'" *Political Theory* 32, no. 1 (2004): 34–60.

55. Malcolm Bull has pointed out the similarities between Arendt and Schmitt and emphasized their shared commitment to political life defined by disruptive conflict. See Bull, "The Social and the Political," 678.

56. For an accessible analysis of society's need for whistle-blowers and contrarians, see Cass Sunstein, *Why Societies Need Dissent* (Cambridge, Mass.: Harvard University Press, 2003).

57. Bull, "The Social and the Political," 678.

58. Villa, "Hannah Arendt," 190–91.

59. James Phillips writes: "The plurality that composes the public space is not the sum of unitary human beings. Just as plurality cannot be subsumed under any unity, it cannot be analysed into unitary beings. It is a question of neither an identifiable whole nor identifiable parts. Totalitarianism is, for Arendt, evidence that the mass convocation of the lonely, each in his or her isolated unitarity, is insufficient to inaugurate the volatile life of the political." See Phillips, "From Radical to Banal Evil: Hannah Arendt Against the Justification of the Unjustifiable," *International Journal of Philosophical Studies* 12, no. 2 (2004): 144.

60. Todd Hedrick, *Rawls and Habermas: Reason, Pluralism, and the Claims of Political Philosophy* (Stanford, Calif.: Stanford University Press, 2010), 185.

61. Ibid., 12.

62. Specter, *Habermas*, 180.

Chapter Six

1. Konrad Jarausch, *After Hitler: Recivilizing Germans 1945–1995* (Oxford: Oxford University Press, 2006), 14.

2. Theodor W. Adorno, *Critical Models: Interventions and Catchwords*, trans. Henry W. Pickford (New York: Columbia University Press, 2005), 90.

3. Alexander Mitscherlich, *Hemmen Tabus die Demokratisierung der deutschen Gesellschaft? Bergedorfer Protokolle,* vol. 12 (Hamburg: G. Schenk, 1965).

4. Jan-Werner Müller, *Another Country: German Intellectuals, Unification, and National Identity* (New Haven, Conn.: Yale University Press, 2000), 31.

5. Koepnick, "Culture in the Shadow of Trauma," 713.

6. For a depiction of the German retreat into the familial sphere during the 1950s, see Axel Schildt, "Bürgerliche Gesellschaft und kleinbürgerliche Geborgenheit: Zur Mentalität im westdeutschen Wiederaufbau der 50er Jahre," in *Kleinbürger: Zur Kulturgeschichte des begrentzten Bewußtseins*, ed. Thomas Althaus (Tübingen: Attempto, 2001), 295–312.

7. Van Laak, *Gespräche in der Sicherheit des Schweigens,* 63–64.

8. Habermas, *Public Sphere*, 202.

9. The immediate postwar period was a time of catch-up growth: countries quickly returned to their own potential levels of output. See Barry Eichengreen, *The European Economy Since 1945: Coordinated Capitalism and Beyond* (Princeton, N.J.: Princeton University Press, 2006), 2.

10. Axel Schildt and Detlef Siegfried, *Deutsche Kulturgeschichte: Die Bundesrepublik von 1945 bis zur Gegenwart* (Munich: Hanser, 2009), 105.

11. Tony Judt, *Postwar: A History of Europe Since 1945* (London: Penguin, 2005), 226.

12. Franz Fühmann, *Das Judenauto* (Rostock: VEB Hinstorff, 1979), 165.

13. For a comparative study of consumption in East and West Germany, see the essays in David F. Crew, ed., *Consuming Germany in the Cold War* (Oxford: Berg, 2003).

14. Judt, *Postwar*, 346.

15. Nathaus, *Organisierte Geselligkeit,* 255.

16. Wolfgang Zapf, *Wandlungen der deutschen Elite: Ein Zirkulationsmodell deutscher Führungsgruppen 1919–1961* (Munich: Piper, 1966), 200.

17. Eckart Conze, "Eine bürgerliche Republik? Bürgertum und Bürgerlichkeit in der westdeutschen Nachkriegsgesellschaft," *Geschichte und Gesellschaft* 30, no. 3 (2004): 534–35.

18. "Since the end of the war," Alexander and Margarete Mitscherlich write, "restoration of the economy is the average German's pet concern." See Mitscherlich and Mitscherlich, *The Inability to Mourn: Principles of Collective Behavior,* trans. Beverley R. Placzek (New York: Grove, 1975), 9. The author Martin Walser called West Germany a state designed to fit a petit bourgeois mentality, for which material well-being is all that matters. See Walser, *Die Alternative oder brauchen wir eine neue Regierung* (Hamburg: Rowohlt, 1961).

19. Arnold Gehlen, "Soziologische Voraussetzungen im gegenwärtigen Staat," in *Rechstaatlichkeit und Sozialstaatlichkeit: Aufsätze und Essays,* ed. Ernst Forsthoff (Darmstadt: Wissenschaftliche Buchgesellschaft, 1968).

20. Cited in Grunenberg, *Die Wundertäter,* 261.

21. Habermas, *Public Sphere,* 164.

22. See Thornhill, *Political Theory in Modern Germany,* 140–41.

23. Habermas, *Public Sphere,* 210.

24. Sheldon Wolin, *The Presence of the Past: Essays on the State and the Constitution* (Baltimore: Johns Hopkins University Press, 1989), 154.

25. I draw the following picture of West Germany from Tony Judt's description of the postwar situation in *Postwar*, 265–77. His overview of the cultural and political conditions in West Germany appears in the chapter titled "The Politics of Stability."

26. Alexander Kluge, *Case Histories*, trans. Leila Vennewitz (New York: Holmes & Meier, 1988).

27. Much of the theoretically guided commentary on Kluge has developed a vocabulary of the "cut" to work out the analogies between his storytelling and techniques associated with film. Readers have argued that Kluge's involvement with cinema predisposed him toward a poetics in which the author splices heterogeneous material to produce an aggregate of fragments and semantically disparate codes. For a representative statement on Kluge's theory and practice of montage, see Miriam Hansen's "Alexander Kluge: Crossings Between Film, Literature, Critical Theory," in *Film und Literatur: Literarische Texte und der neue deutsche Film*, ed. Sigrid Bauschinger, Susan L. Cocalis, and Henry A. Lea (Berlin: Francke, 1984).

28. S. Jonathan Wiesen, "The Modern Guild: Rotary Clubs and Bourgeois Renewal in the Aftermath of National Socialism," in *Conflict, Catastrophe, and Continuity: Essays on Modern German History*, ed. Frank Biess, Mark Roseman, and Hanna Schissler (New York: Berghahn, 2007), 310.

29. Rotary incidentally fits the current conception of a society sustained and invigorated by civic, nonprofit voluntary work of people in small-scale organizations without the direction of the state. For a brief overview of this idea, see John Ehrenberg's introduction to his *Civil Society: The Critical History of an Idea* (New York: New York University Press, 1999), ix–xi.

30. Erik Werner, "Weg und Wille des Rotary Club: Regeln, Pflichte, Ziele," *Aral-Journal: Eine Vierteljahresschrift der BV-Aktiengesellschaft* 10 (1955): 7–8.

31. Ibid.

32. Wiesen summarizes this strain in his recent overview of the postwar history of West German Rotary. Rotarians were "self-avowed 'elites' who saw as their calling the infusion of universal ethical norms into West German Society." In regular meetings, they built a "collective self-image of the international bourgeois citizen, committed to an ethos of philanthropy and responsibility" ("The Modern Guild," 298). Of course, this project was greatly complicated by the Nazi legacy. The Nazi Party had banned the organization, but some Rotarians had made careers in the Third Reich.

33. Kluge, *Case Histories,* 138.

34. Ibid., 139.

35. Ibid., 140.

36. Ibid., 138–42.

37. I draw here on the sociologist Randall Collins. Collins does not restrict the use of the term "ritual" to religious occasions. Building on the works of Erving Goffman and Émile Durkheim, he instead supplies a wider definition applicable to a range of everyday situations, including small-scale conversations. According to him, interaction rituals have four main ingredients: two or more people are assembled, boundaries against outsiders are set, the participants focus their attention on a common object or activity, and they come to take part in a common emotional experience or mood. See Collins, *Interaction Ritual Chains* (Princeton, N.J.: Princeton University Press, 2004).

38. The Rotary meeting's character of identity-confirming ritual is of course only a problem if it is held up as the sole and universal form of interaction in society, or lauded as the reliable medium of rational argumentation. In their critique of Jürgen Habermas from 1972, *Öffentlichkeit und Erfahrung,* Alexander Kluge and his intellectual partner Oskar Negt would claim that a multiplicity of societal groups should be allowed and encouraged to convene in order for their members to share, validate, and collectively articulate the full range of their group-specific experiences. Rather than say that the typical site of bourgeois sociability was not the universally accessible arena it claimed to be, Negt and Kluge thus suggested a dispersal of society into multiple movements and groupings, free to develop their idiolects, elaborate their attitudes, or organize their previously suppressed and sensually lived collective identities. Specifically, they spoke of the *proletarian* public sphere, existing alongside a dominant bourgeois public sphere. See Alexander Kluge and Oskar Negt, *Öffentlichkeit und Erfahrung: Zur Organisationsanalyse von bürgerlicher und proletarischer Öffentlichkeit* (Frankfurt am Main: Suhrkamp, 1972). For a review of Kluge's and Negt's contribution to the discourse on the public sphere, see Miriam Hansen, "Unstable Mixtures, Dilated Spheres: Negt and Kluge's *The Public Sphere and Experience,* Twenty Years Later," *Public Culture* 5, no. 2 (1993): 179–212.

BIBLIOGRAPHY

Adloff, Frank. *Zivilgesellschaft: Theorie und politische Praxis*. Frankfurt am Main: Campus, 2005.

Adorno, Theodor W. *Critical Models: Interventions and Catchwords*. Translated by Henry W. Pickford. New York: Columbia University Press, 2005.

———. *Minima Moralia: Reflexionen aus dem beschädigten Leben*. Vol. 4 of *Gesammelte Schriften*, edited by Rolf Tiedemann. Frankfurt am Main: Suhrkamp, 2003.

Adorno, Theodor W., and Max Horkheimer. *Dialektik der Aufklärung: Philosophische Fragmente*. Vol. 3 of *Gesammelte Schriften*, edited by Rolf Tiedemann. Frankfurt am Main: Suhrkamp, 1981.

Ahbe, Thomas. "Der Kleinbürger als Froschkönig." In *Unsere Feinde: Konstruktionen des Anderen im Sozialismus*, 179–96. Edited by Silke Satjukow and Rainer Gries. Leipzig: Leipziger Universitätsverlag, 2005.

Albrecht, Clemens, et al., eds. *Die intellektuelle Gründung der Bundesrepublik: Eine Wirkungsgeschichte der Frankfurter Schule*. Frankfurt am Main: Campus, 1999.

Anderson, Amanda. *The Way We Argue Now: A Study in the Cultures of Theory*. Princeton, N.J.: Princeton University Press, 2006.

Angerman, Erich. "Das Auseinandertreten von 'Staat' und 'Gesellschaft' im Denken des 18. Jahrhunderts." In *Staat und Gesellschaft*, 109–30. Edited by Ernst-Wolfgang Böckenförde. Darmstadt: Wissenschaftliche Buchgesellschaft, 1976.

Arato, Andrew, and Jean L. Cohen. *Civil Society and Political Theory*. Cambridge, Mass.: MIT Press, 1992.

Arendt, Dieter. "Das Philistertum des 19. Jahrhunderts." *Der Monat* 21, no. 248 (1969): 33–49.

Arendt, Hannah. *Essays in Understanding 1930–1954: Formation, Exile, and Totalitarianism*. Edited by Jerome Kohn. New York: Schocken, 1994.

———. "Es gibt nur ein einziges Menschenrecht." *Die Wandlung* 4, no. 8 (December 1949): 754–77.

———. *The Human Condition*. Chicago: University of Chicago Press, 1958.

———. "Organisierte Schuld." *Die Wandlung* 1, no. 4 (April 1946): 333–44.

———. *The Origins of Totalitarianism*. New York: Meridian, 1958.

———. *Rahel Varnhagen: The Life of a Jewish Woman*. Translated by Richard and Clara Wilson. New York: Harcourt & Brace, 1974.

———. "Über den Imperialismus." *Die Wandlung* 1, no. 8 (August 1946): 650–66.

Arendt, Hannah, and Heinrich Blücher. *Within Four Walls: The Correspondence Between Hannah Arendt and Heinrich Blücher 1936–1968*. Edited by Lotte Köhler. Translated by Peter Constantine. New York: Harcourt, 1996.

Arendt, Hannah, and Karl Jaspers. *Briefwechsel 1926–1969*. Edited by Lotte Köhler and Hans Saner. Munich: Piper, 1985.

Assal, Paul, ed. *Erzählte Zeit—erzähltes Leben: Zehn Gespräche mit Zeitgenossen*. Bremen: Demin, 1999.

Bachmann, Ingeborg. *The Thirtieth Year: Stories by Ingeborg Bachmann*. Translated by Michael Bullock. New York: Holmes & Meier, 1987.

Baehr, Peter. *Hannah Arendt, Totalitarianism, and the Social Sciences*. Palo Alto, Calif.: Stanford University Press, 2010.

Bahners, Patrick. "Der Unterschichtenkerl." *Frankfurter Allgemeine Zeitung*, December 29, 2006, 39.

Baker, Gary L. "German National Character and the Relaxing American." *Germanic Review* 80, no. 2 (Spring 2005): 124–42.

Balakrishnan, Gopal. *The Enemy: An Intellectual Portrait of Carl Schmitt*. London: Verso, 2000.

———. "The Oracle of Post-Democracy." *New Left Review* 13 (January–February 2002): 152–60.

———. "Overcoming Emancipation." *New Left Review* 19 (January–February 2003): 115–28.

———. "States of War." *New Left Review* 36 (November–December 2005): 5–32.

Balke, Friedrich. *Der Staat nach seinem Ende: Die Versuchung Carl Schmitts*. Munich: Wilhelm Fink, 1996.

———. "Gesetz und Urteil: Zur Aktualität einer Problemstellung bei Carl Schmitt." In *Gesetz und Urteil: Beiträge zu einer Theorie des Politischen*, 35–56. Edited by Joseph Vogl. Weimar: Verlag und Datenbank für Geisteswissenschaften, 2003.

———. "Kreuzzug und Kartei: Carl Schmitt und die Juden." *Neue Rundschau* 111, no. 3 (2000): 168–79.

Beech, Dave, and John Roberts, eds. *The Philistine Controversy*. London: Verso, 2002.

Benhabib, Seyla. "Review of *Habermas: An Intellectual Biography*." *Constellations* 18, no. 4 (2011): 589–95.

Bennington, Geoffrey. *Sententiousness and the Novel: Laying Down the Law in Eighteenth-Century French Fiction*. Cambridge: Cambridge University Press, 1985.

Bernstein, J. M. *Recovering Ethical Life: Jürgen Habermas and the Future of Critical Theory*. New York: Columbia University Press, 1995.

Beyme, Klaus von. *Theorie der Politik im 20. Jahrhundert: Von der Moderne zur Postmoderne*. Expanded ed. Frankfurt am Main: Suhrkamp, 2007.

Blanchot, Maurice. *The Book to Come*. Translated by Charlotte Mandel. Stanford, Calif.: Stanford University Press, 2003.

Bösch, Michael. "Pluralität und Identität bei Hannah Arendt." *Zeitschrift für philosophische Forschung* 53, no. 4 (1999): 569–88.

Brady, John S. "No Contest? Assessing the Agonistic Critiques of Jürgen Habermas's Theory of the Public Sphere." *Philosophy and Social Criticism* 30, no. 3 (2004): 331–54.

Breithaupt, Fritz. "The Invention of Trauma in German Romanticism." *Critical Inquiry* 32, no. 1 (2005): 77–101.

Brockmann, Stephen. *German Literary Culture at the Zero Hour.* Rochester, N.Y.: Camden House, 2004.

Brown, Wendy. *Regulating Aversion: Tolerance in the Age of Identity and Empire.* Princeton, N.J.: Princeton University Press, 2006.

Bude, Heinz. *Bilanz der Nachfolge: Die Bundesrepublik und der Nationalsozialismus.* Frankfurt am Main: Suhrkamp, 1992.

Bude, Heinz, Joachim Fischer, and Bernd Kauffmann, eds. *Bürgerlichkeit ohne Bürgertum: In welchem Land leben wir*? Munich: Wilhelm Fink, 2010.

Bull, Malcolm. "The Limits of Multitude." *New Left Review* 35 (September–October 2005): 19–39.

———. "The Social and the Political." *South Atlantic Quarterly* 104, no. 4 (Fall 2005): 675–92.

Calhoun, Craig. "Civil Society and the Public Sphere." *Public Culture* 5, no. 2 (1993): 267–80.

———. "Introduction: Habermas and the Public Sphere." In *Habermas and the Public Sphere,* 1–48. Edited by Craig Calhoun. Cambridge, Mass.: MIT Press, 1992.

Chambers, Simone. "Rhetoric and the Public Sphere: Has Deliberative Democracy Abandoned Mass Democracy?" *Political Theory* 37, no. 3 (2009): 323–50.

Cofalla, Sabine, Friedrich Christian Delius, and Jürgen Schutte. "Gespräch über die Gruppe 47." In *Die Gruppe 47 in Bildern und Texten,* 188–200. Edited by Toni Richter. Cologne: Kipenheuer & Witsch, 1997.

Collins, Randall. *Interaction Ritual Chains.* Princeton, N.J.: Princeton University Press, 2004.

Conze, Eckart. "Eine bürgerliche Republik? Bürgertum und Bürgerlichkeit in der westdeutschen Nachkriegsgesellschaft." *Geschichte und Gesellschaft* 30, no. 3 (2004): 527–42.

Coser, Lewis. *Greedy Institutions: Patterns of Undivided Commitment.* New York: Free Press, 1974.

———. *Men of Ideas: A Sociologist's View.* New York: Free Press, 1965.

Crew, David F., ed. *Consuming Germany in the Cold War.* Oxford: Berg, 2003.

Curtius, Ernst Robert. *Europäische Literatur und Lateinische Mittelalter.* Bern: A. Francke, 1948.

———. "Goethe oder Jaspers?" In *Goethe im Urteil seiner Kritiker: Dokumente zur Wirkungsgeschichte Goethes in Deutschland,* 304–7. Edited by Karl Robert Mandelkow. Vol. 4. Munich: C. H. Beck, 1984.

Dagerman, Stig. *German Autumn.* Translated by Robin Fulton Macpherson. Minneapolis: University of Minnesota Press, 2011.

Dahrendorf, Ralf. *Gesellschaft und Demokratie in Deutschland.* Munich: Piper, 1965.

Deuber-Mankowsky, Astrid. "Nothing Is Political, Everything Can Be Politicized: On the Concept of the Political in Michel Foucault and Carl Schmitt." Translated by Jennifer Bierich and David Pan. *Telos* 148 (Spring 2008): 135–61.

Dews, Peter, ed. *Habermas: A Critical Reader.* Oxford: Blackwell, 1999.

Dudek, Peter. "'Vergangenheitsbewältigung': Zur Problematik eines umstrittenen Begriffs." *Aus Politik und Zeitgeschichte* 3, no. 1 (1992): 44–53.

Duvenage, Pieter. *Habermas and Aesthetics: The Limits of Communicative Reason.* Cambridge: Polity, 2003.

Dyzenhaus, David. *Legality and Legitimacy: Carl Schmitt, Hans Kelsen and Hermann Heller in Weimar.* Oxford: Clarendon, 1997.

Eberan, Barbro. *Die Debatte um die Schuldfrage 1945–1949.* Munich: Minerva, 1983.

Ehrenberg, John. *Civil Society: The Critical History of an Idea.* New York: New York University Press, 1999.

Eichengreen, Barry. *The European Economy Since 1945: Coordinated Capitalism and Beyond.* Princeton, N.J.: Princeton University Press, 2006.

Elster, Jon. "Patterns of Causal Analysis in Tocqueville's *Democracy in America.*" *Rationality and Society* 3, no. 3 (1991): 277–97.

———. "Social Norms and Economic Theory." *Journal of Economic Perspectives* 3, no. 4 (1989): 99–117.

Emden, Christian J. "The Brilliant Fascist: Carl Schmitt and the Limits of Liberalism." *H-German Net Reviews.* June 2005. http://www.h-net.org/reviews/showrev.php?id=10599.

Enzensberger, Hans-Magnus. "Baukasten zu einer Theorie der Medien." *Kursbuch* 20 (1970): 159–86.

———. *Einzelheiten I.* Frankfurt am Main: Suhrkamp, 1962.

Ewald, François. "Die Versicherungs-Gesellschaft." In *Politik in der Risikogesellschaft,* 288–301. Edited by Ulrich Beck. Translated by Mechthild and Thomas Blanke. Frankfurt am Main: Suhrkamp, 1991.

Fischer, Bernard, and Thomas Dietzel. "Zur Geschichte der deutschsprachigen Literaturzeitschriften 1945–1970." In *Deutsche Literarische Zeitschriften 1945–1970: Ein Repertorium,* 1:1–19. Edited by Bernard Fischer and Thomas Dietel. Munich: K. G. Saur, 1992.

Foucault, Michel. *The Birth of Biopolitics: Lectures at Collège de France 1978–1979.* Translated by Graham Burchell. Houndmills: Palgrave Macmillan, 2008.

———. "The Dangerous Individual." In *Politics, Philosophy, Culture: Interviews and Other Writings 1977–1984,* 125–51. Edited by Lawrence D. Kritzman. Translated by Alain Baudot and Jane Couchman. New York: Routledge, 1988.

———. *Discipline and Punish: The Birth of the Prison.* Translated by Alan Sheridan. New York: Vintage, 1977.

Fraser, Nancy. "Rethinking the Public Sphere: A Contribution to the Critique of Actually Existing Democracy." In *Habermas and the Public Sphere,* 109–42. Edited by Craig Calhoun. Cambridge, Mass.: MIT Press, 1991.

———. "Theorie der Öffentlichkeit." In *Habermas Handbuch,* 148–55. Edited by Hauke Brunkhorst et al. Translated by Nikolaus Gramm. Stuttgart: J. B. Metzler, 2009.

Frei, Norbert. *1945 und wir: Das Dritte Reich im Bewußtsein der Deutschen.* Munich: C. H. Beck, 2005.

Freimüller, Tobias. *Alexander Mitscherlich: Gesellschaftsdiagnose und Psychoanalyse nach Hitler.* Göttingen: Wallstein, 2007.

Frow, John. "Genre Worlds: The Discursive Shaping of Knowledge." *Arena Journal* 23 (2005): 129–46.

———. "'Reproducibles, Rubrics, and Everything You Need': Genre Theory Today." *PMLA* 122, no. 5 (October 2007): 1626–34.

Fühmann, Franz. *Das Judenauto.* Rostock: VEB Hinstorff, 1979.

Fuhrmann, Helmut. *Sechs Studien zur Goethe-Rezeption.* Würzburg: Königshausen & Neumann, 2002.

Fuller, Steve. *Kuhn vs. Popper: The Struggle for the Soul of Science.* Cambridge: Icon, 2003.

———. *The New Sociological Imagination.* London: Sage, 2006.

———. *Thomas Kuhn: A Philosophical History for Our Times.* Chicago: University of Chicago Press, 2000.

Furet, François. *Das Ende der Illusion: Der Kommunismus im 20. Jahrhundert.* Translated by Karla Bartsch et al. Munich: Piper, 1996.

Gehlen, Arnold. "Soziologische Voraussetzungen im gegenwärtigen Staat." In *Rechstaatlichkeit und Sozialstaatlichkeit: Aufsätze und Essays,* 321–39. Edited by Ernst Forsthoff. Darmstadt: Wissenschaftliche Buchgesellschaft, 1968.

Gellner, Ernest. *Plough, Sword and Book: The Structure of Human History.* Chicago: University of Chicago Press, 1988.

Gerhardt, Uta. *Soziologie der Stunde Null: Zur Gesellschaftskonzeption des Amerikanischen Besatzungsregimes in Deutschland 1944–1945/1946.* Frankfurt am Main: Suhrkamp, 2005.

Gerken, Heather K. "Second-Order Diversity." *Harvard Law Review* 118, no. 4 (2005): 1099–1103.

Gertenbach, Lars. *Die Kultivierung des Marktes: Foucault und die Gouvernementalität des Neoliberalismus.* Berlin: Parodos, 2008.

Göktürk, Deniz, David Gramling, and Anton Kaes, eds. *Germany in Transit: Nation and Migration, 1955–2005.* Berkeley: University of California Press, 2007.

Greve, Jens. *Jürgen Habermas: Eine Einführung.* Konstanz: UTB, 2009.

Gross, Raphael. *Carl Schmitt und die Juden: Eine deutsche Rechtslehre.* Frankfurt am Main: Suhrkamp, 2000.

———. *Carl Schmitt and the Jews: The "Jewish Question," the Holocaust, and German Legal Theory.* Translated by Joel Golb. Madison: University of Wisconsin Press, 2007.

Grunenberg, Nina. *Die Wundertäter: Netzwerke der deutschen Wirtschaft 1942 bis 1966.* Munich: Siedler, 2006.

Habermas, Jürgen. *Kleine politische Schriften I–IV.* Frankfurt am Main: Suhrkamp, 1981.

———. "Political Communication in Media Society: Does Democracy Still Enjoy an Epistemic Dimension?" *Communication Theory* 16, no. 4 (2006): 411–26.

———. *The Structural Transformation of the Public Sphere: An Inquiry into a Category of Bourgeois Society.* Translated by Thomas Burger. Cambridge, Mass.: MIT Press, 1989.

———. *Strukturwandel der Öffentlichkeit: Untersuchungen zu einer Kategorie der bürgerlichen Gesellschaft.* Neuwied: Hermann Luchterhand, 1962.

———. "Verrufener Fortschritt—verkanntes Jahrhundert." *Merkur* 147 (1960): 468–77.

Hacke, Jens. *Die Bundesrepublik als Idee: Zur Legitimationsbedürftigkeit politischer Ordnung.* Hamburg: Hamburger Edition, 2009.

Hahn, Alois. "Identität und Selbstthematisierung." In *Selbstthematisierung und Selbstzeugnis: Bekenntnis und Geständnis,* 9–25. Edited by Alois Hahn and Volker Kapp. Frankfurt am Main: Suhrkamp, 1987.

———. "Zur Soziologie der Beichte und anderer Formen institutionalisierter Bekenntnisse: Selbstthematisierung und Zivilisationsprozess." *Kölner Zeitschrift für Soziologie und Sozialpsychologie* 3, no. 34 (1982): 407–34.

Hamacher, Werner. "The Right to Have Rights (Four-and-a-Half Remarks)." Translated by Kirk Wetters. *South Atlantic Quarterly* 102, no. 3 (2004): 343–56.

Hansen, Miriam. "Alexander Kluge: Crossings Between Film, Literature, Critical Theory." In *Film und Literatur: Literarische Texte und der neue deutsche Film,* 169–96. Edited by Sigrid Bauschinger, Susan L. Cocalis, and Henry A. Lea. Berlin: Francke, 1984.

———. "Unstable Mixtures, Dilated Spheres: Negt and Kluge's *The Public Sphere and Experience,* Twenty Years Later." *Public Culture* 5, no. 2 (1993): 179–212.

"Hat der deutsche Bürger ausgespielt? Eine Neujahrsumfrage der Frankfurter Allgemeine Zeitung." *Frankfurter Allgemeine Zeitung,* December 30, 1950, 10.

Hauptmann, Emily. "A Local History of 'the Political.'" *Political Theory* 32, no. 1 (2004): 34–60.

Haverkamp, Anselm. *Latenzzeit: Wissen im Nachkrieg.* Berlin: Kadmos, 2004.

Hay, Gerhard, Hartmut Rambaldo, and Joachim W. Storck, eds. *"Als der Krieg zu Ende war": Literarisch-politische Publizistik 1945–1950.* Stuttgart: Ernst Klett, 1973.

Hayek, F. A. *The Road to Serfdom.* Edited by Bruce Caldwell. Chicago: University of Chicago Press, 2007.

Hedrick, Todd. *Rawls and Habermas: Reason, Pluralism, and the Claims of Political Philosophy.* Stanford, Calif.: Stanford University Press, 2010.

Hegel, G. W. F. *Grundlinien der Philosophie des Rechts oder Naturrecht und Staatswissenschaft im Grundrisse.* Vol. 7 of *Werke.* Edited by Eva Moldenhauer and Karl Markus Michel. Frankfurt am Main: Suhrkamp, 1986.

Herdt, Jennifer A. *Putting on Virtue: The Legacy of Splendid Vices.* Chicago: University of Chicago Press, 2008.

Hess, Jonathan. *Reconstituting the Body Politic: Enlightenment, Public Culture, and the Invention of Aesthetic Autonomy.* Detroit: Wayne State University Press, 1999.

Hettling, Manfred. "Bürgerlichkeit im Nachkriegsdeutschland." In *Bürgertum nach 1945,* 7–37. Edited by Manfred Hettling and Bernd Ulrich. Hamburg: Hamburger Edition, 2005.

———. "'Bürgerlichkeit' und Zivilgesellschaft: Die Aktualität einer Tradition." In *Zivilgesellschaft als Geschichte: Studien zum 19. und 20. Jahrhundert,* 45–63. Edited by Ralph Jessen, Sven Reichardt, and Ansgar Klein. Wiesbaden: VS Verlag, 2004.

Hettling, Manfred, and Bernd Ulrich. "Formen der Bürgerlichkeit: Ein Gespräch mit Reinhart Koselleck." In *Bürgertum nach 1945,* 40–60. Edited by Manfred Hettling and Bernd Ulrich. Hamburg: Hamburger Edition, 2005.

Himmelstein, Klaus. "Eduard Sprangers deutsches Bildungsideal auf den Trümmern von 1945." In *Die Schärfung des Blicks: Pädagogik nach dem Holocaust,* 61–75. Edited by Klaus Himmelstein and Wolfgang Keim. Frankfurt am Main: Campus, 1996.

Hirschman, Albert O. *Essays in Trespassing: Economics to Politics and Beyond.* Cambridge: Cambridge University Press, 1981.

———. *Exit, Voice, and Loyalty: Responses to Decline in Firms, Organizations, and States.* Cambridge, Mass.: Harvard University Press, 1970.

———. *A Propensity to Self-Subversion.* Cambridge, Mass.: Harvard University Press, 1995.

Hoffmann, Stefan Ludwig. *Die Politik der Geselligkeit: Freimaurerlogen in der deutschen Bürgergesellschaft 1840–1918.* Göttingen: Vandenhoeck & Ruprecht, 1999.

Hohendahl, Peter Uwe. "Critical Theory, Public Sphere and Culture: Jürgen Habermas and His Critics." *New German Critique* 16 (Winter 1979): 89–118.

———. "Recasting the Public Sphere." *October* 73 (Summer 1995): 27–54.

Huckfeldt, Robert, Paul E. Johnson, and John Sprague. *Political Disagreement: The Survival of Diverse Opinions Within Communication Networks.* Cambridge: Cambridge University Press, 2004.

Jacoby, Wade. *Imitation and Politics: Redesigning Modern Germany.* Ithaca, N.Y.: Cornell University Press, 2000.

Jarausch, Konrad. *After Hitler: Recivilizing Germans 1945–1995.* Oxford: Oxford University Press, 2006.

Jaspers, Karl. "Geleitwort im Auftrag der Herausgeber und des Verlegers." *Die Wandlung* 1, no. 1 (November 1945): 3–6.

———. "Unsere Zukunft und Goethe." *Die Wandlung* 2, nos. 7–8 (October 1947): 559–78.

Joas, Hans. *Sozialtheorie: Zwanzig einführende Vorlesungen.* Frankfurt am Main: Suhrkamp, 2004.

Johnson, Loch K. "Educing Information: Interrogation: Science and Art." *Studies in Intelligence* 51, no. 4 (December 2007): 1–4.

Judt, Tony. *Postwar: A History of Europe Since 1945.* London: Penguin, 2005.

Jung, Werner. *Georg Simmel zur Einführung.* Hamburg: Junius, 1990.

Jünger, Ernst. *Strahlungen*. Tübingen: Heliopolis, 1949.

Kaiser, Paul. "Bürgerlichkeit ohne Bürgertum?" *Aus Politik und Zeitgeschichte* 9–10 (2008): 26–32.

Kalyvas, Andreas. *Democracy and the Politics of the Extraordinary: Max Weber, Carl Schmitt, and Hannah Arendt*. Cambridge: Cambridge University Press, 2008.

Kennedy, Ellen. "Carl Schmitt und die 'Frankfurter Schule': Deutsche Liberalismuskritik im 20. Jahrhundert." *Geschichte und Gesellschaft: Zeitschrift für historische Sozialwissenschaft* 12, no. 3 (1986): 380–419.

Kinkela, Claudia. *Die Rehabilitierung des Bürgerlichen im Werk Dolf Sternbergers*. Würzburg: Königshausen & Neumann, 2001.

Kirkbright, Suzanne. *Karl Jaspers: A Biography—Navigations in Truth*. New Haven, Conn.: Yale University Press, 2004.

Klingwell, Mark. *A Civil Tongue: Justice, Dialogue, and the Politics of Pluralism*. University Park: Pennsylvania State University Press, 1995.

Kluge, Alexander. *Case Histories*. Translated by Leila Vennewitz. New York: Holmes & Meier, 1988.

———. "Die Gruppe 47: Glücksfall einer nicht-öffentlichen Öffentlichkeit." In *Die Gruppe 47 in Bildern und Texten,* 12–15. Edited by Toni Richter. Cologne: Kipenheuer & Witsch, 1997.

———. *Lebensläufe*. Stuttgart: Henry Goverts, 1962.

Kluge, Alexander, and Oskar Negt. *Öffentlichkeit und Erfahrung: Zur Organisationsanalyse von bürgerlicher und proletarischer Öffentlichkeit*. Frankfurt am Main: Suhrkamp, 1972.

Koebner, Thomas. "Die Schuldfrage: Vergangenheitsbewältigung und Lebenslügen in der Diskussion 1945–1949." In *Deutschland nach Hitler: Zukunftspläne im Exil und aus der Besatzungszeit 1939–1949,* 301–29. Edited by Thomas Koebner, Gert Sautermeister, and Sigrid Schneider. Opladen: Westdeutscher, 1987.

Koepnick, Lutz. "Culture in the Shadow of Trauma." In *The Oxford Handbook of Modern German History,* 711–29. Edited by Helmut Walser Smith. Oxford: Oxford University Press, 2011.

Koselleck, Reinhart. *Critique and Crisis: Enlightenment and the Pathogenesis of Modern Society*. Translated by Anon. Cambridge, Mass.: MIT Press, 1998.

———. *Kritik und Krise: Ein Beitrag zur Pathogenese der bürgerlichen Welt*. Freiburg: Karl Alber, 1959.

———. *Vergangene Zukunft: Zur Semantik geschichtlicher Zeiten*. Frankfurt am Main: Suhrkamp, 1979.

König, Helmut. "Von der Diktatur zur Demokratie oder Was ist Vergangenheitsbewältigung." *Leviathan: Zeitschrift für Sozialwissenschaften* 18 (1997): 371–92.

Krauss, Werner. *Briefe 1922 bis 1976*. Edited by Peter Jehle. Frankfurt am Main: Klostermann, 2002.

Kvistad, Gregg. *The Rise and Demise of German Statism: Loyalty and Political Membership*. New York: Berghahn, 1999.

Landry, Jean-Michel. "Confession, Obedience, and Subjectivity: Michel Foucault's Unpublished Lectures *On the Government of the Living.*" *Telos* 146 (Spring 2009): 111–23.

Lau, Jörg. *Hans Magnus Enzensberger: Ein öffentliches Leben.* Berlin: Alexander Fest, 1999.

La Vopa, Anthony J. "Conceiving a Public: Ideas and Society in Eighteenth-Century Europe." *Journal of Modern History* 64, no. 1 (1992): 79–116.

Lenin, Vladimir Ilyich. *Imperialism, the Highest Stage of Capitalism.* Moscow: Progress, 1978.

Lethen, Helmut. *Verhaltenslehren der Kälte: Lebensversuche zwischen den Kriegen.* Frankfurt am Main: Suhrkamp, 1994.

Luhmann, Niklas. *Gesellschaftsstruktur und Semantik: Studien zur Wissenssoziologie der modernen Gesellschaft.* Vol. 1. Frankfurt am Main: Suhrkamp, 1993.

———. *Gesellschaftsstruktur und Semantik: Studien zur Wissensoziologie der modernen Gesellschaft.* Vol. 4. Frankfurt am Main: Suhrkamp, 1999.

———. "Immer noch Bundesrepublik? Das Erbe und die Zukunft." In *BRD ade! Vierzig Jahre in Rück-Ansichten von Sozial- und Kulturwissenschaftlern,* 95–100. Edited by Otthein Rammstedt and Gert Schmidt. Frankfurt am Main: Suhrkamp, 1992.

———. "Öffentliche Meinung." *Politische Vierteljahresschrift* 11 (1970): 2–28.

Maier, Charles S. *The Unmasterable Past: History, Holocaust, and German National Identity.* Cambridge, Mass.: Harvard University Press, 1988.

Mann, Michael. *States, War, and Capitalism.* Oxford: Blackwell, 1988.

Markell, Patchen. *Bound by Recognition.* Princeton, N.J.: Princeton University Press, 2003.

Marx, Karl, and Friedrich Engels. *Werke.* Vol. 1. Berlin: Dietz, 1972.

McCormick, John. *Carl Schmitt's Critique of Liberalism.* Cambridge: Cambridge University Press, 1999.

Meinecke, Friedrich. *Die deutsche Katastrophe: Betrachtungen und Erinnerungen.* Wiesbaden: Brockhaus, 1946.

Menand, Louis. "Woke Up This Morning: Why Do We Read Diaries?" *New Yorker,* December 10, 2007, 106–12.

Missfelder, Jan-Friedrich. "Die Gegenkraft und ihre Geschichte: Carl Schmitt, Reinhart Koselleck und der Bürgerkrieg." *Zeitschrift für Religion und Geistesgeschichte* 58, no. 4 (2006): 310–36.

Mitscherlich, Alexander. *Hemmen Tabus die Demokratisierung der deutschen Gesellschaft? Bergedorfer Protokolle.* Vol. 12. Hamburg: G. Schenk, 1965.

Mitscherlich, Alexander, and Margarete Mitscherlich. *Die Unfähigkeit zu trauern: Grundlagen kollektiven Verhaltens.* Munich: Piper, 1967.

———. *The Inability to Mourn: Principles of Collective Behavior.* Translated by Beverley R. Placzek. New York: Grove, 1975.

Moses, Dirk A. *German Intellectuals and the Nazi Past.* Cambridge: Cambridge University Press, 2007.

Müller, Jan-Werner. *Another Country: German Intellectuals, Unification, and National Identity.* New Haven, Conn.: Yale University Press, 2000.

———. *Constitutional Patriotism.* Princeton, N.J.: Princeton University Press, 2007.

———. *A Dangerous Mind: Carl Schmitt in Post-War European Thought.* New Haven, Conn.: Yale University Press, 2003.

Müller-Doom, Stefan. *Jürgen Habermas.* Frankfurt am Main: Suhrkamp, 2008.

Münkler, Herfried. *Die Deutschen und ihre Mythen.* Berlin: Rowohlt, 2009.

Nathaus, Klaus. *Organisierte Geselligkeit: Deutsche und britische Vereine im 19. und 20. Jahrhundert.* Göttingen: Vandenhoeck & Ruprecht, 2009.

Negt, Oskar. "Mass Media: Tools of Domination or Instruments of Liberation?" Translated by Leslie Adelson. *New German Critique* 14 (Spring 1978): 61–80.

Niehaus, Michael. *Das Verhör: Geschichte—Theorie—Fiktion.* Munich: Wilhelm Fink, 2003.

Niethammer, Lutz. "War die bürgerliche Gesellschaft in Deutschland 1945 am Ende oder am Anfang?" In *Bürgerliche Gesellschaft in Deutschland: Historische Einblicke, Fragen, Perspektiven*, ed. Niethammer. Frankfurt am Main: Fischer, 1990.

Nipperdey, Thomas. *Gesellschaft, Kultur, Theorie: Gesammelte Aufsätze zu neueren Geschichte.* Göttingen: Vandenhoeck & Ruprecht, 1976.

Nolte, Paul. *Die Ordnung der deutschen Gesellschaft: Selbstentwurf und Selbstbeschreibung im 20. Jahrhundert.* Munich: C. H. Beck, 2000.

Norberg, Jakob. "Day-to-Day Politics: Carl Schmitt on the Diary." *Telos* 157 (Winter 2011): 21–42.

Olick, Jeffrey K. *In the House of the Hangman: The Agonies of German Defeat, 1943–1949.* Chicago: University of Chicago Press, 2005.

Palonen, Kari. "The History of Concepts as a Style of Political Theorizing: Quentin Skinner and Reinhart Koselleck's Subversion of Normative Political Theory." *European Journal of Political Theory* 1 (2002): 91–106.

Patten, Alan. *Hegel's Idea of Freedom.* Oxford: Oxford University Press, 1999.

Paxton, Robert. *The Anatomy of Fascism.* New York: Knopf, 2004.

Pensky, Max. "Jürgen Habermas and the Antinomies of the Intellectual." In *Habermas: A Critical Reader*, 211–37. Edited by Peter Dews. Oxford: Blackwell, 1999.

Perrin, Andrew J., and Jeffrey K. Olick. Introduction to Theodor W. Adorno, *Guilt and Defense: On the Legacies of National Socialism in Postwar Germany,* 3–42. Edited and translated by Perrin and Olick. Cambridge, Mass.: Harvard University Press, 2010.

———. "Translators' Introduction: Before the Public Sphere." Introduction to Friedrick Pollock, Theodor W. Adorno, et al., *Group Experiment and Other Writings: The Frankfurt School on Public Opinion in Postwar Germany,* xv–lxi. Edited and translated by Perrin and Olick. Cambridge, Mass.: Harvard University Press, 2011.

Phillips, James. "From Radical to Banal Evil: Hannah Arendt Against the Justification of the Unjustifiable." *International Journal of Philosophical Studies* 12, no. 2 (2004): 129–58.

Pitkin, Hannah. *The Attack of the Blob: Hannah Arendt's Concept of the Social.* Chicago: University of Chicago Press, 1998.

Popper, Karl. *Conjectures and Refutations: The Growth of Scientific Knowledge.* New York: Basic, 1962.

———. *The Open Society and Its Enemies.* London: Routledge, 1945.

Pourciau, Sarah. "Bodily Negation: Carl Schmitt on the Meaning of Meaning." *MLN* 120 (2005): 1066–90.

Quaritsch, Helmut, ed. *Carl Schmitt: Antworten in Nürnberg.* Berlin: Duncker & Humblot, 2000.

———. "Theorie der Vergangenheitsbewältigung." *Der Staat* 31, no. 4 (1992): 519–51.

Rabinbach, Anson. "Restoring the German Spirit: Humanism and Guilt in Post-War Germany." In *German Ideologies Since 1945: Studies in the Political Thought and Culture of the Bonn Republic,* 23–39. Edited by Jan-Werner Müller. New York: Palgrave Macmillan, 2003.

———. "Eichmann in New York: The New York Intellectuals and the Hannah Arendt Controversy." *October* 108 (Spring 2004): 97–111.

Reese-Schäfer, Walter. *Jürgen Habermas.* Frankfurt am Main: Campus, 2001.

Reginster, Bernard. "Nietzsche on Ressentiment and Valuation." *Philosophy and Phenomenological Research* 57, no. 2 (1997): 281–305.

Reichel, Peter. *Vergangenheitsbewältigung in Deutschland: Die Auseinandersetzung mit der NS-Diktatur von 1945 bis heute.* Munich: Beck, 2001.

Riedel, Manfred. *Studien zur Hegels Rechtsphilosophie.* Frankfurt am Main: Suhrkamp, 1969.

Ritter, Joachim. *Hegel und die französische Revolution.* Frankfurt am Main: Suhrkamp, 1965.

Roberts, David. "Die Formenwelt des Zusammenhangs: Zur Theorie und Funktion der Montage bei Alexander Kluge." *Zeitschrift für Literaturwissenschaft und Linguistik* 12, no. 46 (1982): 104–19.

Runciman, David. *Political Hypocrisy: The Mask of Power from Hobbes to Orwell and Beyond.* Princeton, N.J.: Princeton University Press, 2008.

Safranski, Rüdiger. *Ein Meister aus Deutschland: Heidegger und seine Zeit.* Munich: Carl Hanser, 1994.

Sanders, Willy. *Gutes Deutsch—besseres Deutsch: Praktische Stillehre der deutschen Gegenwartssprache.* Darmstadt: Wissenschaftliche Buchgesellschaft, 1996.

Santner, Eric L. "The Trouble with Hitler: Postwar German Aesthetics and the Legacy of Fascism." *New German Critique* 57 (Winter 1993): 5–24.

Scheuerman, William E. "Unsolved Paradoxes: Conservative Political Thought in Adenauer's Germany." In *Confronting Mass Democracy and Industrial Technology: Political and Social Theory from Nietzsche to Habermas,* 221–42. Edited by John P. McCormick. Durham, N.C.: Duke University Press, 2002.

Schildt, Axel. "Bürgerliche Gesellschaft und kleinbürgerliche Geborgenheit: Zur Mentalität im westdeutschen Wiederaufbau der 50er Jahre." In

Kleinbürger: Zur Kulturgeschichte des begrentzten Bewußtseins, 295–312. Edited by Thomas Althaus. Tübingen: Attempto, 2001.

Schildt, Axel, and Detlef Siegfried. *Deutsche Kulturgeschichte: Die Bundesrepublik von 1945 bis zur Gegenwart*. Munich: Hanser, 2009.

Schleiermacher, Friedrich. "Versuch einer Theorie des geselligen Betragens." In *Schriften aus der Berliner Zeit 1796–1799*, vol. 2 of *Kritische Gesamtausgabe*. Edited by Günter Meckenstock. Berlin: Walter de Gruyter, 1984.

Schmitt, Carl. *Der Begriff des Politischen. Text von 1932 mit einem Vorwort und drei Corollarien*. Berlin: Duncker & Humblot, 1963.

———. *Ex Captivitate Salus: Erfahrungen der Zeit 1945/47*. Cologne: Greven, 1950.

———. *Gesetz und Urteil: Eine Untersuchung zum Problem der Rechtspraxis*. Munich: C. H. Beck, 1969.

———. *Glossarium: Aufzeichnungen der Jahre 1947–1951*. Ed. Eberhard Freiherr von Medem. Berlin: Duncker & Humblot, 1991.

———. *Der Leviathan in der Staatslehre des Thomas Hobbes: Sinn und Fehlschlag eines politischen Symbols*. Hamburg: Hanseatische Verlagsanstalt, 1938.

———. *The Leviathan in the State Theory of Thomas Hobbes: Meaning and Failure of a Political Symbol*. Translated by George Schwab and Erna Hilfstein. Westport, Colo.: Greenwood, 1996.

———. *Politische Theologie: Vier Kapitel zur Lehre von der Souveränität*. Berlin: Duncker & Humblot, 2004.

Schönborn, Sibylle. *Das Buch der Seele: Tagebuchliteratur zwischen Aufklärung und Kunstperiode*. Tübingen: Max Niemeyer, 1999.

Schulz-Buschhaus, Ulrich. *Moralistik und Poetik*. Hamburg: LIT, 1997.

Schumpeter, Joseph. *Aufsätze zur Soziologie*. Tübingen: J. C. B. Mohr, 1953.

———. *Capitalism, Socialism, and Democracy*. New York: Harper & Brothers, 1942.

Seligman, Adam B. "The Fragile Ethical Vision of Civil Society." In *Citizenship and Social Theory*, 139–61. Edited by Bryan S. Turner. London: Sage, 1993.

Shaw, Tamsin. *Nietzsche's Political Skepticism*. Princeton, N.J.: Princeton University Press, 2007.

Siegel, Elke. "Remains of the Day: Rainald Goetz's Internet Diary *Abfall für alle*." *Germanic Review* 81, no. 3 (Summer 2006): 235–54.

Siegrist, Hannes. "Bürgerlichkeit und Antibürgerlichkeit in historischer Perspektive." In *Der Aufstand gegen den Bürger: Antibürgerliches Denken im 20. Jahrhundert*, 35–50. Edited by Günter Meuter and Henrique Ricardo Otten. Würzburg: Königshausen & Neumann, 1999.

———. "Ende der Bürgerlichkeit? Die Kategorien 'Bürgertum' und 'Bürgerlichkeit' in der westdeutschen Gesellschaft und Geschichstwissenschaft der Nachkriegsperiode." *Geschichte und Gesellschaft* 20, no. 4 (1994): 549–83.

Simmel, Georg. "Soziologie der Geselligkeit." In *Aufsätze und Abhandlungen 1909–1918*, vol. 12 of *Gesamtausgabe*. Edited by Rüdiger Kramme and Angela Rammstedt. Frankfurt: Suhrkamp, 2001.

Sombart, Nicolaus. *Rendezvous mit dem Weltgeist: Heidelberger Reminiszenzen 1945–1951*. Frankfurt am Main: S. Fischer, 2000.

Specter, Matthew G. *Habermas: An Intellectual Biography*. Cambridge: Cambridge University Press, 2010.

Sperber, Jonathan. "*Bürger, Bürgertum, Bürgerlichkeit, Bürgerliche Gesellschaft:* Studies of the German (Upper) Middle Class and Its Sociocultural World." *Journal of Modern History* 69, no. 2 (1997): 271–97.

Stanitzek, Georg. *Essay—BRD*. Berlin: Vorwerk 8, 2011.

Stehr, Nico. *Die Moralisierung der Märkte: Eine Gesellschaftstheorie*. Frankfurt am Main: Suhrkamp, 2007.

Sternberger, Dolf. "Aspekte des bürgerlichen Charakters." *Die Wandlung* 4, no. 6 (June 1949): 474–86.

———. "Bürgerlichkeit." *Die Wandlung* 3, no. 3 (April 1948): 195–200.

———. *Über den Jugendstil und andere Essays*. Hamburg: Claassen, 1956.

———. "Versuch zu einem Fazit." *Die Wandlung* 4, no. 8 (December 1949): 699–710.

———. "Vorbemerkung der Redaktion." *Die Wandlung* 1, no. 4 (April 1946): 333.

Stirk, Peter. *Twentieth Century German Political Thought*. Edinburgh: Edinburgh University Press, 2006.

Strum, Arthur. "Bibliography of the Concept Öffentlichkeit." *New German Critique* 61 (Winter 1994): 161–200.

———. "Öffentlichkeit von der Moderne zur Postmoderne: 1960–1999." In *Öffentlichkeit: Geschichte eines kritischen Begriffs*, 92–123. Edited by Peter Uwe Hohendahl. Stuttgart: J. B. Metzler, 2000.

Sunstein, Cass. *Why Societies Need Dissent*. Cambridge, Mass.: Harvard University Press, 2003.

Taylor, Charles. "Modes of Civil Society." *Public Culture* 3, no. 1 (1990): 95–118.

Tenfelde, Klaus. "Stadt und Bürgertum im 20. Jahrhundert." In *Wege zur Geschichte des Bürgertums*, 317–53. Edited by Klaus Tenfelde and Hans-Ulrich Wehler. Göttingen: Vandenhoek and Ruprecht, 1994.

Theweleit, Klaus. *Männerphantasien*. Frankfurt am Main: Roter Stern, 1977.

Thornhill, Chris. *Political Theory in Modern Germany: An Introduction*. Cambridge: Polity, 2000.

———. "Carl Schmitt and Early Western Marxism." Vol. 5 of *The History of Continental Philosophy*, 19–45. Edited by David Ingram. Chicago: University of Chicago Press, 2010.

Tollefsen, Deborah Perron. "Group Deliberation, Social Cohesion, and Scientific Teamwork: Is There Room for Dissent?" *Episteme: A Journal of Social Epistemology* 3, no. 1 (2006): 37–51.

Tönnies, Ferdinand. *Community and Civil Society*. Edited by Jose Harris; translated by Margaret Hollis. Cambridge: Cambridge University Press, 2001.

Trilling, Lionel. *Sincerity and Authenticity*. Cambridge, Mass.: Harvard University Press, 1972.

Tsao, Roy T. "The Three Phases of Arendt's Theory of Totalitarianism." *Social Research* 69, no. 2 (2002): 579–619.

van Laak, Dirk. *Gespräche in der Sicherheit des Schweigens: Carl Schmitt in der politischen Geistesgeschichte der frühen Bundesrepublik*. Berlin: Akademie, 1993.

Vilarós, Teresa M. "The Spirit of the Beehive: On Carl Schmitt's 'The New *Nomos* of the Earth.'" *South Atlantic Quarterly* 104, no. 2 (Spring 2005): 359–70.

Villa, Dana. "Genealogies of Total Domination: Arendt, Adorno, and Auschwitz." *New German Critique* 34, no. 1 (2007): 1–45.

———. "Hannah Arendt: Modernity, Alienation, and Critique." In *Hannah Arendt and the Meaning of Politics,* 179–206. Edited by Craig Calhoun and John McGowan. Minneapolis: University of Minnesota Press, 1997.

Vogl, Joseph. "Asyl des Politischen: Zur Topologie politischer Gelegenheiten." In *Das Politische: Figurenlehren des sozialen Körpers nach der Romantik,* 23–38. Edited by Uwe Hebekus, Ethel Matala de Mazza, and Albrecht Koschorke. Munich: Wilhelm Fink, 2003.

———. *Kalkül und Leidenschaft: Poetik des ökonomischen Menschen*. Zürich: Diaphanes, 2004.

Vogl, Joseph, and Alexander Kluge, *Soll und Haben: Fernsehgespräche*. Zürich: Diaphanes, 2009.

von Essen, Gesa. "Max Weber und die Kunst der Geselligkeit." In *Heidelberg im Schnittpunkt intellektueller Kreise,* 462–84. Edited by Hubert Treiber and Karol Sauerland. Opladen: Westdeutscher Verlag, 1995.

Waldmüller, Monika. *Die Wandlung: Ein Bericht*. Marbach am Neckar: Deutsche Schillergesellschaft, 1988.

Walser, Martin. *Die Alternative oder brauchen wir eine neue Regierung*. Hamburg: Rowohlt, 1961.

Wedemeyer, Arnd. "Herrschaftszeiten! Theopolitical Profanities in the Face of Secularization." *New German Critique* 35, no. 3 (Fall 2008): 121–41.

Wehler, Hans Ulrich. "Deutsches Bürgertum nach 1945: Exitus oder Phönix aus der Asche?" *Geschichte und Gesellschaft* 27 (2001): 617–34.

———. *Deutsche Gesellschaftsgeschichte 1949–1990*. Munich: C. H. Beck, 2008.

Werner, Erik. "Weg und Wille des Rotary Club: Regeln, Pflichte, Ziele." *Aral-Journal: Eine Vierteljahresschrift der BV-Aktiengesellschaft* 10 (1955): 7–8.

Wetters, Kirk. *The Opinion System: Impasses of the Public Sphere from Hobbes to Habermas*. New York: Fordham University Press, 2008.

Wiesen, S. Jonathan. "The Modern Guild: Rotary Clubs and Bourgeois Renewal in the Aftermath of National Socialism." In *Conflict, Catastrophe, and Continuity: Essays on Modern German History,* 297–317. Edited by Frank Biess, Mark Roseman, and Hanna Schissler. New York: Berghahn, 2007.

———. "Service Above Self? Rotary Clubs, National Socialism, and Transnational Memory in the 1960s and 1970s." *Holocaust and Genocide Studies* 23, no. 1 (2009): 1–25.

Wolfe, Robert. "Revival of Democratic Culture During the American Occupation of Heidelberg, 1945–1949." In *Heidelberg 1945,* 15–29. Edited by Jürgen C. Heß, Hartmut Lehmann, and Volker Sellin. Stuttgart: Franz Steiner, 1996.

Wolin, Sheldon S. "Hannah Arendt: Democracy and the Political." In *Hannah Arendt: Critical Essays,* 289–306. Edited by Lewis P. Hinchman and Sandra K. Hinchman. Buffalo: SUNY Press, 1994.

———. *Politics and Vision: Continuity and Innovation in Western Political Thought*. Princeton, N.J.: Princeton University Press, 2004.

———. *The Presence of the Past: Essays on the State and the Constitution.* Baltimore: Johns Hopkins University Press, 1989.

Wood, Allen. Introduction to *Elements of the Philosophy of Right* by G. W. F. Hegel, vii–xxxii. Translated by H. B. Nisbett. Cambridge: Cambridge University Press, 1991.

Zapf, Wolfgang. *Wandlungen der deutschen Elite: Ein Zirkulationsmodell deutscher Führungsgruppen 1919–1961*. Munich: Piper, 1966.

Zeruvabel, Eviatar. "The Social Sound of Silence: Toward a Sociology of Denial." In *Shadows of War: A Social History of Silence in the Twentieth Century,* 32–44. Edited by Efrat ben-Ze'ev, Ruth Ginio, and Jay Winter. Cambridge: Cambridge University Press, 2010.

INDEX

absolutism, 110–14, 121–22
Adenauer, Konrad, 159
Adorno, Theodor, 20, 71, 159, 199n54
affability and companionableness (*Umgänglichkeit*), 8, 33, 40–41, 161, 167, 172, 174
anti-Semitism, 86, 112–13, 208n17
Arato, Andrew, 212n17, 212n25, 213n39
Arendt, Hannah, 6–7, 11–13, 16, 20, 21–22, 24–25, 79–105, 108, 123–24, 129, 133–34, 141, 148–52, 154, 163, 168, 206n61, 206n62, 213n39, 214n47; *The Human Condition,* 103, 123, 149; "On Imperialism," 85–93, 100; "Organized Guilt," 93–99; *The Origins of Totalitarianism,* 84, 93, 104–5, 202n16, 202n23, 203n33, 207n5
argumentation, social and political, 13, 19, 66, 104, 115, 135, 137–47, 145–46
aristocratic class, 35–36, 98, 142
art consumption, 144–45, 169–70
associations: defined, 15; historical importance of, 15; postwar emergence of, 46–47; social integration and cohesion through, 15–16, 47, 183n27
aura, of art, 144–45
authority: hegemonic wielding of, 12, 23–24; Schmitt on, 63–64; skepticism about, 30, 52; social cohesion in absence of, 8, 9, 11, 12, 23, 33, 43, 49, 81; societal forms of, 119–24, 150–51

Bachmann, Ingeborg, 157
Baehr, Peter, 202n18
Balke, Friedrich, 196n26
Balzac, Honoré de, 86, 87
Baudelaire, Charles, 86
Becher, Johannes, 204n37
Benjamin, Walter, 145
Benn, Gottfried, 57
Bild-Zeitung (newspaper), 167
Bismarck, Otto von, 36
blood, social cohesion through, 48–49, 60
Blücher, Heinrich, 85, 104
body, the: the bourgeoisie and, 35–37, 130; sociability and, 144
Böll, Heinrich, 45
bon mots, 141, 145, 146
Bösch, Michael, 206n60
bourgeois society: Arendt's criticisms of, 24–25, 81–105, 154, 163, 168; aristocratic class vs., 35–36, 98, 142; and art, 144–45; characteristics of, 35–36, 96–97, 167, 205n53; comfort of, 38–39; communal formation in, 82–84, 88–101, 122–23 (*see also* and politics); conflict avoided by, 11–12; crises affecting, 39; and criticism, 115–17; criticisms of, 11–12, 151, 168, 202n28, 205n50; guilt of, for Nazi actions, 93–99; Habermas on, 131–55, 168–72; Hegel on, 181n12, 183n20, 205n51; historical German critique of, 100, 183n20; and imperialism, 85–93; individuals in, 11, 12, 82–84, 89–93, 141, 171, 203n33; Koselleck on, 109–11, 114–18, 122–24, 131–32, 135–36, 162, 208n27, 209n37; maintenance of lifestyle of, 4–5; mob likened to, 81, 84–85, 88–92, 163, 201n3; morality of, 35–36; National Socialism and, 98–99, 204n37; and politics, 12, 36, 43, 83, 99–101, 114–15, 129, 132–38, 154–55, 168, 203n33, 208n27, 212n22, 213n37 (*see also* communal formation in); postwar status of, 39–42; public sphere grounded in, 135; and responsibility, 100–101, 115–16, 122–23; security as value of, 96–98, 113–14; the self in, 116–17; and sexuality/sensuality, 36–38; sociability grounded in, 6–13, 33–34, 40–42, 58, 114, 137, 161; state in relation to, 114–18, 136–38, 212n25; status within, 141–42, 213n31; Sternberger's criticisms of, 35–37; unsuitability of, for politics, 12; *Die Wandlung* on,

bourgeois society, *continued*
201n6; in West Germany, 167–68. *See also* civil society; sociability
Breithaupt, Fritz, 213n37
Brown, Wendy, 197n40
Bude, Heinz, 184n32
Bull, Malcolm, 183n21
Burkhardt, Jakob, 86

capitalism, 85–88, 202n18, 202n22
Christian Democratic Party, 173
civil society, 42, 182n13. *See also* bourgeois society
class distinctions, 3–5, 41, 141–43
Club der Freunde von 1927, 47
Club zu Bremen, 57
coffeehouses, 141–42, 148
Cohen, Jean, 212n17, 212n25, 213n39
Cold War, 116–17, 151
collective. *See* social integration and cohesion
Collins, Randall, 218n37
companionableness. *See* affability and companionableness
confessional discourse, 69–72, 76, 78, 196n27
conflict: bourgeois avoidance of, 11–12, 130; political role of, 12, 151–52; sociability and, 48–51, 60, 130, 145–48, 172–73
conformity and conformism, 83, 98, 110, 119, 122–24, 141, 147–51
consciousness industry, 149, 215n50
conspiracy thinking, 125–26, 210n55
constitutional patriotism, 10
consumerism, 166, 168–71
conversation: art as instigation for, 144–45, 169–70; circles of, 44–46; interrogation and, 24, 66–68, 197n37; principles of, 142; Schmitt on, 63–67. *See also* discursive interactions
conviviality. *See* sociability
Conze, Eckart, 167
Coser, Lewis, 46, 148
criminals and gangsters, 89–92, 94–95, 202n23. *See also* mob, bourgeois society likened to
criticism and critique, 115–18, 138, 148
culture, as basis for sociability, 13–16, 52–54
culture industry, 149, 214n50
Curtius, Ernst Robert, 53–54, 193n77, 194n80

Dagerman, Stig, 3–5, 41
Dahrendorf, Ralf, 14, 18, 35
decisionism, 132
democracy: obstacles and threats to, 149; as postwar German goal, 7, 9, 17, 18, 23, 26, 33, 48, 58, 82, 104, 130, 158–59, 169
Deuber-Mankowsky, Astrid, 196n26
diaries, Schmitt and, 72–79
Dirks, Walter, 44
discursive interactions: bourgeois society grounded in, 40; genres of, 62–63, 69–70; in postwar Germany, 17–18; Schmitt's critiques of, 23–24, 58–79; social integration and cohesion through, 29–30; study of, 19. *See also* conversation; interrogation; public sphere
disenchantment, 139, 144
domination, political, 30, 31, 87, 92, 109, 121, 125, 127, 132, 135, 143, 151, 212n20

Eberan, Barbro, 201n6
economy: Arendt's criticisms of, 103–4; bourgeois place in, 39–40; postwar, 5, 21, 165–66, 168, 173; social integration by means of, 21, 186n45. *See also* market
Elias, Norbert, 189n28
Enlightenment, 107, 117–18, 121, 125–26, 127, 135, 142, 144, 148, 151, 209n29
Enzensberger, Hans Magnus, 45
Erhard, Ludwig, 168
expressionism, 188n9
exteriority, 77

focus groups, 71
Foucault, Michel, 186n45, 198n40, 198n41
Frankfurter Allgemeine Zeitung (newspaper), 39
Frankfurt School, 20, 71
Fraser, Nancy, 212n20, 213n30
Freemasons. *See* Masonic lodges
French Revolution, 86, 100
Frow, John, 196n23, 196n24
Fühmann, Franz, 166

gangsters. *See* criminals and gangsters
Gehlen, Arnold, 132, 168
genres, 62–63, 69–70, 147, 196n23, 196n24

Germany: division of, 43, 54–55; national character of, 55; pathologies of, leading to National Socialism, 34–36, 94–95; postwar political transition of, 17, 158; postwar psychology of, 70–71. *See also* culture, as basis for sociability; guilt; social integration and cohesion; state; *Vergangenheitsbewältigung;* West Germany
Gertenbach, Lars, 186n45
Geselligkeit. See sociability
Gesellschaft Imshausen, 44
Goebbels, Joseph, 98
Goering, Herrman, 98
Goethe, Johann Wolfgang von, 51–54, 193n76, 194n80
Goethe congregations, 13–15, 161
Goethegesellschaft, 15
grandeur, social and political displays of, 134, 139
Grass, Günter, 45
greedy institutions, 46
gregariousness, 42, 48, 58, 83, 158, 172
Greve, Jens, 212n24
Gross, Raphael, 208n17
Group Experiment, 71
Grunenberg, Nina, 5
Gruppe 45, 47, 161, 191n51
guilt: Arendt on, 24, 81, 82; German attitudes toward, 71, 158–59, 204n42, 205n43; German collective, 93–99, 204n42, 205n43; German discussion of, 18, 31; organized, 93–99, 204n42; types of, 204n39; *Die Wandlung* as forum for discussion of, 31, 81, 93. *See also Vergangenheitsbewältigung* (coming to terms with the past)

Habermas, Jürgen, 6–7, 9–10, 12–13, 16, 20, 21–22, 44, 105, 126, 127–55, 162–63, 165, 168–72, 182n16, 184n32; *The Structural Transformation of the Public Sphere,* 9–10, 16, 17, 25–26, 55, 127–29, 132–55, 169, 184n31
Hacke, Jens, 182n14
Hamacher, Werner, 202n28
Hauptmann, Emily, 215n54
Hayek, Friedrich, 20
Hedrick, Todd, 153
Hegel, G.W.F., 88, 145, 181n12, 183n20, 190n41, 205n51
hegemony, 12, 24, 67, 212n20
Heidegger, Martin, 57–58
Heidelberger Aktionsgruppe zur Demokratie und zum freien Sozialismus, 44–45
Hettling, Manfred, 41
Hilferding, Rudolf, 86
Himmler, Heinrich, 96, 98
Hitler, Adolf, 98, 196n25
Hobbes, Thomas, 86, 87, 90–91, 111–13, 208n26
Hobson, J. A., 86
Hoffmann, Stefan Ludwig, 37
Höflichkeit. See politeness
Hohendahl, Peter Uwe, 128, 185n33
Horkheimer, Max, 20
human rights, 102
hypocrisy, 117, 122–23, 208n26. *See also* self-deception and -delusion

imperialism, 85–93, 202n16, 202n18, 202n22
individuals: associations formed by, 15, 46–47; in bourgeois society, 11, 12, 82–84, 89–92, 141, 171, 203n33; in mobs, 89–92; in modern institutional society, 170; and private property, 40; in relation to community, 102–3, 152; social cohesion of, 6, 9, 11, 33, 38, 42, 46, 48, 53, 83; in society, 90–92; in totalitarian societies, 95. *See also* the self
institutionalism, 132
institutions, characteristics of, 141
interiority, 77
interrogation: conversation and, 24, 66–68, 197n37; and reeducation, 66–69, 197n38; relationship of parties in, 198n44; Schmitt's, by United States, 23, 58, 62–63, 79, 195n4, 196n25; and the self, 66–69, 197n37

Jacoby, Wade, 188n8
Jarausch, Konrad, 158
Jaspers, Karl, 8, 11, 22–24, 29–34, 37–38, 49, 51–54, 57, 59–60, 85, 104, 108, 187n2, 188n16, 193n76, 194n80, 204n39, 207n5; *Die Schuldfrage,* 94
Jews, social and political role of, 112–13
Jünger, Ernst, 73–74

Kalyvas, Andreas, 72, 208n16
Kempner, Robert W., 196n25
Klingwell, Mark, 186n40
Kluge, Alexander, 26–27, 45, 174–75, 177–79, 217n27, 218n38

Koepnick, Lutz, 183n25
Kogon, Eugen, 44
Koselleck, Reinhart, 7, 11–13, 20, 22, 25, 104–5, 107–26, 131–33, 135–36, 146, 148, 150–51, 154; *Critique and Crisis,* 107–10, 113–26, 128, 131–32, 151, 162
Krauss, Werner, 50–51, 55
Kvistad, Gregg, 182n18

La Vopa, Anthony, 111
Lenin, Vladimir, 85, 86, 87
Lethen, Helmut, 199n60
liberalism: Arendt's criticisms of, 83–84; German lack of, 35; German striving for, 7, 9, 16, 18, 20, 58, 186n45; Schmitt's criticisms of, 61, 72, 195n16, 195n17, 208n16
licenses, 23, 24, 32, 50, 59
Locke, John, 119–20
Luhmann, Niklas, 210n47, 213n38

market: Arendt's criticisms of, 141, 149; individual relations in, 20, 103–4, 136–39; political sphere in relation to, 20, 138, 147. *See also* economy
Marx, Karl, 202n28, 205n50
Marxism: anti-bourgeois stance of, 104; Arendt and, 83, 86, 93, 99–100; on Germany, 20; on imperialism, 87, 89, 202n18
Masonic lodges, 37, 107–8
media: postwar growth of, 166–67, 169; as threat to democracy, 149–50
Meinecke, Friedrich, 13–16, 161
Mitscherlich, Alexander, 17, 44, 159, 184n33, 185n36
Mitscherlich, Margarete, 17, 184n33
mob, bourgeois society likened to, 81, 84–85, 88–92, 163, 201n3. *See also* criminals and gangsters
modernity: Arendt's critique of, 154; German deficiencies concerning, 35; Nazi statehood and, 94–95; pathologies of, 21
morality, bourgeois, 35–36
Moses, Dirk, 21, 187n48
Müller, Jan-Werner, 182n19
Münkler, Herfried, 186n44

Nathaus, Klaus, 46, 167, 195n4
National Socialism: associations declined under, 46, 47; and the bourgeoisie, 98–99, 204n37; elite of, 98–99; explanations of, 201n6; German pathologies leading to, 34–36, 94–95; identification of, with German people, 94–96; and imperialism, 85–86; postwar allegiance to, 70–71; postwar ruminations on, 16–17, 21; and Rotary Club, 218n32; Schmitt and, 11, 23, 58, 67, 79, 196n25; and state formation, 94–99; as totalitarian, 93
Negt, Oskar, 218n38
Nietzsche, Friedrich, 86, 209n28
Nipperdey, Thomas, 15, 183n27

Oelze, F. W., 57
Olick, Jeffrey K., 70
openness, political and social, 17–19, 158–59, 185n39
Ordoliberalism, 186n45
organized sociability, 46–47, 57, 167, 195n4

Palonen, Kari, 209n29
Pensky, Max, 211n14
Pepys, Samuel, 73, 200n69
Perrin, Andrew J., 70
Phillips, James, 216n59
pluralism. *See* political pluralism
politeness (*Höflichkeit*), 5–6, 8–9, 23–24, 33, 34, 40–41, 48, 51, 58, 146, 160–61, 167, 174
political pluralism, 17, 18
politics: Arendt's conception of, 83, 100–104, 133, 152, 206n61, 206n62; bourgeoisie and, 12, 36, 43, 83, 99–101, 114–15, 129, 132–38, 154–55, 168, 203n33, 208n27, 212n22, 213n37; Habermas's conception of, 134–40, 152–53; Koselleck on, 109–10, 113–26, 124, 209n29, 209n36, 210n51; left vs. right, 20; paradoxical character of, 210n47; "the political" vs., 215n54; reason and, 152–55; Schmitt's conception of, 134; silence and consensus as means of, 60–61; sociability in relation to, 49, 55, 58, 60–61, 124–25, 137, 140–48, 172–74; *Die Wandlung* and, 50. *See also* public sphere
Popper, Karl, 20, 185n39, 210n55
postwar historical and political thought: chief concerns of, 16–17; on sociability, 6–13; typical themes in, 20–22

private realm, 111–12
property, 40–41, 101, 171, 190n41
Psychological Warfare Division, U.S. Army, 70
public opinion, 214n47
public sphere: Arendt's conception of, 101–4, 206n62; bourgeois basis of, 135; bourgeois sociability and, 16, 20, 25–26; concept of, 128, 184n31; defined, 127; emergence of, 9–10; Habermas on, 9–10, 13, 25–26, 127–28, 133–55; market as basis of, 136–39; monitoring of, 59; proletarian, 218n38; as site for politics, 134–40; sociability as forerunner to, 140–47; status within, 142–43, 213n30

Rabinbach, Anson, 16–17
race, social cohesion through, 48–49, 60
racism, 86–87
reason: and political order, 152–53; public exercise of, 137–47
reeducation: conflict avoided in, 60; interrogation and, 66–69, 197n38; Schmitt on, 64, 66; and the self, 66; sociability as means of, 34, 37, 49, 64, 68, 71–72, 81, 130; U.S. oversight of, 31, 68, 81; *Die Wandlung* and, 23, 30–31
Reese-Schäfer, Walter, 213n31
refugees, 102
responsibility, bourgeois failures of, 100–101, 115–16, 122–23
ressentiment, 209n28
Richter, Hans Werner, 45
Romanticism, 100
Rotary Club, 47, 175–79, 217n29, 218n32
Rousseau, Jean-Jacques, 120–22
Der Ruf (journal), 188n9
Runciman, David, 208n26

salons, 37, 48, 103–4, 141–42, 149
Die Sammlung (journal), 188n9
Schmitt, Carl, 6–7, 11–13, 16, 20–25, 58–79, 108, 124, 129, 132–34, 151, 154, 161–62, 195n4, 196n25, 207n5, 208n17; *Ex Captivitate Salus,* 64–70; *Glossarium,* 75–76, 199n57; *The Leviathan in the State Theory of Thomas Hobbes,* 111–12
Schumpeter, Joseph, 88, 202n22, 212n22
self, the: in bourgeois society, 116–17; diaries and, 72, 76–78; interrogation, reeducation, and, 66–69, 197n37. *See also* individuals
self-adjustment, 42, 110, 124
self-deception and -delusion, 25, 78, 118–19, 122, 124–26, 154. *See also* hypocrisy
self-legislation, 110, 120, 151
self-management. *See* self-regulation and -management
self-organization, 15, 42, 43, 58, 61, 82, 161
self-regulation and -management, 6, 11–12, 48, 51, 82, 109, 114, 120, 122, 163
sexuality and sensuality, 36–38, 130, 144
Shaw, Tamsin, 207n14
Simmel, Georg, 213n33
sociability (*Geselligkeit*): Arendt's criticisms of, 103–4, 149; art as instigation for, 144–45, 169–70; bourgeois, 6–13, 33–34, 40–42, 58, 114, 137, 161; characteristics of, 5, 8–9, 48, 107, 157; and conflict, 48–51, 60, 130, 145–48, 172–73; and conformity, 147–51; criticisms of, 11–12, 150–51, 161–64; culture as basis for, 13–16, 52–54; debates about, 129–40; decline of, 165–72; examples of postwar, 44–47; functions, purposes, and value of, 6–9, 38, 160–64, 174; Habermas's engagement with, 20, 128–29, 131–55, 162–63, 168–72; Kluge and Negt on, 218n38; Koselleck on, 107–26; male, 37, 157; obstacles to, 49–50; organized, 46–47, 57, 167, 195n4; politics in relation to, 49, 55, 58, 60–61, 124–25, 137, 140–48, 172–74; postwar political thought and, 6–13; rationality and, 142–44; and reeducation, 34, 37, 49, 64, 68, 71–72, 81, 130; Rotary Club as example of, 175–79; the salon as site for, 37, 48; Schmitt's criticisms of, 59, 68, 161–62; significance of, 6, 18–19; social integration through, 9, 13–16, 33–34, 38, 42–43, 48, 57–58, 61, 81–83, 112, 129–30, 147–50, 160–64; and status, 141–43; Sternberger and, 33–51; therapeutic function of, 34–37, 58; venues for, 107; *Die Wandlung* as example of, 33–34, 49–51, 60. *See also* discursive interactions

social integration and cohesion: absence of, 29; apart from the state, 8, 9, 15–16, 23, 30, 33, 42–43, 49, 58, 61, 119–24, 130–31; Arendt on, 101–4; associations as means to, 15–16, 46–47, 183n27; bourgeois society and, 82–84, 88–101, 122–23; discourse as means of, 29–30; discredited means of, 8; economy/market as means of, 21, 103–4, 136–37, 141, 186n45; hegemony and, 12; Koselleck on, 118–24, 131–32, 135–36; Nazi methods of, 94–96; Rotary Club as example of, 176; sociability as means of, 9, 13–16, 33–34, 38, 42–43, 48, 57–58, 61, 81–83, 112, 129–30, 147–50, 160–64; U.S. role in, 32
Sombart, Nicolaus, 108
Soviet Union, 93
Specter, Matthew G., 128, 182n16
Spengler, Oswald, 86
Der Spiegel (magazine), 167
Spranger, Eduard, 64–67, 197n31, 197n38
Stalin, Joseph, 93
Stalinism, 100
state: bourgeoisie in relation to, 114–18, 136–38, 212n25; characteristics of, 182n18; Hobbes on, 90–91, 111–13; institutionalization and, 170; Koselleck on, 110–11, 113–14, 119–20; modern, 94–95, 207n14; Nazi formation of, 94–99; private realm vs., 111–12; Schmitt on, 111–13; social integration and cohesion apart from, 8, 9, 15–16, 23, 30, 33, 42–43, 49, 58, 61, 119–24, 130–31
Sternberger, Dolf, 8–12, 20–24, 30, 32–51, 57–58, 60–61, 64, 68, 72, 81, 83, 85, 93, 104, 108, 130, 140, 144, 145, 147, 154, 161, 163, 167, 181n12, 194n80, 207n5
Stirk, Peter, 181n10
Streicher, Julius, 98
surveys, 70–71
Swinburne, Algernon, 86
Syndicalism, 3

Taylor, Charles, 182n13
Tenfelde, Klaus, 39
Theweleit, Klaus, 189n28
Thornhill, Chris, 134, 195n17
Tollefsen, Deborah Perron, 214n42
Tönnies, Ferdinand, 182n17
totalitarianism, 86, 87, 122, 202n16, 202n18
Tsao, Roy T., 201n3, 202n16
Turgot, Anne-Robert-Jacques, 120

Umgänglichkeit. See affability and companionableness
United States: oversight and control exerted by, 23, 30–32, 50, 59, 70–71; and reeducation project, 31, 68, 81; Schmitt's interrogation by, 23, 58, 62–63, 79, 195n4, 196n25
upper-middle class. *See* bourgeois society

Van Laak, Dirk, 44, 59, 198n45
Vergangenheitsbewältigung (coming to terms with the past), 17, 159, 184n31, 185n36
Vogl, Joseph, 205n53, 215n54
Volk, 8, 23, 43, 58, 160

Waldmüller, Monika, 194n82
Walser, Martin, 45, 168
Die Wandlung (journal), 8, 9–11, 17, 23–25, 29–34, 37–38, 43, 48–55, 57, 59–60, 68, 80, 81–82, 84–85, 92–93, 99, 102–5, 129–30, 145, 147, 154, 160, 163, 188n8, 188n10, 188n16, 194n82, 201n6, 207n5
Weber, Alfred, 44, 108
Wehler, Hans Ulrich, 41
West Germany: bourgeois society in, 167–68; decline of sociability in, 165–72; demographics of, 173, 187n49; Rotarian sociability in, 175–79
Wolfe, Robert, 31
Wolin, Sheldon, 206n61

ISLAMIC AFRICA